Identity Reset
The Future of Black Wealth

The New House of Jacob

By

Anthony B. Cornish CPA, MBA

D1500912

Copyright © 2014 by Anthony B. Cornish

United Black Wealth

ISBN: 978-0615730059

First Edition

ALL RIGHTS RESERVED.

TheSocietyofJacob.com

"I wonder how you gonna save your soul?" - AMFP

To

Michelle

Stay focused on the
Most High. - Ant

TABLE OF CONTENTS

Read this first

This book is an effort to uplift a people that has been economically and spiritually destroyed. This task is complicated by the wide spread denial and confusion that exists within this same community.

What is the meaning of Identity Reset? The following statement sums up the issue that we are dealing with:

There is no greater destruction that can come upon a people than to lose their identity.

To destroy something means to change its form, function, or definition. Using the above statement as a gauge, we have to accept the unfortunate conclusion that the black community is destroyed. Why? Because we are not operating from a clear collective identity. Instead we have submitted ourselves to the definitions provided by the historical enemies of our people. The above highlighted statement also gives the uncomplicated explanation of why the black community is destroyed and what we can do about it.

Until we regain a collective and consistent identity, we will continue to be a destroyed people and remain as spiritual captives in the lands where our ancestors were physically enslaved.

Our community remains powerless because we are not operating from the truth. The truth is that we are still in the process of waking up from centuries of brutal enslavement and the complete dismantling of our knowledge of ourselves, our heritage and the world around us.

Any group of people that does not have a clearly defined identity will automatically become the spiritual and economic slaves of whoever they let define their identity for them.

The good news is that we have all the resources that are needed to regain our individual and collective power. These tools, however, must be properly understood and defined. They must then be properly redirected in order to solve our unique problems. This book gives the blueprint to accomplish this task.

Is there a difference between black wealth and white wealth?

We are going to unequivocally show you that if you think that there is no difference, you have been brainwashed. This brainwashing is the reason for the continued wealth and income gap that exists in the world. Undoing this brainwashing is the key to unlocking the massive wealth that is contained within the black community. This book is going to show you exactly how to do it.

The current situation

We live in a world that is dominated by a small white minority. The white race as a whole makes up roughly only 10% of the world's population but is still able to physically and spiritually dominate the world. Through violence and deception, this small minority has been able to force their definitions and standards onto the majority population of the world. The deception is so thorough that most people do not even realize that what they call information, education, and entertainment is really just an indoctrination into the definitions and standards created to benefit this small minority group.

The description of every subject that is taught in schools and universities around the world should really have the term "white" put in front of them. More accurate labels for these subjects would be white science, white psychology, white economics, white politics, white business, white history, and white religion. Because this distinction is not made, the masses of people are tricked into believing that the definitions and standards set by the white community are universal.

There is a vast difference between the definitions created by the white supremacy system and reality. Most of these definitions can easily be proven to be false, but it seems that the world is still under the spell of the 500 year deception created by the system of white supremacy.

What this deception does to the 90% majority in the world is to create spiritually dead people who can be easily manipulated through false information and emotions.

The solution

Money, luxury, and the trappings of wealth are useless to a spiritually dead people just as they are useless to a physical slave. Material things can offer temporary relief but they do not solve the underlying problem. Money and status gained under a vague identity and false definitions will eventually lead to physical and spiritual corruption. We see this over and over again in our community.

The future of black wealth therefore hinges on us returning to a consistent identity and correct definitions. A collective consistent identity tied to a consistent belief system is the only way to effectively deal with the unique problems that have been thrust onto our community by colonization, slavery, and economic oppression.

2

An inconsistent identity eventually translates into economic problems, personal relationship problems, family problems, social problems, physical health problems, and mental health problems. How you identify yourself and what you identify with ultimately determines your quality of life.

Confusion and stress

Stress is the real cause of the problems that we face as a community. The white supremacy system causes unnatural stress not only on our community, but on the entire planet. A consistent identity eliminates confusion because it leads to predictable action. Predictability combats confusion and stress. Predictable action is not possible under a confused identity.

Some of the many things that we are confused about include: who we are, what to do, how to deal with each other, how to deal with other cultures, how to be healthy, how to organize, how to protect ourselves, how to be happy, how to obtain and pass on wealth and resources to the next generations.

If you ask the average person of color where they came from, they have no clue. If you ask them how they identify themselves, you will get dozens of different answers even among people in the same family. Most likely you will get a vague reference to Africa, or maybe they will say they are a "child of God", many will say it doesn't matter because they don't see color, and some will say it doesn't matter because "we are all in this together now".

The wrong focus

There is no way that you can say that you love all people if you have no real love for yourself or your own people. This is the major problem that people who do not have a clear identity face when they claim that they "love everybody". When you have no clear identity rules, you develop an inverse relationship between loving other cultures and hating yourself and your own. In order to be accepted by the oppressors of our people, we have developed the same disdain for our own people that other cultures have. There is truly no way to love anyone else until you love yourself and your own.

In our community, we have people in the same immediate families who don't share the same ideas about spirituality, God, religion, or the same basic worldview. Most of us don't even have the same understanding of our own recent family and cultural history.

Because we have no real identity, we have developed inconsistent and ineffective ways of dealing with the mental, spiritual, and physical attacks that are still being carried out on an institutional level against our community.

This identity confusion can be found in black and brown people from all walks of life; from business and political leaders, millionaire celebrities, religious leaders, highly educated scholars, down to the average person on the street.

We know that this is not by accident. The former slaves of the European powers are still being mentally and spiritually dominated in the places of their ancestors' physical captivity. They are still being mis-educated and misled about their true place in history. Many of us are so deep in denial that we think that none of this even matters. But we are forced back into reality when we see the devastating reoccurring problems that show up in our communities on a daily basis.

The only way to create unity and restore our people is under a consistent belief system that is based on the truth.

The problem solved in the book

This book deals with a series of unique dilemmas that affect so-called people of color, but the question we are dealing with is universal: <u>How do you find prosperity without falling victim to the corrupt state of the world in which we live?</u>

To answer this question we are going to deal with multiple crises that are unique to our community:

(1) Power and wealth crisis, (2) Identity crisis, (3) Definitions and rules crisis, (4) Time and energy crisis, (5) Unity and harmony crisis, (6) Truth and justice crisis.

These crises present a series of dilemmas that we need to solve in order to eliminate each crisis. Each chapter of the book will deal with solving a dilemma related to one of these crises.

Power and wealth crisis

What is power? Power is the ability to resist unwanted circumstances – to resist evil. This kind of power translates into living a stress free lifestyle. This is the definition of wealth that we are using in this book.

With this definition, wealth is not dependent on your circumstances. It is only dependent on how you emotionally deal with the circumstances that come your way; whether or not you let circumstances destroy you through stress.

If having money and material things adds to your stress, or forces you into evil or unjust schemes, it cannot be considered wealth. The key word here is force. If in order to live like you want, you are forced into an unnatural identity, you are not wealthy, you are a slave. Unless you are using clear identity definitions and boundaries, there is no way to tell the difference between slavery and freedom.

Identity crisis

It does not matter how much money you make or what social status you are able to attain, if you have an unnatural or inconsistent identity you will not be able to live a stress free lifestyle. You will eventually bring stress to yourself or inflict stress on other people. Inflicting stress on other people is the definition of evil.

A consistent identity means that temporary physical circumstances do not change who you are. It means that you do not let your physical circumstances dictate your mental state. Under this definition, the powerful, wealthy person is the one who is in charge of his own mental state. This mental state is dictated by the rules of your identity.

Even under the worse physical circumstances, when you have clear identity rules, you can still manifest power. You can still resist the negative mental effects that come along with a negative physical environment.

Definitions and rules crisis

When you do not have a clear identity, you cannot clearly define anything else. Without a self defined identity, you are forced to define yourself in relation to other people and things that you come into contact with. This means that you are being overly controlled by outside influences. These influences may or may not have your best interest at heart.

Truly spiritual people are the ones who can accurately define things and what things mean. Clear definitions mean that meanings are consistent and do not cause contradictions and confusion.

Whoever controls your definitions has rulership over you.

Time and energy crisis

All wealth is manifested through human energy. Definitions are needed in order to control human energy. Directing and redirecting human energy is how people gain power over others. This is done by controlling information and what things mean.

Because of the enormous potential contained in human energy and the fact that the amount of energy we can manifest is constrained by the undefined factor of time, you should consider your personal energy to be the most valuable commodity on the face of the earth.

The only real commodity that can be "spent" in the human experience is time. This is the only real economy on earth. How you use and direct your energy is what is in question. The consequences that result from how you use your energy is the real scorecard that we are dealing with when we talk about wealth.

The ability to direct your personal energy as you see fit is the definition of freedom. But to understand freedom you must understand the natural boundaries that define humanity. The boundaries that you live by are what define your identity. Keep in mind that these are mental, not physical concepts.

Harmony and unity crisis

Part of your personal renewal has to deal with answering the question: How do we correct the broken state of our community?

A community of individuals who face the same common threats needs to follow a common set of rules in order to defend itself against the unique threats that it faces. It must unify its efforts in order to prevent individual and collective energy loss. Energy loss equates to the loss of wealth. Unity and harmony can only be achieved through shared definitions and rules.

You must come to terms with the fact that there is no way to individually escape the low spiritual state of your own people. Money can't do it. Status can't do it. Only unified thought and action can do it.

Our community seems lost in this world because we are not operating from common principles that can keep order within our community. We are not standing on any sound doctrine that can provide unified wisdom and guidance in all areas of our lives. As a result, we are following all kinds of different foreign philosophies that leave us disorganized, confused, and powerless.

No one person has the energy to deal with the concentrated energy of an organized structure. The only thing that can effectively resist organized structures is another organized structure.

A lack of clear identity makes collective structure and order impossible. This unstructured state creates confusion and stress throughout our entire community.

Because we do not have clear identity boundaries as a community, instead of joining together, we allow our individual energy to be redirected and used in economic schemes that take power from our people.

Instead of combining our own energy together, many of us believe that the way out is to join forces with oppressive schemes. By joining with these oppressive schemes, we help transfer energy out of our own community and provide even more power to the controllers of the institutions of oppression.

There is no such thing as economic, spiritual, or any other kind of unity when a people lacks a common belief system. Nothing will improve as long as we refuse to adopt a common belief system that is specific to our own people and our own situation.

Truth and justice crisis

We have tried various movements and various leaders to solve our on going problems but there is no possible way to bring about justice under vague identity definitions. When you do not have a clear belief system, you do not have an objective standard to clearly evaluate what is right and what is wrong behavior.

Because we do not have a clearly defined identity or belief system, the leaders of our community falsely equate equality with justice. Equality and justice are not the same thing. We should never try to gain an equal footing in unjust schemes. We should never spend our energy fighting for inclusion in things that are evil.

Because we are not operating from a clear belief system built on consistent definitions, instead of seeking justice, we wind up seeking to be equal with the oppressors of our people. It is justice, not equality that will bring about peace and prosperity. There can never be any real prosperity in trying to become one with an oppressor and trying to imitate his ways.

Trying to convince yourself that none of this matters is the strongest evidence of a broken and destroyed spirit. The truth always matters and justice always matters. Period.

The bottom line

> And go, get thee to them of the captivity, unto the children of thy people, and speak unto them, and tell them, **Thus saith the Lord God**; whether they will hear, or whether they will forbear. - Ezekiel 3:11

We are going to show that on the earth today, we are left with only two alternative world views in dealing with the dilemmas that we face:

1) Thus said the white man
   Or
2) Thus saith the Lord

These two world views have been proven to be completely opposite philosophies. In any situation you can only choose one philosophy or world view.

The stance of this book of course is "Thus saith the Lord".

I can already hear your questions and objections. "But how do we know Thus saith the Lord? Don't we all have free will to do whatever we want? How is this intelligent? What about science and logic? What's so wrong with the way things are? Can't a white man speak for the Lord? My God says we are the same and to love everybody. Who are you to say these things? I got my own personal relationship with God, etc, etc, etc."

Some of these objections may be legitimate but many of the questions and objections that will pop into your head are the direct result of your denial of the truth.

In order to deprogram yourself and renew your mind you are going to have to admit that you have been the target of mental and spiritual manipulation. Your community is unique because it has lost its identity which means that it does not have a value system that can effectively defend itself against this kind of manipulation.

As long as we are following thus said the white man, we will have no wealth or power, no identity, no accurate definitions and rules, little control over our own time and energy, no harmony and unity, and no peace or justice.

The bottom line is that we have been made to blindly follow thus said the white man, and are in total rebellion against Thus saith the Lord.

How do we know Thus saith the Lord?

> **Study to shew thyself approved unto God**, a workman that needeth not to be ashamed, **rightly dividing the word of truth**. - 2 Timothy 2:15

We have to study and rightly divide things into two basic categories, truth and untruth.

Opening exercise

When you finish this introduction you should turn to the Identity Survey in the Appendix. These questions show the nature of the identity problem that has a hold on our community. These questions help you see for yourself that most of us are using inconsistent definitions that create more stress than they solve.

Many of the beliefs that we hold are just a result of us trusting someone else's opinion without any logical proof. This book does not ask you to do that. You should take what you learn here and go investigate for yourself.

Group exercise

Have you ever discussed these types of questions at length with your loved ones? Is it even possible to discuss these things without causing confusion, division, and hostility? How can you predict your loved ones' responses to various life situations without knowing their responses to these types of questions?

You will probably find out that you and those closest to you will give very different answers to these questions. This situation highlights the problem that this book attempts to solve.

You were not put on this earth as an individual. You belong to a nation. Today we mistakenly lump ourselves into a bunch of fictitious nationalities that were created to obscure history and keep us enslaved. Because of this we are unable to rightly divide truth from falsehood.

Re-educating ourselves is the first step in resetting our identity and truly regaining our freedom. We must humble ourselves to the truth that we have been purposely mis-educated and be willing to reexamine history with an open mind.

Arguments and counter arguments

We must evaluate things rationally and avoid becoming overly emotional. Emotionalism clouds good judgment and is actually the chief weapon that is being used against us. We must evaluate arguments and counter arguments in a logical fashion until we arrive at the truth.

To make the analysis easier, whenever you may "feel" that you disagree with the logic of something that you read in this book, ask yourself one or two simple questions:

1. Does what I'm feeling advance the cause of MY people or not?
2. Does the point being made create justice for MY people?
3. Have I investigated all sides of this issue?

It's just that simple. It doesn't take endless debate to figure this out. In the end you must study to show yourself approved not by man but by the Creator.

Take away from this chapter:

1. So-called people of color are being ruled by false definitions including the definition of who we are.

2. We must put everything up to scrutiny to prove if it is true or false.

3. To gain our freedom, we must recognize the truth.

My people are destroyed for lack of knowledge: because **thou hast rejected knowledge**, I will also reject thee, that thou shalt be no priest to me: seeing thou hast forgotten the law of thy God, I will also forget thy children. - Hosea 4:6

1 Nationhood Reset

The unity dilemma

> **Prove all things**; hold fast that which is good. Abstain from
> all appearance of evil. - 1 Thessalonians 5:21-22

1. What is nationality?
2. What is the true nationality of people of color?
3. How do you gain power under your true nationality?
4. What are the accurate indicators of success and progress under
   your true nationality?

Nationhood and nationality are the chief instruments of global wealth
and power. Your nationality ultimately adds to or subtracts from your
ability to manifest personal wealth and personal power.

Since slavery and colonization, so-called people of color have struggled
to define who we really are and what nation we actually belong to. In
our attempt to reclaim dignity for ourselves we have tried on various
labels and philosophies. None of these labels and philosophies has
been able to provide a real explanation or real solutions to the unique
problems that plague our community.

African, African American, Negro, West Indian, Hispanic, Latino,
Nubian, Moor, Muslim, Christian; we have been all these things at one
time or another. History has proven, however, that identifying with
these labels does not provide us with a way out of our cultural
confusion. None of these philosophies has been able to provide a way
out of our spiritual captivity under the historical enemies of our people.
This is because none of these labels can provide a useful explanation of
our history in relation to our current condition.

All of these labels and philosophies must be held accountable for the
low economic and spiritual state of our people. This is the only way to
get to the bottom of our inability to create unified effort in solving our
own ongoing problems.

We are at the point where we must test all philosophies and institutions
to see if they are helping or hurting our community; if they are based
on the truth, or just remnants of the brainwashing that we received
from the enemy of our people through slavery.

Many of us refuse to understand that there is another people who is opposed to our progress whether they or the other people admit it to themselves or not. The misguided among us truly believe that equality is the answer and that we are just "all in this together".

When you ask people who are under this kind of denial how it is that our people are still suffering at the bottom, they most likely reply with something like: "We bring it on ourselves"or "we need to vote more" or "we need more jobs" or "it's the Republicans".

Yes we do bring it on ourselves but it is our lack of understanding of identity that has caused us to become our own worst enemy.

We have to return to a nationality that provides us with clear definitions, clear rules, and predictable outcomes. We cannot make ANY progress under the colonial labels, political titles, and corporate fictions by which we are currently identifying ourselves.

We have to teach the next generations the importance of nationality because recognizing our true nationality is the only way to restore good order, peace, and prosperity; not only for ourselves, but for the entire world.

Nationality is not where you were born

The first thing that you must do to truly understand and accept the truth is to realize that the current notion of nationhood is an invention of the white supremacy system. The government that is ruling over you is not a nationality.

Because of colonialism, almost anywhere that you go in the world, there are at least two or more nations residing on the same land under the same government. This is where the confusion starts. Although they may be under the control of the same government and residing on the same land, these are still separate nations that have different agendas, needs, goals, and desires.

Your real nationality is determined by genetics, not geographic locations. In most parts of the world, governments are nothing more than corporate fictions that are a part of a global corporate empire that is controlled by just a few families. At this point, everything is controlled under these corporate titles, even the governments themselves. The corporate identities that we are using, in effect, make us the property of these controlling families.

The Bible shows the original genetic nationality groupings of all of mankind. The origin of every person on earth can be traced back to the original 18 bloodline nationalities of the Bible.

There is really no such nationality as African American, West Indian, Dominican, Puerto Rican, Brazilian and the other names that people of color are called today. These names are colonial labels and corporate fictions, not true identities. The problem with these colonial labels is that they create a confused identity that leads to the self destructive behavior patterns that we see in our community today.

One of the main deception tactics of white supremacy is to rename groups of people after the government of the lands that the white supremacists have stolen. Before this tactic came into being, land was always named after an actual genetic bloodline. By reversing this common sense practice, white supremacy has been able to confuse the identities of its victims. It has also been able to disguise the true origins of white people. Diversity and the "melting pot" are promoted as feel good ideas but they really are a part of a divide and conquer strategy.

As the victims are busy trying to "melt in", they lose the ability to organize any defense against the organized, systematic attack that is launched by those who act along family bloodline preference.

Individual versus the group

There can be no group without the individual and no individual without the group.

The diagram below shows that identity is a trade off between the individual and the group.

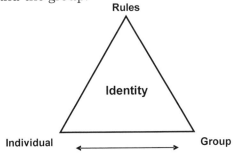

The diagram also shows that identity has boundaries. Finally, it shows that identity stems from rules and points back to rules in order to maintain structure. These rules are the definitions that define who you are.

Wealth and nationhood

All wealth involves the relationship between the individual and a group. There is no such thing as individual wealth. All wealth is a function of how society is arranged and what society deems to be important.

Make no mistake, no matter how much money or power or material resources that you are able to gain within the white supremacy system, you are still a slave as long as you are confused about who you are and your true nationality.

If you think that we are "all in this together" or "we are all just Americans" or "everybody should just do their own thing" or "we just need to work harder", you are still a spiritual captive of your colonial masters.

Nothing that you do while you are under this kind of mindset can create real progress for you or your community. All of your so-called hard work and industrious effort will most likely end up benefiting the offspring and assigned beneficiaries of the men who set up the white supremacy system.

Just look at the track record of our black capitalists, entertainers, athletes, politicians, and preachers. You can add hustlers, drug dealers, and criminals to this list also. White supremacy turns money, power, and influence over to these individuals, yet more often than not, these talented but misguided people are usually of no use to their community as a whole, and many of them wind up destitute themselves even though they may have earned hundreds of millions of dollars over the course of a career.

Why?

Because they do not understand that all economics is based on bloodline survival. Economics is naturally organized around bloodline, not white supremacy created labels. In the end, it is brethren looking out for brethren.

So you can call yourself an American or anything else that they allow you to, but when it comes down to where you focus your energy and resources, any sane individual is going to deal with his blood first. That's the way it is and that's the way it was created by God from the beginning.

Because our so-called powerful people of color do not recognize who their brethren actually are and what bloodline that they belong to, they are easy prey for those who understand how the system actually works.

The House of Jacob

"Afro" in front of a name such as in Afro American, Afro Caribbean, or Afro Latino or Afro Hispanic really denotes a distinct bloodline nationality. The true bloodline nationality of these people is <u>Israelite</u>. They make up the true tribes of Israel. Israel was a flesh and blood man named Jacob, his bloodline descendants are Israelites and they are NOT the Caucasians that call themselves "Jewish".

> And he said, **Thy name shall be called no more Jacob, but Israel**: for as a prince hast thou power with God and with men, and hast prevailed. - Genesis 32:28

The overwhelming evidence shows that people of color are the Biblical Israelites by bloodline nationality. In the coming chapters, we are going to prove that the Biblical description of the Israelites (The House of Jacob) undoubtedly links perfectly to the history, archaeology, physical appearance, character, and condition of people of color. This is a real nationality that does not change by your physical location, the government that controls you, the customs you follow, or the language that you speak.

Many people who read and preach the Bible, draw parallels between the struggles of people of color and the Israelites of the Bible because the comparisons are unavoidable. The parallels between the people of the Bible and people of color are not a coincidence; the Bible points to the real history of a real people.

History shows that the people of the Bible are not by any stretch of the imagination the Caucasians who call themselves Jewish.

The people in the State of Israel today are not the Biblical Israelites. There is not one shred of evidence that links the Caucasians that call themselves "Jewish" to the Biblical Israelites. Those who call themselves "Jewish" are Caucasians who were converted into a religion called Judaism that is based on the customs of the Israelites, but they are not the Israelites. There is really no disputing this fact at this point.

White supremacy propaganda has created this deception and it has been accepted across the earth but there is no logical evidence to

15

support the claim that Caucasians could be the bloodline of Israel. Again Israel was a man (Jacob), not a place. We are going to show that any claim that Caucasians are Israelites is both physically and logically impossible.

History does show that the people who were taken into slavery in Africa as well as the ones who were conquered to create the Americas and Caribbean Islands are actually the scattered Biblical Israelite nation. This nation of people is dispersed throughout the world but through multiple wars and captivities had become concentrated in West Africa and the Americas.

As the white supremacy system finally took over most of the world, the Israelites were sought out and destroyed as a people through colonization and slavery. Ironically, much of this destruction has been carried out in part by the Caucasians who have now assumed the identity of Israel.

The House of Jacob versus the House of Esau

> And the Lord said unto her, **Two nations are in thy womb, and two manner of people shall be separated from thy bowels**; and the one people shall be stronger than the other people; and **the elder shall serve the younger**.
> - Genesis 25:23

As we have stated, people of color who are now located in the Americas and the Caribbean have a prehistory and an identity that predates Africa, the Americas, or the Caribbean. It is also true that the Caucasians that carried out slavery and colonialism have a prehistory that predates Europe.

Focusing on this prehistory is how you will gain the understanding of the fundamental nature of what is happening on the earth today. This fundamental nature is an ancient spiritual war that has gone on since Biblical times.

The prehistory shows that Western slavery and colonization involved two ancient nations. The Transatlantic Slave Trade and colonization of the Americas was carried out by the House of Esau against the House of Jacob. What does this mean?

1. The so-called Negros, Afro Natives, and Latinos of North America, South America and the Caribbean are actually one race of people, Israelites; The House of Jacob. These are the descendants of the people who actually wrote the Bible.

2. The true historical name of the Caucasian race that created the white supremacy system is Edomites; The House of Esau.

These two national identities are traceable from Biblical times to today. The Bible is the key historical record that you need in order to understand this history. Contrary to what most of us have been taught to believe about the Bible, it is not a white mans religious book, it also is not a fairytale book, and it definitely is not our slave masters' book; what it really is, is the national records of the Israelite nation.

The Bible shows us that the House of Jacob is the spiritual system that will ultimately destroy the system of white supremacy.

If you have never heard all of this before it probably sounds totally ridiculous to you. But the brainwashing involved in racism is about more than discriminating against certain people. It is also about obscuring the history of all the races and about keeping all people from remembering the historical truths about their identity. This confusion is why racism has been so difficult to understand and root out.

The white supremacy system has used deceptive propaganda in an attempt to repurpose the Bible for its own benefit, but the Scriptures tell the real story. White supremacy has tried to turn the Bible into a fairytale book that can be interpreted different ways by different people. This is not true. We are going to show you that when you read the scriptures with the understanding of whose history is being documented, there is no room for interpretations of words that you can read plainly for yourself.

This missing historical information is the link that allows us to understand the whole story behind what is really going on in the world today.

Competing kingdoms

Nationhood is about rulership. Rulership is about who sets the definitions. The definitions that you use set the rules.

> When the righteous are in authority, the people rejoice: but **when the wicked beareth rule, the people mourn.**
> - Proverbs 29:2

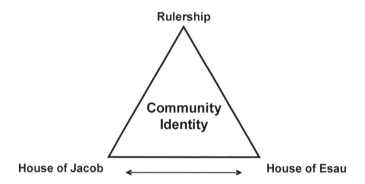

For Esau is the end of the world, and Jacob is the beginning of it that followeth. - 2 Esdras 6:9

The diagram shows the two groups that we need to be concerned with in dealing with the future of the wealth problem. The House of Jacob and The House of Esau are the two basic rivals that you must consider in order to understand the true nature of race and our current reality.

The House of Jacob and the House of Esau are two opposite spiritual philosophies with very different definitions. The definitions of the House of Jacob are found in the Bible. The House of Esau makes up its own definitions through national constitutions and organizations like the United Nations.

The major difference is that the rules of the House of Esau change almost daily. They are totally dependent on the whims of the human mind and human emotions.

The House of Jacob's rules do not change and have not changed since the beginning of time. Why? Because the House of Jacob is ruled by Thus saith the Lord. Any system that claims to be about truth and justice that changes everyday cannot be what it says it is. It cannot produce stability. The truth does not change.

The law of the Lord is perfect, converting the soul: the testimony of the Lord is sure, making wise the simple.
- Psalm 19:7

As much as religions have tried to make it so, unlike the laws of the House of Esau, the Bible cannot be amended and cannot be changed. The truth requires no amendments.

Each kingdom has its own systems. Each has a:

- System of justice
- System of education
- System of government
- System of economics
- System of social order
- System of warfare
- System of science
- System of health

A good tree cannot bring forth evil fruit, **neither can a corrupt tree bring forth good fruit.** – Mathew 7:18

When we look at the inner workings of each system you will find that The House of Jacob is an all around superior system to the injustice of the white supremacy system that was created by the House of Esau.

How this identity solves our problems

Keep therefore and do them; for this is your wisdom and your understanding in the sight **of the nations, which shall hear all these statutes, and say, Surely this great nation is a wise and understanding people.** - Deuteronomy 4:6

We have tried this philosophy or that philosophy, this thing or that thing, this leader or that leader. We have tried voting, higher education, working along side white folks, fighting wars for white folks, spending money with every other culture, and adopting the various religious practices and customs of other people, but none of these things have seemed to change the position of the black community as a whole.

Before we go deeper into the identity issue we should look at some background information to understand the practical importance of focusing on the competing kingdoms.

The theories and strategies of our great leaders must be amended based on what we have found out from their work. That is how we honor them.

History through another lens

Throughout the entire 20th century various black leaders tried to rectify the ills and injustices that are built into the white supremacy system.

In the United States, arguably the two greatest political and economic movements of the last century were The Garvey Movement of the early 1900s and The Civil Rights Movement of the 1950s and 1960s.

These movements were effective to a point, but neither really was able to accomplish the task of freeing our people from economic and spiritual captivity under the enemies of our people. In many ways our community is even worse off spiritually than we were at the start of these movements.

Looking back at these movements through the lens of our true identity we can see that uniting as Israelites under the House of Jacob would have brought these two justice movements into total agreement. This identity is the missing link that returns our historical value system and our verifiable place in history that predates the white supremacy system.

We are going to show you how this is absolutely the antidote to defeating the white supremacy system.

The Garvey Movement

The Garvey Movement's approach to dealing with economic injustice was to launch an economic unity campaign among people of color around the world. His organization was called the United Negro Improvement Association (UNIA). When black people were just one generation out of slavery, Garvey promoted separate economic development among black and latino people across the earth. Garvey's motto was "Africa for Africans".

In the early 1900s, at the height of his movement, Garvey had created black funded and operated businesses that culminated in a shipping line that attempted to economically connect people of color in North America, South America, the Caribbean, and West Africa.

Garvey issued stock throughout the black and latino community worldwide. The proceeds from this stock sale were used to fund his Black Star shipping line. At its height, the Garvey organization had over 2 million members and stockholders.

But as the movement gained in popularity, the U.S. Justice Department and FBI under J. Edgar Hoover attacked and infiltrated the UNIA. Eventually Garvey was framed by the FBI for an alleged $25 mail fraud. For this minor offense, Garvey was sentenced to 5 years in prison in 1922.

Garvey served two years of his sentence and then was deported to his native country, Jamaica. The United States then personally bankrupted him and his organization and blacklisted anyone who continued to claim membership in the UNIA. In 1940, Garvey died broken and penniless having never set foot in Africa.

The Garvey organization was over in the 1920s but his movement spawned other Black Nationalist and Black Power organizations including the Nation of Islam and the Black Panthers.

When you look back at The Garvey Movement you see that it should have been applauded by the so-called freedom loving United States government and its "free market" system. The Garvey Movement was a genuine and dignified attempt by the victims of slavery to fix the doomed economic system of white supremacy for both black and white people. Within a few years after Garvey was shut down by the U.S. government, the United States went into "the Great Depression" and has been in a downward boom and bust economic spiral ever since.

Garvey and the people involved in his movement were simply trying to provide the restitution and justice that the white supremacy system has proven to be incapable of producing. Why was Garvey attacked by the United States government? What was unjust or illegal about what Garvey and his followers were doing?

Even more shameful is the fact that many of the black men who participated in the Garvey Movement were war veterans returning from World War I where they were told they were fighting to keep the world safe for freedom, democracy, and the capitalist way of life; none of which they had ever experienced or would ever experience under the wicked nature of the white supremacy system.

Was the injustice inflicted on the Garvey movement ever righted? How would the wealth landscape look across the globe had the United States government not attacked the Garvey movement? Is this a part of the "free market system" that we are supposed to strive to make work for us?

We are going through this as a brief reminder to show that this type of ridiculous hypocrisy and injustice is how the white supremacy system attempts to create an advantage for its preferred beneficiaries even to this day. Many of us seem to forget these important facts as we try to figure out what to do about the wealth problem that exists today.

This highlights the spiritual nature of the economic war. Garvey was an Israelite whether he knew it or not. The people who were attacking him were Edomites whether they knew it or not. This was a part of a physical and spiritual war between the House of Jacob and the House of Esau.

The Civil Rights Movement

The Civil Rights Movement actually got its start around the time of the Garvey Movement. It was developed as a competing philosophical approach to that of the Garvey movement.

The National Association for the Advancement of Colored People (NAACP) was the leading civil rights organization involved in the Civil Rights Movement.

What many people do not realize is that the NAACP was actually founded, funded, and headed by members of the Jewish community. In fact, the NAACP did not have a black president until 1975, some 60 years after its founding.

The NAACP in many ways seems to have been founded to directly oppose the economic and educational ideology of Booker T. Washington who was Garvey's greatest inspiration.

Black scholars and leaders like W.E.B. Dubois and A. Phillip Randolph were major critics of first Washington and later Garvey and his call for separate economic development for people of color with a focus on Africa.

The NAACP and The Civil Rights Movement that it spawned was to focus on providing safety and security for people of color by acquiring full inclusion into the promised "American way of life"; the American Dream.

Inclusion and integration was seen as the answer to the lynching, beatings, lack of economic opportunities, and the segregated public and private institutions in the Southern United States. The culmination of these rights was to be the Voting Rights Act of 1964 and the desegregation of schools, public accommodations, and private businesses.

White immigration

It should be noted that in between The Garvey Movement and the height of the Civil Rights Movement more than 12 million white European immigrants were admitted into the United States as new citizens.

White immigration created an additional white population that was roughly equivalent to half of the entire black population of the United States today. This eventhough the black population has been expanding in the United States for at least 400 years.

Because of this immigration wave and the white supremacy propaganda associated with it, it is easy to overlook the fact that 90% of the black population has been in the Americas longer than 90% of the white population.

After one or two generations these new white immigrants took on the full arrogance of the American superiority narrative, eventhough they had nothing to do with the founding or building of America. Many even count themselves as "the greatest generation" of Americans.

The secret of non violence

As the Civil Rights Movement moved forward into the 1950's and 60's, it produced many brave heroes and leaders. But by far the most prominent leader was Dr. Martin Luther King, Jr. In the 1960s, his leadership, speeches, marches, and demonstrations earned Dr. King the Nobel Peace Prize and worldwide respect and acclaim.

Not only did he become the most recognized leader of civil rights but Dr. King became probably the greatest moral leader of the last millennium, certainly in the history of America. His non-violent approach confounded those who called for physical confrontation against the brutality of the white supremacy system.

Many of the Black Power organizations that came out of the Garvey Movement took issue with the non violent approach promoted by Dr. King.

Logically, it seemed that the only way to protect the community from the violent warlike white supremacy system was to separate from it or go to physical war with it.

As many Black Power organizations have found out, white supremacy welcomes violence because it thrives off violence. It is operating over the entire globe using violence and deception as its chief methods.

Despite the criticisms and the horrific violence committed against he and his fellow freedom fighters, Dr. King never waivered from his nonviolent approach.

Gradually the non-violent approach seemed to do something different to the white supremacy system that has historically thrived on violence, murder, war, and all other types of inhumane behavior.

By resisting it with a high moral standard, Dr. King and his fellow freedom fighters had finally inflicted some level of shame on the white supremacy system.

Technology also played a part in the success of the non violent approach. Television, airplanes, and other technological advances had come into existence since the days of Marcus Garvey. These advances connected people to each other and current events more quickly.

Because of this new connectivity, Dr. King was able to show the entire world the hypocrisy of the so-called American Dream. In case they didn't already know, the non violent movement also showed white people in America what their beloved prideful and self righteous country is really about.

In 1968, Dr. King the nonviolent practitioner, who spoke of nothing but love, peace, and brotherhood of all people, was finally murdered by the violent system of white supremacy; but not before he helped bring about sweeping civil changes across the United States which in fact changed the entire world.

It is not by chance that at the time that he was murdered, Dr. King had turned his attack to the economic injustice that is built into the white supremacy capitalism system.

In his last speech, given the day before he was gunned down, Dr. King called for a boycott of Coca Cola and Wonder Bread. He also called for black people to remove their money from white banks and white insurance companies. This coupled with the fact that he was just about to launch a program called he Poor Peoples Campaign should show the seriousness about which Dr. King was set to attack white supremacy concerning the role that economic injustice plays in the low condition of not only black people, but the entire world.

Eventhough FBI Director J. Edgar Hoover and the United States government did their best to find something to pin on Dr. King; they were unable to find a way to criminalize his message like they did with Garvey. This time the white supremacy system could do nothing but turn to its original tried and true tactic, murder.

Accurate indicators and measuring progress

The chief weapon of the House of Esau is the concept of white supremacy. Because it is just a concept, white supremacy can be hard to define which makes it an elusive target to fight against.

Understanding the truth behind the Biblical nationalities unmasks the deception of white supremacy, but we still need some objective measure in order to gauge our progress in defeating white supremacy and creating justice.

Dr. King gave us such a measure.

Exactly one year to the day that he was murdered, Dr. King profoundly laid out the major tool that we need to use in order to measure our progress under our true nationality.

Lost in the romanticism and the nostalgia of Dr. King's "I have a dream" speech is the fact that the Dream speech was not the reason that he became a marked man.

Dr. King gave the Dream speech in 1963 in an effort to show a vision of what a just world could be like. But four years later in 1967 he gave a very different speech entitled "Beyond Vietnam" in which he expressed that he felt that he had a moral obligation to tell the truth about the evil that his country also commits around the globe.

Beyond Vietnam was one of Dr. King's most moving and poignant speeches, and from that day forward the analysis that he laid out should have been the marching orders for people of color and anyone else who is serious about justice.

In Beyond Vietnam, Dr. King perfectly and unapologetically foretold the bleek future of the white supremacy system. Not only did he call for blacks not to serve in the military, he called for clergy to give up their exemptions and allow themselves to be jailed rather than serve in the war.

Quoted below is the part of the speech where he lays out the main measuring stick of justice and success of the movement:

"We must rapidly begin the shift from a "thing-oriented" society to a "person-oriented" society. When machines and computers, profit motives and property rights are considered more important than people, the giant triplets of racism, materialism, and militarism are incapable of being conquered."

Dr. King puts forth that the major components of the opposition facing people of color, the giant triplets of:

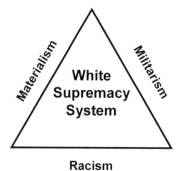

1. **Racism**
2. **Materialism**
3. **Militarism**

This is a devastatingly accurate description of the working components of the white supremacy system. If any of these components is still operating we know that the system has not been defeated.

More importantly we know that any strategy that coincides with or complements these components is a false strategy. Any person or institution that promotes one of these strategies is knowingly or unknowingly working in support of white supremacy. These are the objective measures that we must use in order to evaluate our direction, strategies, and leadership.

Dr. King then lays out in no uncertain terms what is at stake for the people of the world under the white supremacy system:

"A nation that continues year after year to spend more money on military defense than on programs of social uplift is approaching spiritual death."

"History is cluttered with the wreckage of nations and individuals that pursued this self-defeating path of hate."

The dismal results of an undefined identity

After Dr. King's death the Poor Peoples Campaign collapsed. As a result of the Civil Rights Movement, many more black people did enter into politics. Black people were able to get a lot better government jobs and some of us are now able to attend majority white schools.

These social changes sound great on the surface but it seems somehow in the mist of all of this "progress", we have fallen under the spell of the political and economic corruption of the white supremacy system. In our attempts to assimilate and integrate we have become practicing white supremacists ourselves.

The jails are full of our young men and have become the new Jim Crow system; we have the highest unemployment and drop out rates; income inequality is widening; our family structures are in disarray. Our politicians are many times just as corrupt and ineffective as white politicians.

The split between the Black Power separation ideology and the Civil Rights assimilation ideology still continues to this day. The split became even more complicated by the introduction of Islam into the black community by the Nation of Islam. Now not only do you have two political ideologies but we have two or more spiritual approaches within the same community—often within the same family. This has all led to one thing, confusion.

We have formed identities that do not create the social responsibility to each other that is absolutely necessary in order to combat the giant triplets.

Out of the two great movements of the 20th Century, former Black people, Negros, and Colored people settled on "African American". It seems that we got the "African" from the Garvey vision of returning to control Africa and the "American" from the Civil Rights notion of full inclusion in America.

We even got an "African American" President of the United States.

To show how ironic all of this is; the "black" President can claim this black identity eventhough he shares little racial, cultural, or philosophical background with the average black man in America. He is considered black only by virtue of his skin tone and mannerisms that he has learned by contact with the black community in Chicago. Even more ironic is, unlike most black men in America, the black President is actually an "African American", since one of his parents was actually an African and the other was a white American.

What is not ironic is that with all of this confusion, we still have many of the same problems that we had when Dr. King, a non elected leader was making headway against the system. What happened?

Are we focused on the giant triplets?

The power to resist

Deploying the giant triplets is the basic strategy of the white supremacy system. The overall strategy involves using deception and violence to aid in the ultimate goal of theft and control. The whole white supremacy economic system is built on this process.

The masses of people are tricked into aiding the giant triplets by being indoctrinated into extreme individualism and competition. They confuse individualism, narcissism, and competition with personal freedom.

The only way that a few can rule the many is with the help of the many. This can only happen when people in the larger group become confused and corrupted. The purpose of the giant triplets is to create this confused situation. The process works like this:

1. People become confused as to the truth about who they are (racism).
2. People develop a corrupted value system (materialism).
3. People become afraid to resist (militarism).

People become confused, corrupted, or scared into going along with their own enslavement. Through this process, they are put into a state of spiritual possession.

Solving the white supremacy dilemma

The answer to defeating the giant triplets is to develop a belief system that guards against confusion and corruption.

Below is a chart of the giant triplets and the corresponding defense to each one.

The Triplets		**Defense**
Racism	Vs	(1) Identity
Materialism	Vs	(2) Guiding Values
Militarism	Vs	(3) Resistance

The general steps are:

1. Know who you are and the truth about your situation
2. Develop incorruptible definitions, rules, and values
3. Resist without fear (faith)

These steps seem simple enough but the difficulty is that we are dealing with abstract concepts that need to be clearly defined. A consistent identity and belief system requires a clear understanding based on accurate information.

The war against us can be summed up as follows:

Racism = Corrupt definitions
Materialism = Greed, covetousness, scarcity mindset
Militarism = Aggression and destructive emotions

Unless you are completely clear about the definitions and meanings that you are using, you could easily get trapped into believing that you are carrying out an effective strategy when you have really fallen into a trap that keeps the system going. Gaining your support through deception is the only way that the system can function.

Unified resistance can only be achieved with a proper guiding value system that is connected to a defined identity. These three solutions are linked just as the three triplets are linked.

There can be no true prosperity or peace until justice is done. Justice and injustice are also concepts that are tied to nationality.

The giant triplets of racism, materialism, and militarism are directed against a certain people and carried out by a certain people. Unless you can identify the people who are carrying out and benefiting from these actions as well as the people who are being attacked and victimized, there is no chance of bringing about justice.

Take away from this chapter:

1. Nationhood is the chief instrument of wealth and power.

2. Nationality is tied to your bloodline NOT a country or physical location.

3. Nationality has been purposely obscured by the white supremacy system as a confusion and control tactic.

4. The war against our nationality was defined by Dr. Martin Luther King as the giant triplets of racism, materialism, and militarism. Success or failure has to be measured by these three factors.

And ye shall know the truth, and **the truth shall make you free.** - John 8:32

2 Wealth and Power Reset

The classification dilemma

> Study to shew thyself approved unto God, a workman that needeth not to be ashamed, **rightly dividing the word of truth**. - 2 Timothy 2:15

1. What does it mean to be conscious?
2. How do you determine what is valuable?
3. How do you define wealth and power?
4. What are the economic formulas that lead to wealth and power?

	Assets	**Liabilities**
Real Value (physical)	**Tangible Assets** 1.	**Tangible Liabilities** 3.
+		
Perceived Value (spiritual)	**Intangible Assets** 2.	**Intangible Liabilities** 4.

= Wealth

Buy low and sell high. This simple statement describes the basic method of any sustainable business activity.

Because high and low are relative terms and can involve perception, you need to be able to clearly define what things mean in order to make sound decisions. You have to be able to rightly divide and label things in order to place a proper value on them.

To understand buy low, sell high, value, wealth creation, and power you need to understand the following formula:

Wealth = Real value + Perceived value

The chart above, along with the Wealth Formula gives you an accurate representation of the battlefield of economic and spiritual warfare. Everything and every activity can be categorized into one of the four categories on the chart. When you do this, you have an accurate way of determining true value. Wealth is nothing more than value creation.

Substance versus style

> **There is a way that seemeth right unto a man**, but the end thereof are the ways of death. - Proverbs 16:25

The reason why all of this is important is because most of us have not been taught to rightly divide things into proper categories. Also the masses of people are taught that all that matters is the tangible or physical world. This creates a warped world view.

Again the formula for wealth is:

Real value + Perceived value = Total value

We can further breakdown the analysis to state that real value and perceived value relate to substance and style.

Real value = Substance
Perceived value = Style

Substance - real value- are those things that are absolutely required for survival. Food, water, shelter, and clothing equate to these basic needs.

Real value is contained in things that have utility value, meaning they have some usefulness in overcoming the challenges of the physical world, in overcoming some physical liability.

There is little question that humans eventually need food, water, shelter, and clothing to survive. This is the only real truth or reality that is involved in the physical world. Everything else that we experience is a matter of our own thoughts and perceptions.

Style - perceived value - is where the power and wealth problem begins. Perceived value involves the imagination of human beings. Style is completely influenced and controlled by emotions. Emotions are just persistent thoughts. Thoughts all originate in the mind. So all perceived value exists only in the mind of human beings.

The dilemma of style and substance is the key to understanding wealth and power. In modern times, value, and therefore wealth, is almost completely a matter of style. Power and wealth is totally dependent on perceptions of the human mind. These perceptions produce the labels and definitions that are used by humans to regenerate the thoughts and actions that define what is valuable and who has power.

The problem is that perception is not necessarily reality. Perception only exists in the minds of people. This perception does not necessarily coincide with the way that the world is supposed to work. Man is the only creation that can attempt to change the natural use of himself and other creations. When this happens, man becomes a destructive force to himself and the earth. This is the current corrupted state of the world.

> **The foolish shall not stand in thy sight**: thou hatest all workers of iniquity. - Psalm 5:5

The false definitions that are being used by those who are in power are not based on the truth therefore the idea of value, power, and wealth are all totally corrupted. This produces unnecessary human suffering and chaos across humanity.

The wealth formula can be restated as follows:

Substance + Style = Power

When style and substance are brought together under the truth (proper definitions), lasting power is created. This balance creates lasting peace and prosperity.

Consciousness and mis-education

Consciousness is the awareness and recognition of both the tangible and intangible sides of reality. That both substance and style matter. It means that you understand the total value formula.

Many of us are baited into focusing only on either real value or perceived value. Even worse, we may be mistaking perceived value for real value. When you mix up the two you can be made to believe that something is valuable when it is in reality worthless. This is how the power and wealth game is played.

The real purpose of any proper education is to give you the tools and ability to rightly divide things into one of the four categories. To help you understand how to balance substance and style.

To say someone has been mis-educated means that they do not have the understanding to properly divide things into the right categories. This is the problem that we face when dealing with power and wealth creation.

Most of us have been purposely misled and confused into making decisions that are not in our best interest because we are confused as to how to rightly put things into their proper categories. This mis-education serves those in power because the people who are currently in power are only able to rule by attempting to change the natural use and purpose of things.

Time, purpose, labels, and value

To properly understand the value of something, you have to be able to properly identify and understand its purpose. Everything has a particular and proper purpose that it was created to fulfill. Knowing the purpose and place of things is the definition of wisdom.

> **To every thing there is a season, <u>and</u> a time to every purpose** under the heaven:

> A time to be born, and a time to die; a time to plant, and a time to pluck up that which is planted; A time to kill, and a time to heal; a time to break down, and a time to build up; A time to weep, and a time to laugh; a time to mourn, and a time to dance; A time to cast away stones, and a time to gather stones together; a time to embrace, and a time to refrain from embracing; A time to get, and a time to lose; a time to keep, and a time to cast away; A time to rend, and a time to sew; a time to keep silence, and a time to speak; A time to love, and a time to hate; a time of war, and a time of peace. - Ecclesiastics 3:1-8

Time is the main boundary in the human experience. We all have some unknown amount of time in which to live in our current physical form. This makes time the chief hurdle in any endeavor in the real and perceived value dilemma.

Our ongoing physical liabilities (hunger and thirst) are a function of time. Gain and loss can only be expressed in terms of a period of time. The question always is: How do you properly divide your time? On what should you focus your time and energy?

If everything has a time and season, then right and wrong are tied to when and where something is. This can further complicate our understanding. Not only must we identify what something is and its natural purpose, we must also understand when it should be used or discarded according to the time and its natural purpose. What we do know for sure is that everything has value according to its time and purpose. If these two definitions are not consistent, the thing becomes corrupted.

Conversely, things that have little or no value in one time period may suddenly have value at a different time. This is the function of a market. People are willing to pay money not only for currently useful things but for things that are perceived as being able to provide value in the future eventhough they may have little or no current useful value.

The subtle nature of value is why being able to rightly divide things is absolutely necessary in carrying out the basic business method of "buy low, sell high".

The social nature of value

In any wealth building pursuit, you are dealing with a series of trade offs and dilemmas that must be solved. What you trade and how you trade is a function of your concept of value.

Is gold valuable? Can you eat it? Can you use it for shelter? Can you make clothing with it? For all practical purposes, gold has little or no useful value to the average person. If you were on a deserted island by yourself, which would you rather have, twenty pounds of gold or twenty pounds of nuts and berries? Why then is gold considered to be valuable?

What we are showing here is that value creation is always a social activity. It involves perception. Once you get beyond basic survival, the value of things depends purely on human perception. Perceived value is a social not physical phenomenon.

The social nature of value requires that you identify your own value in relation to other people. It requires that you understand the motivations of other people. The purpose of understanding the motivations of other people in value creation is to understand how you can help people solve their problems and how other people can help you solve your problems. The simple formula for lasting wealth, therefore, is to successfully solve the problems of a large number of people.

The simple wealth formula is complicated by the fact that problems can be real or imagined. This goes back to the substance or style dilemma. The fact that problems can be imagined or not real means the solutions can also be imagined or not real. This fact can cause confusion regarding true value.

To deal with the illusionary characteristics of wealth, you need to be able to identify things using clear and concise definitions. To properly identify something means that you are properly dealing with it according to its natural definition, form, function, and meaning.

How you attach value and how close your assessment is to the reality of the situation determines your effectiveness and whether you gain or lose value.

Because of perceived value, total value can be heavily influenced by mental manipulation. Being able to clearly define perceived value is the key skill in overcoming this mental manipulation.

Money

Contrary to what most of us may think, money does not and can not determine wealth. Money is only an idea. Physical money is a neutral object that needs some sort of social arrangement in order to have any value. Someone has to be willing to accept your money before it can be said to have any value at all. All that money can do is facilitate a flow of human energy. That flow of human energy is really a social arrangement between two or more people. Money can store energy but only as it relates to shared ideas between people.

The more perceived value something has the more people are willing to pay for it. The less perceived value something has, the less people are willing to pay for it.

Wealth is the accumulation of things that are valuable. These valuable things are what create income.

All of this means that money has a spiritual quality that is tied into our thoughts and emotions. If we can control our thoughts and our emotions and our interactions between each other, we can create instant wealth.

Economic decisions

When you rightly divide things you are making a prediction of the likelihood that a threat or an opportunity will manifest into physical reality -- whether or not intangibles will become tangible. Most of this process takes place in our own imagination. This means that the true power in the world is spiritual, not physical. Potential power is unlimited but we must align our minds in a way that can manifest it.

Your economic decisions reflect your perceived values. Your physical choices as expressed through these economic decisions determine your quality of life. The spiritual aspect of wealth and economic warfare is mostly ignored when we try to deal with the wealth problem. The spiritual aspects of wealth contain vastly more opportunities and threats than what the capitalistic white supremacy system leads you to believe.

When intangible liabilities become a part of your basic needs-- you become weak. This is what propaganda marketing under corporate capitalism does. People are made to believe that worthless things are valuable and valuable things are worthless.

Assets strengthen you while liabilities weaken you, so you must prioritize your decision making to focus on maximizing assets and minimizing liabilities.

Power, adversaries, and boundaries

When we talk about wealth, we are really talking about the ability to overcome problems. Power is a measure of the energy that can be used to accomplish this task. This translates into the ability to overcome stress.

In the end, the wealthy person or group of people are the ones who have little or no stress.

People working together are assets to each other. People working in opposition to each other are liabilities to each other. In the struggle for wealth and power you have to be able to define your group.

You must also be able to define any opposition and properly classify this opposition as a current or potential liability. You must be able to classify your allies as current or potential assets. Then you must be able to predict the impact of your decisions on your group and the opposing group.

The number one strategy in dealing with economic and spiritual warfare is: **Do not let false authority cause stress in your life.**

> Eat thou not the bread of him that hath an evil eye, neither desire thou his dainty meats: **For as he thinketh in his heart, so is he**: Eat and drink, saith he to thee; but his heart is not with thee. - Proverbs 23:6-7

In order to recognize opposition and allies, you have to understand boundaries. You must understand and identify your allies as well as the opposing forces. It is impossible to defend yourself if you are operating under false information or artificial boundaries.

Violating natural boundaries is a recipe for destruction. The war of wealth and power is being waged by distorting perception and obscuring boundaries. We are going to prove to you that the boundaries are set by the Creator of all and can not be changed by man.

Take away from this chapter:

1. You must understand the difference between assets and liabilities.

2. You must further break down assets and liabilities into their real value and perceived value components. Real value plus perceived value equal wealth.

3. If we can control our thoughts and our emotions and our interactions between each other, we can create instant wealth.

He that trusteth in his own heart is a fool: but whoso walketh wisely, he shall be delivered. - Proverbs 28:26

3 House of Jacob Reset

The identity dilemma

He sheweth his word unto Jacob, his statutes and his judgments unto Israel. **He hath not dealt so with any nation**: and as for his judgments, they have not known them. Praise ye the Lord. - Psalms 147:19-20

1. What is the House of Jacob?
2. How do you identify the House of Jacob?
3. What is the proof of the House of Jacob?

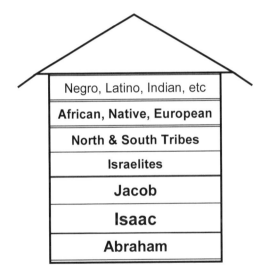

Racism is nothing more than the creation of false definitions. Identity is the most powerful defense to these false definitions.

To defeat racism we must look at the labels that we are using to define ourselves and the world around us. The false labels and false nationalities that white supremacy has created is the key indication that racism is still the number one problem facing the entire earth today.

Racism is about obscuring the historical identity of the white race and redefining other races. This allows the white race to dominate and rule by falsely defining what things mean. The entire earth is still under this spell in clear opposition to common sense and the natural order set by the Creator.

The Bible shows that there are not really races but nationalities. It documents the original names of all of these nationalities.

Whether you want to believe it or not, the identity, meaning the nationality, of so-called people of color has been stolen by another people. We have been renamed according to the whims of the controllers of the white supremacy system in direct opposition to the natural order set by the Creator.

The identity of the House of Jacob

> **He sheweth his word unto Jacob**, his statutes and his judgments unto Israel. **He hath not dealt so with any nation**: and as for his judgments, they have not known them. Praise ye the Lord. - Psalms 147:19-20

The above verse indicates that if you do not identify the House of Jacob on the earth today, the spiritual system that is contained in the Bible has no effect. The controllers of the white supremacy system know this. This is why the religions that we are following are not able to defend our communities against the devastating problems that we see happening every day. In the black and latino communities we have four of five churches on every block but they seem to have no positive spiritual affect on the community as a whole.

According to the Bible, the distortion of the identity of the Israelites is the very reason why people of color have come to be so easily oppressed and dominated by other seemly weaker people and nations. It is also the reason why the world is being dominated and controlled by the immoral people and nations that created the white supremacy system.

To understand the importance of the House of Jacob and why other people would claim to be Israelites when they are really another people, you must understand the Bible.

The Bible is the Book of the Israelites. It characterizes the Israelites as God's chosen people. Both the Old Testament and the New Testament contain the prophecy of the final battle between the forces of righteousness and the forces of unrighteousness across the whole of humanity.

Israel literally means "Prince of the Power" or "Prince of God".

> **For Jacob my servant's sake, and Israel mine elect, I have**
> **even called thee** by thy name: I have surnamed thee,
> though thou hast not known me. - Isaiah 45:4

There are no lost tribes of Israel. The children of Israel exist on the earth today, but they are definitely NOT the Caucasians who claim that they are Jewish. Even so-called Jewish scholars are forced to admit this when confronted about the true history of the Israelites.

The Bible

The Table of Nations presented in the Book of Genesis chapter 10 provides the most detailed and complete understanding of the true nationalities of every person alive on the planet today.

The Bible is not a fairytale book. And it is really NOT a book of religion. You can call it a spiritual book, but it is actually the national historical records and Constitution of the House of Jacob—the bloodline that is the true nation of Israel. The Bible is a nationalistic book and can only be understood when it is read as such.

> **Even the mystery which hath been hid from ages and**
> **from generations**, but now is made manifest to his saints:
> - Colossians 1:26

The reason why the Bible becomes more and more relevant everyday is because it tells the story of human nature and the history of empires throughout world history. Biblical prophesy is accurate because human nature does not change. The same issues that existed 4,000 years ago still exist on the earth today. Predictably, descendants exhibit the same characteristics as their forefathers. The bloodlines on the earth today are exhibiting the same characteristics as they did since the beginning of time.

The Bible is a true and prophetic book because it predicted, thousands of years ago, the very condition that the House of Jacob is in today. Just as the prophecy foretold, no matter who has tried to claim it, change it, or misuse it, the Scriptures have found their way into the hands of the remnants of the House of Jacob, even though they have lost the memory of who they really are.

THIS IS NOT SCIENCE FICTION. OPEN YOUR EYES.

The Bible and the name Israel have been stolen, repackaged, and promoted as another people's nationality and another people's work.

But this too is prophetic since the Bible states that the truth of the House of Jacob must be spread to reach all four corners of the earth for the prophecy to be fulfilled.

> And the gospel must first be published among all nations.
> - Mark 13:10

So through the theft and misuse of both the Bible and the people of the Bible, everyone on the planet has now been exposed the book of The House of Jacob; even if they have never read it or understood what it really is.

King James the last black ruler of Europe

Every Scripture that is quoted in this book comes out of the King James 1611 Bible. The King James 1611 version is the most accurate English Bible in existence today. How is this so? Because King James himself was from the House of Jacob. He was not a white man as falsified history may lead you to believe. The rein of King James of England is called the "Jacobean" period.

King James VI came out of the Stuart line of rulers of Scotland. Stuart comes from the Norrish word for black, Svart. The word "swarthy" is the word that is used to describe the black rulers of Europe. Swarthy also means black. King James became King James I of England and ruled over England, Scotland, and Ireland at the same time. He was the last black ruler of Europe.

King James seemed to have sensed the onslaught of the newly created doctrine of white supremacy. White supremacy was being ushered in around the globe and being financed by a new phenomenon of the earth, global corporations. Throughout Europe, these global corporations under the name "The East India Companies" began to take on the characteristics of kingdoms within themselves. They had their own armies and their own local governors that colonized and exploited India and China. By the time of King James' rulership the global corporations had begun to rival the kings themselves for control of their home countries.

As King James foresaw, the white supremacists finally took control during the rein of his son Charles I. In 1650, as a result of the English

Civil War, King James's son Charles I was beheaded and Germans have had control of the Monarchy of England up until today.

If there is still any doubt in your mind as to the race of King James, consider the fact that his grandson Charles II who unsuccessfully fought to bring the Stuart bloodline back into power was known as "Black Boy" by his subjects. This name is still used by a chain of pubs in England today to commemorate the rein of Charles II.

Again, this is not science fiction, it is real history.

Different versions of the Bible

In the early 1600s King James commissioned the Bible to be translated from the original Hebrew and Greek into English. The Bible like most other high knowledge of the time was produced mainly in Latin in order to keep the masses of people from actually reading the text. The Church controlled society's understanding of the Bible and most other information. King James bypassed the Latin to produce a pure version of the Scriptures that could be read by the masses of people. The King James 1611 Bible is the result of this translation.

If you look at other versions of the Bible side by side with the King James translation you will find that the subtle differences in the other versions all have to deal with obscuring the identity and the true doctrine of the House of Jacob. We are told these "translations" make it easier to read but this is just a cover for changing and removing verses that do not agree with the religions that white supremacy has created.

Every version of the Bible shows that the fleshly children of Israel are God's chosen people. This is even stated in the Quran that is used by the Muslim religion.

The real reason for so many versions of the Bible is that all of the versions that have come after the King James 1611 are an attempt to obscure the race of the Israelites. They also try to obscure the fact that the Bible is a book of the Israelites, not European created religions. When you look at translations done in recent times in the United States such as the New International Version or World Translations, you find that entire verses have been removed. The NIV is missing at least 17 verses. Here is an example of two important missing verses:

> Howbeit this kind goeth not out but by prayer and fasting.
> - Matthew 17:21

> For the Son of man is come to save that which was lost.
> - Matthew 18:11

These omissions are not arbitrary, but are a purposeful and deliberate falsification of the Scriptures. Of course the excuse is made that these translations are needed because it is hard to read the English of the King James translation. This is utter non sense.

The race of the Israelites

What do these scriptures mean?

> **My skin is black** upon me, and my bones are burned with heat. - Job 30:30

> **I am black**, but comely, O ye daughters of Jerusalem, as the tents of Kedar, as the curtains of Solomon.
> - Song of Solomon 1:5

> Their visage is **blacker than a coal**; they are not known in the streets: their skin cleaveth to their bones; it is withered, it is become like a stick. - Lamentations 4:8

> **Our skin was black like an oven** because of the terrible famine. - Lamentations 5:10

All of these scriptures reference the skin color of the House of Jacob, the children of Israel.

When you look at these verses in the so-called new translations, you will find that the words and the meanings have been obscured in order to add obscurity and ambiguity as to the race and skin color of the Israelites.

Below is a slice of the geology chart of Jacob. It shows the two paths that the children of Jacob took to get to the Americas.

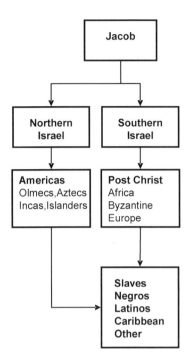

When you have a proper understanding of the Bible and world history, you find out that the majority of so-called Negros and Latinos of the Americas and the Caribbean (so-called people of color) are in fact Israelites; the bloodline sons and daughters of The House of Jacob.

These lost and disconnected peoples are actually a part of one bloodline and are one distinct nation of people, one "House". This is the House whose ancestors created the Scriptures that would become the Bible. These are God's chosen people according to the Bible.

> 8 When the Most High divided to the nations their inheritance, when he separated the sons of Adam, he set the bounds of the people according to the number of the children of Israel. 9 **For the Lord's portion is his people; Jacob is the lot of his inheritance.** - Deuteronomy 32:8-9

The above Scripture explains that the bloodline of Jacob is the chosen bloodline of God. This is the reoccurring theme throughout the whole Bible. The House of Jacob is favored by God but repeatedly turns away from the power of God and becomes enslaved over and over again by the other nations and their false gods.

This leads us to the real explanation of modern slavery. The people who were taken into slavery, colonized, and victimized in the Americas are Hebrews, not Africans or Indians. It is the House of Jacob that was taken captive in Africa and the House of Jacob that was colonized and virtually wiped out in the Americas as native "Indians" by the so-called European Royal Houses.

The aboriginal people and the slaves are one nation of people. The white invaders are one people whether they called themselves Spanish, Portuguese, French, Dutch, or British.

The people of color who are now called African Americans, Jamaicans, Puerto Ricans, Dominicans, Haitians, Cubans, Hondurans, Brazilians, Panamanians, Mexicans, South Americans, and Native American Indians, and the various other names are the true House of Jacob – the children of Israel. They have not only been a victim of physical theft but the evidence shows that they have also been a victim of a massive identity theft.

Because of white supremacy propaganda and racism, most if not all of these peoples live in complete confusion and denial concerning their connected heritage. Because of this deception, the entire world is in turmoil.

Historical proof of Jacob

We are going to show you how the so-called Negro slaves and the so-called Native Americans took two different paths to the Americas but originated from the same progenitor, Jacob whose name was changed to Israel according to the Bible.

The nation of Israel is not a land, it is a people. It is a genetic bloodline. Like all lands in ancient times, the lands that this bloodline settled were called after the father of the bloodline, but the nation is the people not the land.

In 900 BC the bloodline split into two kingdoms; the Northern Kingdom and the Southern Kingdom.

The original so-called Americans are actually the Northern Kingdom of Israel that was exiled in 720 BC by the Assyrians. They escaped Assyrian captivity and found their way to what is now called the Americas. They are the so-called 10 lost tribes.

The slaves of so-called Negro descent who were taken from West Africa are the Southern Kingdom of Israel. This Southern Kingdom migrated to West Africa after the final fall of Jerusalem 700 years after the Northern Kingdom fell. This was shortly after the time of Christ in 70 AD.

The Southern Kingdom is comprised of the tribes of Judah (the true Jews), Benjamin, and part of the tribe of Levi. These tribes were collectively called the Jews because they resided in the country of Judea.

Where is the real House of Jacob today?

The following list is the approximate location of the various tribes of Israel today based on world history and the prophecy of Genesis chapter 49.

```
1. JUDAH.................AFRICAN AMERICANS, BRAZILIANS
2. BENJAMIN............WEST INDIANS
3. LEVI....................HAITIANS
4. SIMEON...............DOMINICANS
5. ZEBULON.............GUATEMALA TO PANAMA
6. EPHRAIM.............PUERTO RICANS
7. MANASSEH..............CUBANS
8. GAD........................AMERICAN INDIANS
9. REUBEN...................SEMINOLE INDIAN
10. NAPHTALI...............ARGENTINA
11. ASHER....................COLUMBIA TO URUGUAY
12. ISSACHER...............MEXICANS
```

Note: This chart lists the approximate locations of the 12 tribes of the House of Jacob. As we have said, the House of Jacob is spread throughout the entire earth. Physical appearance or physical location is not the only indicator, so don't get bogged down in this list. It is the spirit that ultimately bears witness of who is the core of the House of Jacob.

Black slaves – the Southern Kingdom

We know that the black slaves that were brought into slavery in North America, South America, and the Caribbean Islands beginning in the 1600s were taken from West Africa. White historians like to point out that Africans sold their own people into slavery as if the whole continent of Africa is one people. The question is; how were certain Africans targeted for sale to European slavers? Why would a nation sell its own sons and daughters into slavery especially when it resides on the most resource rich continent on earth?

Africans selling other Africans into slavery is generally true, but it is also a purposely vague generality. The truth is that Hamite African tribes that had converted into Islam sold Israelite tribes into slavery.

Much of the strife in Africa today in places like Nigeria and Sudan exists because of the ethnic difference between the people that we lump together as "Africans".

The Israelite tribes had migrated into Africa fifteen hundred years before the European slave trade. Hamite and Israelites are the Bible names of two different dark races who live on the African Continent.

You can see the Israelite stamp in the names of various townships across West Africa. One of the largest slave ports is called Oudah or in Portuguese Ajuda, this translates to Judah in English. This port was the main feeding point to Brazil where half of all West African slaves wound up. The Ashanti people are named after a town in Israel— Ashan. Ashan"ti" means people of Ashan. Ashan is the name of a city located in southern Israel (Joshua 15:42 - 19:7 / 1st chronicles 4:32 - 6:59). Most North American slaves were from Igboland. Igobo or "Heebo" is a corruption of the word "Hebrew". Still today tribes like the Dogon, who remained largely remote from European influence, practice customs that are very similar to the Hebrew customs of the Old Testament.

None of these facts is a coincidence.

The Israelites began to permanently settle in West Africa when the Roman-Israelite War ended in the final Roman destruction of Jerusalem in 70 AD. The reason that Israelites fled into Africa was simple; the Southern Kingdom of Israel could blend in among the native African populations because they, like the Africans, are dark skinned people.

Throughout history, Israelites have always been mistaken for native Africans.

If we look at the Biblical account of Jacob --the father of the Israelite nation – we find that his own son Joseph became one of the rulers of Ancient Egypt. When, after many years apart, Joseph's brothers saw him, they thought that he was an Egyptian. They could not tell the difference between their own brother and an Egyptian. This tells us that the Ancient Egyptians and the Israelites looked so similar that even Israelites had a hard time telling them apart. This important Biblical account alone should be enough to convince you that Israelites could not be Caucasian.

There is also the Biblical account of Moses, the Israelite who is credited with writing down the first five Books of the Bible. Moses' story took place 400 years after the time of Jacob. The story tells us that when he was born, Moses had to be hidden inside of Egypt to escape the genocide that was being carried out against Israelite male children.

How could Moses be hidden among Egyptians unless he looked similar to the Egyptians? Even more interesting is the fact that this narrative tells us that Moses was able to actually pose as the Egyptian Pharaoh's own flesh and blood grandson until age 40.

These Biblical accounts are why white supremacy propaganda tries to make the world believe that the Ancient Egyptians were white skinned people. The problem with this "white lie" is that there are too many statues, wall paintings, and tombs that show otherwise. Every ancient statue, figurine, painting, and carving shows that the Ancient Egyptians had what we would now call Negro features.

White supremacy has put forth movie fantasy to create the illusion of a white race of Egyptians. The secret, however, is not that the controllers of white supremacy care that the Egyptians were black. The bigger issue is that if the world understands that the Egyptians were dark people, there is no way that the fictional identity of the Caucasian Jewish identity can hold up. The next logical question would have to be, if the Caucasian Jewish people are not the real Jews, who is? Who are these Biblical stories referencing? We are answering these questions right now.

The Roman historian Cornelius Tacitus (56-118 AD) gave his opinion on where the Israelites from the Southern Kingdom (the Jews) came from. He is writing this at the time right before Israel was finally destroyed by the Romans in 70 AD.

Here is how Tacitus described the speculation as to the origin of the Jews:

"Others assert that in the reign of Isis <u>the overflowing population of</u> **Egypt**, led by Hierosolymus and Judas, discharged itself into the neighbouring countries. <u>Many, again, say that they were a race of</u> **Ethiopian** <u>origin</u>, who in the time of king Cepheus were driven by fear and hatred of their neighbours to seek a new dwelling-place."

This Roman historian Cornelius Tacitus, an eyewitness of the time period, described the Israelite race by comparing them with the obviously dark skinned people of Africa. At the time when the Israelites fled Jerusalem for good, this eyewitness compared the race of the Israelites (the Jews) of the Southern Kingdom to black Egyptians and Ethiopians.

Is there any wonder why after the final fall of Jerusalem the Israelites would flee into Africa to escape Roman persecution? The Israelites of the Southern Kingdom were able to seamlessly blend in with the native African peoples as they always had because they had a similar look and skin color.

After existing side by side with Africans in various locations but still practicing Hebrew based customs for hundreds of years, the disbursed Southern Tribe, was eventually again conquered and forced into the slave markets of the Americas.

Israelites in Africa

Christ prophesized about the coming destruction of Jerusalem in 70 AD when he said:

> And when ye shall see Jerusalem compassed with armies,
> then know that the desolation thereof is nigh. Then let them
> which are in Judaea **flee to the mountains**; and let them
> which are in the midst of it depart out; and let not them that
> are in the countries enter thereinto. - Luke 21:20-21

And it did come to past that the last of the Israelites fled Jerusalem when it fell to the Roman Empire in 70 AD. Also during this time, Greek speaking Israelites became a part of the Eastern Roman Empire that would later become the Byzantine Empire.

Approximately one million Israelites of Jerusalem fled into Yemen and then migrated into West Africa eventually founding the Empire of Ghana.

The Romans never crossed the Sahara Desert so these Israelites remained undisturbed by Roman persecution for a thousand years. The original Ghanaian Empire was built by the Israelites. The crown jewel of the 1000 year Ghanaian Empire was the Kingdom of Timbuktu.

The Israelites built and controlled their own kingdom and prospered until 1000 AD when Islam swept through West Africa.

Separate Israelite identity in Africa

The easiest way to identify the Israelite tribes in Africa is to look at the customs that they were following when the Arabs and Europeans arrived. These tribes practiced Biblical Israelite rituals long before any contact with either Islam or white Christians.
Such Biblical rituals include:

- Circumcision
- Division of tribes into twelve
- The king is also the high priest
- Blood sprinkling on alters and post
- Marrying of a brother's wife after his death
- Separation and purification after child birth
- Uncleanness during menstruation
- New moon celebrations
- Patrilineal lineage system

The point is that within West African society, there were tribes that were ethnically different and carried on very different social structures and cultural practices from the majority populations. This different ethnic makeup is the reason why Africans were willing to sell other dark skinned people who appeared to be their own people to Arabs and white Europeans.

The evidence also shows that the Europeans knew who these ethnically different "Africans" really were.

Israelite tribes had continued with their own customs and traditions which made them a target for slave trafficking in the thousand years before the European slave trade.

With powerful Arab backing, the newly converted Muslim African tribes began to dominate West Africa. They also began to sell Israelites to Arab slavers. This was the sub Saharan slave trade.

Native Americans – the Northern Kingdom of Israel

At the same time that Spain and Portugal started attacking the "New World" and its inhabitants, they were also expelling their Jews and exiling them to West Africa. Why? Because the Jews of Portugal were dark people also.

Many of the early accounts of European contact with the Native peoples of the Americas confirm the identity of these Israelites.

William Penn was one of the first prominent white colonizers. The state of Pennsylvania is named after him. When you read his accounts of his time in early America you see that he knew that the so-called Natives were Israelites and he also knew that the language that they spoke was a form of Hebrew.

In a letter dated August 1683, Penn gives conclusive evidence about who he believed the Natives were as well as what they looked like. Penn writes:

"The natives I shall consider in their person, language, manners, religion, and government, with my sense of their original. For their persons, they are generally tall, straight, well built, and of singular proportion; they tread strong and clever, and mostly walk with a lofty chin. Of complexion black, but by design, as the gipsies in England."

He goes on to describe their language:

"Their language is lofty, yet narrow; but, like the Hebrew in signification, full. Like short-hand in writing, one word serveth in the place of three, and the rest are supplied by the understanding of the hearer, imperfect in their tenses, wanting in their moods, participles, adverbs, conjunctions, interjections."

Penn then shows not only that the Natives practiced Hebrew customs but also that the Jews in a section of London looked and acted similar to the Natives proving that the Jews in London were also of black complexion:

"For their original, I am ready to believe them of the Jewish race, I mean of the stock of the ten tribes, and that for the following reasons: first, they were to go to a land not planted nor known, which to be sure Asia and Africa were, if not Europe; and He who intended that extraordinary judgement upon them might make the passage not uneasy to them, as it is not impossible in itself, from the easternmost parts of Asia to the westernmost of America. In the next place, I find

them of the like countenance, and their children of so lively resemblance, that a man would think himself in Duke's Place or Berry Street in London, when he seeth them. But this is not all: they agree in rites; they reckon by moons; they offer their first fruits; they have a kind of feast of tabernacles; they are said to lay their altar upon twelve stones; their mourning a year; customs of women; with many other things tat do not now occur."
- Quoted from Samuel Janney's Life of William Penn, 6th edition, 1882.

Artifacts

There are major ancient artifacts that have been uncovered in North and South America that point to the Israelite identity of the original inhabitants. We will list just a few of the more irrefutable pieces of evidence, namely: Word inscriptions, physical statues, and architectural structures.

In Los Lunas, New Mexico there is a carving of the Ten Commandments in Hebrew that has been dated to be thousands of years old. As the truth has come out about this stone, of course white supremacy scientist have rushed to call it a fake.

There are the Pyramids of South America. No other place on earth has parallel pyramid building and architectural know-how that rivals ancient Egypt. Despite wild theories that have been put forth by white supremacy scientists, the obvious answer is that the people who were in Egypt brought the knowledge of pyramid building with them when they came to the Americas.

There are the Olmec colossal structures in Mexico. These statues are 10 feet tall stone statues of heads that have distinctively Negro features. These giant statues also rival the colossal structures of Egypt. They obviously are portrait sculptures of the rulers of ancient America.

You can attempt to dismiss these obvious clues or try to provide all kinds of alternate theories but all of the artifacts put together with eyewitness accounts leave little doubt.

Biblical historical explanation

William Penn's account conclusively proves multiple points in one eyewitness narrative. Penn's account proves:

1. The Jews of America and the Jews of Europe were the same people and they were both black.

2. The reason why European invaders could communicate with the natives is because they could use Hebrew as a common language.

3. William Penn and the early "settlers" had a firm grasp on the Biblical account of the Jews and knew who they were dealing with.

4. The part of the Bible that Penn is referencing was removed from later common printings of the Bible by the Protestant Church.

In his explanation, William Penn was referencing the Book of Esdras. Esdras is one of the 14 Books that are generally missing from most Bibles that are in use today. These Books were a part of the original King James 1611 Version. Today these Books are mostly printed separately and are called the Apocrypha or hidden books. They were always a part of the King James Bible before the 1800s. These Books fill in the blanks between the Old Testament and the New Testament in terms of historical context and prophetic understanding.

To prove this, we first find the story of what happened to the Northern Tribes of Israel in 2 Kings in the "normal" Bible--the Bible that most people are reading today.

The verse below tells what happened to the 10 Northern Tribes. In the 8th century B.C. the Northern Tribes were conquered by Assyria.

> In the ninth year of Hoshea **the king of Assyria took Samaria, and carried Israel away into Assyria**, and placed them in Halah and in Habor by the river of Gozan, and in the cities of the Medes. - 2 Kings 17:6

To get further clarification however, you must find the explanation in the Book of 2 Esdras in the Apocrypha:

> <u>Those are the ten tribes, which were carried away prisoners</u> out of their own land in the time of Osea the king, whom Salmanasar the king of Assyria led away captive, and he carried them **over the waters**, and so came **they into another land**. - 2 Esdras 13:40

It goes on to state:

> But they took this counsel among themselves, that they would leave the multitude of the heathen, and go forth into a further country, **where never mankind dwelt**,
> - 2 Esdras 13:41

A land "where never mankind dwelt" suggest the "New World". The Europeans went searching for these lost 10 tribes that had disappeared into a land where they had never known.

The Book of Esdras even goes on to tell the name of the land:

> For through that country there was a great way to go, namely, of a year and a half: and the same region is **called Arsareth**. - 2 Esdras 13:45

The Bible gives the original name of the Americas as Arsareth.

William Penn used this Biblical account to relate to his readers who the natives were. When he stated "I am ready to believe them of the Jewish race, I mean of the stock of the ten tribes", he was using the above scripture as his reference. He would never have referenced this passage had it not been a commonly known scripture at the time.

Penn's account leaves no doubt that the so-called Europeans knew who they were dealing with when they came to the "New World". It also leaves no doubt as to the racial makeup of the Israelites.

Other parts of the world

> I said, I would scatter them into corners, I would make the remembrance of them to cease from among men:
> - Deuteronomy 32:26

The House of Jacob is spread to all four corners of the world. We are highlighting the Americas because it has been ground zero in the war against the true children of Israel.

Jewish converts

Where did those who call themselves Jewish come from?

The name "Jewish" is never used in the Bible to describe the children of Israel (The House of Jacob). So who are the people who say they are Jewish?

The people that the world calls Jewish are the followers of the religion called Judaism. Judaism is not a real nationality.

> Therefore thus saith the Lord God; Surely in the fire of my jealousy have I spoken against the residue of the heathen, and against all **Idumea, which have appointed my land into their possession** with the joy of all their heart, with despiteful minds, to cast it out for a prey. - Ezekiel 36:5

Jewish people are so-called Europeans who adopted the ways of the bloodline nation of Israel. They are religious converts. They are NOT descendants of the people known as Israelites. They are NOT the House of Jacob. They have been persecuted by other Europeans because they would not forcibly convert to Christianity like other Europeans.

The current Jewish state was founded in 1948 by Great Britain after World War II. The people who live in this state are Caucasians not Jews. They are not Jews by racial origin by any stretch of the imagination. They are Jew"ish", not Jews.

Common sense evidence

The Bible is what is being used to designate these "Jewish" people as the chosen people of God. Incredibly, none of the history of the "European Jew" even remotely matches up with history or Bible prophesy.

Here are just a few questions that highlight the preposterous nature of the claim of the so-called Europeans that profess to be Jewish by birth. They have used this claim not only to take control of the State of Israel but also to receive billions of dollars in reparations that rightly belong to the true children of Jacob.

1. Why do Jewish people follow another book, the Talmud, that has nothing to do with the Bible?

2. Where do you find any white skinned people on the walls of the Ancient Egyptian tombs where Israelites first went into slavery?

3. How did Jacob's son, Joseph and later Moses (both Israelites) blend in and hide amongst the dark peoples of Ancient Egypt at various points in history if the Israelites were white people?

4. Why do so-called Jewish people deny Jesus, when Jesus is actually from the tribe of Judah (a real Jew)?

5. Why does the Bible describe Jesus and the various prophets as being dark skinned people?

6. Why can't Jewish people tell you what happened to the other ten tribes?

7. Why aren't the "Israelis" seeking to reunite with the other tribes as the Old and New Testament prophesy commands?

8. According to the Bible the priests of the Israelites wear mitres, a head covering that keeps the top of the head uncovered. Jewish people wear yamakas, a hat that covers the top of the head. This is the same cap that muslims and catholic priests wear. This head covering is the custom of the Greeks, the Bible calls it blasphemy.

The list of inconsistencies could fill a whole other book. But you get the picture. This is one of the biggest hoaxes in world history.

Converted Jewish population

These unanswered questions should lead you to understand that the people who call themselves <u>Jewish</u> are definitely NOT who they say they are. They are NOT from the bloodline of Israel and are NOT the people that are written about in the Bible. They are NOT Israelites. They are converts to a religion called Judaism which is loosely based on the customs of the true Israelites. You can follow another man's customs but you cannot convert into another man's nationality.

You should note the words that followers of Judaism use. They call themselves Jew"ish" meaning kind of like Jews. They call themselves Israeli, NOT Israelites. Israelite means you are from the genetic blood line of Jacob.

Israeli and Jewish only mean that you subscribe to a political and religious ideology. Adopting an ideology is not the same thing as being an actual descendent of the specific person, Jacob, whose name was changed to Israel according to the Bible.

Finally, the Bible says that when the Jews return to their land, the whole earth would follow the laws statutes and commandments of the Bible and there would be no more war (Isaiah 2:2-4).

Has that been the case since the 1948 founding of the State of Israel? Of course not, it has been the exact opposite. It has been nothing but war, strife, racism, turmoil, and phony politics that creates new laws daily, all of which go against the laws, statutes, and commandments of the Bible. Its time we wake up from this massive hoax.

Prophetic Biblical proof of the House of Jacob

The Bible tells us how we can find the House of Jacob even when they lose their identity and become enslaved and scattered around the world. In fact, one of the defining marks of the House of Jacob is that they would go into captivity, lose the knowledge of their heritage, and forget their true identity and their God.

Bible prophecy says that the other Houses would conspire together in an attempt to take the House of Jacob "out of remembrance". American slavery and colonization fulfilled that prophecy.

> They have taken crafty counsel against thy people, and consulted against thy hidden ones. 4 **They have said, Come, and let us cut them off from being a nation;** that the name of Israel may be no more in remembrance. - Psalms 83:3-4

Even during modern Western slavery, some of the Children of Jacob were able to figure out our situation by reading the Bible.

Gabriel Prosser, Denmark Vesey, Nat Turner and other slaves who learned to read, immediately recognized the prophecies and the parallels between themselves and the Israelites of the Bible.

It was because of Nat Turner's uprising in 1831 that it became illegal for slaves to read the Bible or hold religious services if a white person was not present. These laws have contributed to the confused doctrine that is being preached in our churches today.

And they shall be upon thee for a sign and for a wonder, and upon thy seed for ever. - Deuteronomy 28:46

The Bible tells us that the condition of the people is the sign of the identity of the House of Jacob forever. Who does the Bible describe? Who has suffered the curses spoke of in the Bible?

The Book of Deuteronomy the 28th chapter lays out the unique signs that would identify the House of Jacob if they turned away from the Law that was given to them by Moses. These signs tell the story of the House of Jacob.

Curse	Scripture
Judgment will occur against the Israelites because they were given the law. If they do not follow the law they will be cursed.	Deuteronomy 28:15 & 28:63
The land and the people shall become cursed	Deuteronomy 28:16-31
They will become ruled by an oppressive nation	Deuteronomy 28:36
Go into bondage in a new Egypt on slave ships	Deuteronomy 28:68
Have a fierce and evil enemy come from afar	Deuteronomy 28:49-53
Be cut of from being a nation and become scattered across the entire earth	Deuteronomy 28:64

Curse	Scripture
Serve strange gods of wood and stone	Deuteronomy 28:64
Be called by different derogatory names and forget who they are	Deuteronomy 28:37
Economically serve their enemies and be dominated economically by their enemies	Deuteronomy 28:48
Have their sons and daughters sold to enemies	Deuteronomy 28:32 & 28:41
Woman and children rule over the men	Deuteronomy 28:56
Have no power to resist enemies	Deuteronomy 28:65
Build civilizations but not prosper from them	Deuteronomy 28:33
Strangers will rule over their community	Deuteronomy 28:43-44
There will be no unity among the people	Deuteronomy 28:54
They shall live in constant stress	Deuteronomy 28:65-67
The curses shall follow their descendants until the descendants repent	Deuteronomy 28:46

Deuteronomy chapter 28 gives the clear explanation of the condition of so-called people of color. It also gives the explanation of why this condition continues to this day. We continue to ignore the truth.

> They have moved me to jealousy with that which is not God;
> they have provoked me to anger with their vanities: and I will
> move them to jealousy with those which are not a people; **I
> will provoke them to anger with a foolish nation.**
> - Deuteronomy 32:21

We are being judged and punished as a nation, not as individuals. The individual mindset is what is keeping us spiritually destroyed and under the yoke of a godless people.

> **You only have I known of all the families of the earth**:
> therefore I will punish you for all your iniquities. - Amos 3:2

Because we continue to follow definitions that go against the word of the Lord, we are under the total control of the enemies of the word of God.

The solution is to return to the truth.

We must come together as a nation in order to end these curses and set the world back in order.

Take away from this chapter:

1. History shows that the so-called people of color in the Americas are Israelites, the descendants of Jacob.

2. The Israelites wrote the Bible. The Bible is the history and Constitution of the Israelites.

3. The world is in turmoil because of the deception concerning the identity of the Israelites.

> **For the Lord will have mercy on Jacob**, and will yet choose
> Israel, and set them in their own land: and the strangers
> shall be joined with them, and they shall cleave to the house
> of Jacob. - Isaiah 14:1

4 House of Esau Reset

The injustice dilemma

> As it is written, Jacob have I loved, but **Esau have I hated**.
> - Romans 9:13

1. Who created racism?
2. What is the white supremacy system?
3. Where did racial hostility come from?

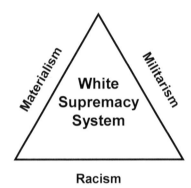

Racism

The above diagram shows that racism is one leg of the system of white supremacy. Without the other two legs, racism has no power. Without economic or physical force, racial prejudice means nothing. There is nothing wrong with preferring your own race. There is something wrong when you use this preference to injure other races. Preference and injury is the legacy of the white supremacy system. By attempting to force other races to submit to the unjust terms and conditions of the white supremacy system, the white race continues to injure all other races.

Racism = Corrupt definitions
Materialism = Greed and covetousness, scarcity mindset
Militarism = Aggression and destructive emotions

Racism is organized through political systems. Materialism is played out through the economic system. Militarism is carried out through law enforcement and military force. These institutions compliment each other. Neutralizing the power of one of the legs does not necessarily destroy the system.

The white supremacy system of so-called democracy and capitalism are institutions that are used to distribute the accumulated effects of crimes against humanity. The effects of the crimes of the white supremacy system will continue to accumulate until restitution has been made or the white supremacy system is destroyed.

So although the masses of white people can claim that they "did not do it", history shows that the middle class immigrants to the Americas as well as the existing white population of the Americas, Great Brittan, France, Germany and the other so-called European powers are the economic beneficiaries of the crimes against humanity and the accumulated theft that is embedded in the global economic system.

The injustice dilemma

White denial is the main reason why the white supremacy system has no chance of being reformed. White people can not figure out a way to fix the system because no current generation of the white race wants to take responsibility for the crimes that have been carried out on their behalf by their ancestors and the current leaders of their race.

Lack of responsibility is the hallmark of white supremacy. Because it is an institutionalized system no one personally has to take responsibility for it. Those who believe in and celebrate the so-called greatness of the white race also desperately seek to relieve the white race of any responsibility for the evil results that continue to be produced by their rule. They want all of the glory and credit but none of the shame and responsibility.

Even well meaning white folks can't bring themselves to admit that they are a party to an extreme form of evil and have inherited the benefits of bloody crimes against humanity. Until real repentance and restitution has been made, the beneficiaries of the white supremacy system are just as guilty as their forefathers who committed the original crimes. This may be tough to deal with but it is the truth. Focusing on this truth is the only way to bring about justice. Justice is the only way to bring about peace.

The truth is that we are all charged with the unpaid injustices of our fore parents and therefore must attempt to atone accordingly. Not surprisingly, this is a major Biblical principle that is glossed over in all white supremacy created religions. The Bible, which is really the story of the multiple captivities of the House of Jacob, is meant to show this important fact to the rest of the world.

There is no such thing as equality without justice. Equality is not the same thing as justice. We are not all equally at fault for the crimes of the white supremacy system. The victims of white supremacy are not to be equated to the beneficiaries, nor should they ever want to be. When you buy into the so-called greatness of the systems created by white supremacy, you are also liable for the crimes that it has committed and continues to commit. You cannot accept the benefits without accepting responsibility for the massive spiritual and economic debts that are embedded in the crimes. This may be hard for white people to accept, but their forefathers set this in motion and they will somehow have to make real repentance and restitution. That is justice.

To make matters even more complicated, because of white supremacy indoctrination, many of the victims of white supremacy join in on the denial. In the United States for example, if you ask many so-called African Americans if they have an economic enemy, they will either say no or refuse to name the enemy. Most will deny that the white race is their historic economic enemy and that it continues to be a major factor in their economic and social problems. Those that will admit the adversarial nature of their economic relationship with whites most likely will still be unable to identify the true nature of the attack.

Religion-the beginning of the race problem

Racism was created under the cover of religion. In 1452, six imperial powers began a perpetual war against the House of Jacob and other nations of the world. These imperial powers are the English, French, Portuguese, Spanish, Dutch, and Danish. Their quest to colonize and enslave the rest of the world was called the "Discovery Age".

Where did the imperial powers get the "authority" to carry out their crimes? They got it from the Pope and the Catholic Church.

The white supremacy international constitution

Unknown to most people, the white supremacy system has an international constitution that is upheld across the globe under the authority of the Roman Catholic Church. In the year 1452 Pope V of the Roman Catholic Church issued a decree that the King of Portugal could steal the lands that Portugal "discovered" and enslave the people on those lands forever. This international law has never been repealed eventhough it has been repeatedly challenged in international courts by indigenous people whose land was stolen to create the global white supremacy system.

To this day this criminal doctrine called "The Discovery Doctrine" is the basis for all European, American, and African law. The Supreme Court of the United States has repeatedly upheld this doctrine as the basis for U.S. land claims. So anyone who claims that there is a separation of church and state in the United States is a liar. The church is the state when it comes to the entire legal foundation of the United States.

It should be noted, that it is church doctrine not the Bible that is the basis for this immoral policy. Ironically, the Bible strongly condemns the House of Esau and the very nature of creating these kinds of oppressive empires. The prophets of the Bible prophesized that these events would come to pass because the House of Jacob refused to follow its own laws, statutes, and commandments.

The first decree of the Discovery Doctrine entitled "Dum Diversas" was issued by the Pope V to Portugal in 1452. In 1454 Pope V issued the follow up confirmation "Romanus Pontifex" which in part reads:

"...granted among other things free and ample faculty to the aforesaid King Alfonso -- to invade, search out, capture, vanquish, and subdue all Saracens and pagans whatsoever, and other enemies of Christ wheresoever placed, and the kingdoms, dukedoms, principalities, dominions, **possessions, and all movable and immovable goods** whatsoever held and possessed by them and **to reduce their persons to perpetual slavery**,.."

In 1493 Pope Alexander VI issued "Inter caetera" that stated that one white "Christian" could not take dominion over a land already stolen by another white "Christian". This was issued in response to Christopher Columbus' conquests. This decree was meant to settle disputes among the various white supremacy imperial nations.

The two decrees together are referred to as the Discovery Doctrine. This was nothing more than a church sponsored decree of murder, theft, and slavery. It was, and still is, organized crime on the highest level. As we already stated, the Discovery Doctrine has never been rescinded and is still upheld by the United States and the other European nations. The Discovery Doctrine is the international constitution of white supremacy.

Who is Esau?

The question is why? Why would the church that claims to be the keeper of Christ's word call for perpetual land theft and perpetual enslavement of literally billions of people?

How can these billions of people follow a religion that is responsible for the invention of the white supremacy system? The answer can only be found in the Bible.

The six imperial powers: the English, French, Portuguese, Spanish, Dutch, and Danish; along with the other so-called European nations are really one Biblical bloodline. They are the bloodline of Edom, they are Edomites. The father of the Edomite nation is Esau.

The only way to understand current events or world history is to trace the steps of The House of Esau. The only way to track The House of Esau is through understanding the Bible.

No matter how many times you have read the Bible, if you did not understand the House of Esau and its relationship to the House of Jacob, you could not have gotten a proper understanding. If you thought that the Europeans who call themselves Jewish are the people of the Bible, you do not have a true understanding of the Bible or history.

Both Dr. King and Marcus Garvey fell prey to this common misunderstanding that our slave fore parents were taught about the Scriptures.

Many of us today, dismiss the Bible because of this identification misunderstanding. Even worse, the religion that declared war on the House of Jacob has misled many of us into acting in direct opposition to the Bible because of this misunderstanding.

Nearly all of the slaves who rose up against slavery figured out who they were and the true situation at hand by reading the Bible. This is the real reason why slaves were eventually forbidden from learning to read. It was also the reason why white controlled theology schools were set up to steer our preachers away from identifying the actual people of the Bible.

The House of Esau

Esau is the Biblical name of the so-called white race. No matter what political names they may be using in the earth today, the majority of those who the world recognizes as Caucasian are <u>Edomites</u> whose progenitor is Esau according to the Bible (Genesis 25:25).

> And the first came out red, all over like an hairy garment; and they called his name Esau. - Genesis 25:25

Esau literally means "wasted away is he" in Hebrew which is a reference to the lack of pigmentation in his skin.

If you trace the white race back from anywhere they are today, you find that they can all be generally traced to Germany, before that Rome, before that Greece, and before that, to their real home of <u>Edom</u>. The nations of the white race are Edomites according to the Bible.

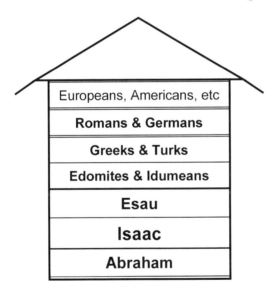

The father of the Edomites is Esau (Genesis 36:1). Esau's sons – Edomites -- created multiple tribes that eventually spread across Europe to create what we now call the Caucasian race. This transition is recorded in the Bible.

> Now these are the generations of Esau, who is Edom. - Genesis 36:1

The name Edomite is a Biblical name that you rarely, if ever, hear uttered today, even in churches. This should strike you as odd since there is a whole book in the Bible dedicated to the prophecy of Edom - The Book of Obadiah.

History has been so well confused by the House of Esau that it will just take you around in circles. But we can get a general understanding of what we are dealing with by tracing what is happening today and working back through history.

The House of Esau has done a good job of obscuring its tracks through history mainly by refusing to call itself the House of Esau – by shunning the name Edomites. They accomplished this by calling themselves after various conquered lands and peoples and then absorbing their customs, knowledge and traditions. The House of Esau has been able to all but write the name of Esau out of history even as it continues the same historical stance of creating war and chaos across the earth.

The Bible gives us a means to put the pieces back in place, to understand the history of how Edomites came to call themselves after the land masses of Europe instead of their original bloodlines.

The Book of Obadiah leaves no doubt that the House of Esau (the Edomites) is going to be the mortal enemy of the House of Jacob in the last days.

The House of Esau is the creator and controller of the current corporate global empire that rules the earth today. To trace Esau's history we have to use common sense and our understanding of the divisions that exist between the so-called Europeans in modern times.

The first thing you must understand is that Europe was originally the land of the Japhetic people. This was a dark race of people who most likely became the Asian and East Indian people. These people were either pushed out of Europe or killed much in the same way that the natives of the Americas have been dealt with by the House of Esau.

The House of Esau invented white supremacy
Why does the world need to recognize The House of Esau?

> **And Esau hated Jacob because of the blessing wherewith his father blessed him**: and Esau said in his heart, The days of mourning for my father are at hand; then will I slay my brother Jacob. - Genesis 27:41

68

The House of Esau created the white supremacy system.

By hiding the identity of the Edomites (the House of Esau), history loses its instructive importance. When you follow the historical path of the Edomites you can clearly see the folly in the current path that it has evolved into -- the destructive corporate empire of the white supremacy system.

By failing to acknowledge the identity of the House of Esau, even well meaning people are tricked into serving the mission of the House of Esau as put forth by Pope Nicholas V in 1452.

> O Lord, my strength, and my fortress, and my refuge in the day of affliction, the Gentiles shall come unto thee from the ends of the earth, and shall say, **Surely our fathers have inherited lies, vanity, and things wherein there is no profit.** - Jeremiah 16:19

The descendants of Edom must understand what is going on in order to have any hope of avoiding total destruction. They must recognize that they have inherited lies from their forefathers. These lies will not go unpunished. Their forefathers did not get away with anything. The punishment has been transferred to the current generations. The current generations must either repent or face the punishment that was due to their forefathers. That is justice.

White supremacy and propaganda

White supremacy ideology was created by the House of Esau as a tactic of confusion and corruption. It confuses the historical identity of various peoples and corrupts your perception of what is actually happening. If you do not understand white supremacy, you will automatically be trapped in a world of illusions and false perceptions.

White supremacy is purely a propaganda tool. It proposes that a deficiency, skin without pigmentation, is actually a superior trait. In modern times this fantasy has become the defining characteristic of the structure of the global world system of control. This clearly irrational notion is the main cause of mental confusion in the world. When you deliberately or inadvertently use the white supremacy fallacy in your reasoning, it is impossible to develop any serious solutions to the problems that exist in the world.

To keep up the farce of white supremacy; history had to be falsified to show that anyone of historical significance had to have white skin.

This false doctrine is coupled with the doctrine that people with skin pigmentation are inferior to people without skin pigmentation. This astonishing and ridiculous false logic is the fabrication that is holding the global corporate plantation system together.

The skin color fantasy has become so engrained through propaganda, icons, and idols that many people are not aware that they build white supremacy and its propaganda and false definitions into their search for solutions to the worlds problems.

White supremacy is the recognized standard by which the entire world filters methods, solutions, and outcomes. This flawed circular thinking keeps solutions from materializing from within the system. This is what keeps the system alive.

Attempting to acquiesce to the system of white supremacy in anyway perpetuates the idea that founded the system and inadvertently gives legitimacy to the false premise. This is the greatest secret of racism. In trying to fight against it you can inadvertently affirm the premise that it is built upon – that you need to prove your worth to white people and be approved by white people, because they are the standard of right and wrong.

By refusing to recognize the truth that white people are in no moral position to judge anything or anybody, you try to fight the system by buying into it instead of creating alternatives systems that have a foundation in truth. A truthful system REQUIRES justice not equality.

The "equality" angle is a trick of white supremacy. Equality makes us all equally guilty for the crimes committed by white supremacy. If a crime was committed, someone has to be the victim and someone has to be the perpetrator. The two are not equal and can never be equal until the perpetrator stops the crime, repents, and restores the victim if possible.

Having this kind of conversation with black people or white people will surely uncover another interesting trick of white supremacy -- the cry of "reverse racism".

The facts show that white supremacy is an ongoing unprovoked attack against a people based on an obvious lie. So-called reverse racism is something altogether different. If it even can exist, it is a logical response to the original unprovoked attack.

If the victims of white supremacy do not want to associate with white people or do not trust white people, they have at least 500 years of real facts on which to base these conclusions. The facts and logic make "reverse racism" seem like a very rational, logical reaction to the truth. It would seem that the irrational position would be NOT taking a cautious even discriminatory posture toward a group of people that has declared perpetual war on your people and have been the historical purveyors of violence and injustice throughout the world.

The white supremacy system does an excellent job of taking the personal responsibility out of racism. If you ask anyone does racism exist, they will say yes. If you ask them who the racist are, they have a much harder time coming up with an accurate answer, at least in public.

Very few if any of the controllers of the white supremacy system will ever admit that they are a racist. This is definitely one of the unintended downsides to the shame that the Civil Rights Movement thrust upon the agents of racism. They were forced to hide. This forced deception actually makes dealing with them that much harder.

The renaissance, false history, and the House of Esau

The original people of Europe, which was called Asia Minor, its rulers, and its people were what we would call black people.

During what Europeans now call the Renaissance Period (1300s-1600s) these original black people were systematically exterminated and removed from the history of what is now called Europe.

During the so called Renaissance, all of the historical accomplishments of the original dark races were then rewritten to erase the truth about the periods when the white race was not in rulership. They named the period which lasted a thousand years from the 400 AD -1500 AD "The Dark Ages".

After this period, white skin and white features was put up as the standard for human beings even though thousands of years of history prove otherwise.

The Renaissance means "rebirth". This "rebirth" of Europe in actuality appears to have been about the remaking of world history in the image of white skinned people. The Renaissance was the beginning of the previously unheard of and ridiculous doctrine called "white supremacy"- the superiority and entitlement of people because of their skin color.

71

It was at this time that paintings and sculptures were produced to reinvent world events and ancient history to include so-called white skinned people. The images of Jesus, all the prophets of the Bible, the kings and queens of Europe, and any remnants of rule by the dark races were remade by white artist such as Michael Angelo and Leonardo da Vinci to make it appear that all of these people and events of history were the work of the white race.

The European Renaissance is billed as a cultural revolution but it is really just a discovery and repackaging of other culture's knowledge and history by people who had little culture of their own. Historians pretend that the Renaissance was about nostalgia for the past but it was really a reinvention of the past in the image of the white race.

Just like the Renaissance artist, Hollywood continues the white washing of history by portraying historical figures such as Moses, Noah, and Christ as white, rewriting the Native American narrative, and putting out movies that show questionable white people in history in a favorable light.

The symbolism of Esau

To see the symbols of the House of Esau you have to look no further than the United States. The United States is nothing more than a copy of the Roman Empire which is a copy of the Babylonian, Egyptian, Assyrian, Persian, and Greek empires.

This is not surprising since the U.S. was founded by the continuation of the Roman Empire through the German Empire which was split into the various countries in Europe. The U.S. was set up by the British arm of the German Empire.

It is quite easy to see the Edomite roots in the symbolism of the U.S. From the adoption of the eagle as the national symbol, to the Egyptian obelisk that they call the Washington Monument, to the pyramid on the back of the dollar, to the adoption of the Roman Catholic pagan religious practices and holidays, to the adoption of the Roman calendar, to the governmental structure. These are all the clues of the House of Esau.

The eagle

The eagle is used by the U.S. as it was in Rome, Greece, and Nazi Germany.

> **Though thou exalt thyself as the eagle**, and though thou set thy nest among the stars, thence will I bring thee down, saith the LORD. - Obadiah 1:4

What did the U.S. astronauts say when they supposedly reached the moon? "The eagle has landed."

The goat of Mendes

The goat is the symbol of the Greek Empire. This symbol is used in the design of the U.S. Pentagon, in flags, company logos, satanic hand gestures and many other places that you may have not noticed.

> And the **rough goat is the king of Grecia**: and the great horn that is between his eyes is the first king. - Daniel 8:20

The pyramid

One of the first places the Greek Edomite Empire took knowledge from was Egypt. The pyramid and the eagle both appear on the back of the dollar bill. Here is what the Bible says about Egypt and its practices and symbols:

> And **the spirit of Egypt shall fail** in the midst thereof; and I will destroy the counsel thereof: and **they shall seek to the idols, and to the charmers, and to them that have familiar spirits, and to the wizards.** - Isaiah 19:3

Most people who celebrate Easter have no idea that Easter is loosely based on the Israelite Passover. What is the Passover Celebration?

> **For I will pass through the land of Egypt this night**, and will smite all the firstborn in the land of Egypt, both man and beast; **and against all the gods of Egypt I will execute judgment: I am the Lord**. - Exodus 12:12

The God of the Bible is against the symbols and practices of Egypt. Why would officials in America place the symbols of Egypt on their money yet proclaim to be a nation that believes in the God of the Bible? The money even says on the top of it "In God We Trust". Obviously the money is referencing another god that is not the God of the Bible.

Because of the House of Esau, this Egyptian symbolism is front and center on the money that passes through the hands of billions of people throughout the world. What is the point of forcing this symbolism on billions of mostly unsuspecting people?

The trinity of Esau

Below is the flag for Washington, D.C. Officially it is said that this is the coat of arms for George Washington's family in England. But why would a country that supposedly fought to be independent from England use an English coat of arms as the flag of its capital city?

Even stranger, Washington D.C. is the capital of the so-called model for democracy yet no resident of Washington D.C. really has ANY representative in Congress. The citizens have NO real voting rights at all and are not attached to any state yet they pay some of the highest taxes in the country. Was this not the very thing that George Washington supposedly fought England against; taxation without representation?

The United States of Rome

> And it was given unto him to make war with the saints, and to overcome them: and power was given him over all kindreds, and tongues, and nations. - Revelation 13:7

The D.C. flag is actually representative of the real power structure of the House of Esau. This is the Vatican in Rome, The City of London in England, and Washington D.C. All of these cities are really city states that operate totally differently from the countries where they are located. They are separate in their governance and control because they are the power centers of the controllers of the House of Esau.

The Vatican is the spiritual center. The Pope controls everything through pagan demon worship. The Vatican steers people away from the Bible and into pagan theology. The Roman system of laws and government practiced through out the world are in direct opposition to the Bible. The laws coming directly from the Vatican are the basis for all land theft and slavery that is practiced throughout the House of Esau.

In order to keep the law in place, you will find pagan Egyptian/Babylonian worship throughout all the religions of the House of Esau, but it starts with the Vatican.

Washington is the military arm. Notice that the center piece of the murderous military complex is the Pentagon which is a pentagram shaped building after the Goat of Mendes.

London City is the financial arm. Notice while the rest of Europe moved to Euro dollars, England still uses the British Pound as its currency.

The only Israelite controlled country in the world

To conclude our study of the House of Esau, let's take a look at the only Israelite controlled country in the world today and how the House of Esau deals with it.

Before reading this book and understanding real history, like most people, you probably believed that the State of Israel is a country inhabited and run by Israelites. We have proven this to be a blatant falsehood. The State of Israel is not an Israelite state. It is in truth a state that is both inhabited and controlled by Edomites, not Israelites. It is part of the House of Esau operating under one of its assumed identities-the identity of the Israelites.

But there is one and only one Israelite controlled country in the world today that fought against the House of Esau to gain its freedom. That country is Haiti. You have to look no further than Haiti to observe the economic war and spiritual war that is still being waged against the Israelites.

Shortly after the American Revolution in 1789, Haitian slaves fought their French masters in armed conflict to win their freedom. The Haitians are the only victims of the Trans-Atlantic slave trade that were able to defeat their masters in armed warfare and forcibly take their freedom. In 1804 the former Haitian slaves took over what was at the time the most profitable plantation country in the world. These Israelites had gained control over a country that was producing 50% of the sugar and 60% of the coffee in the entire world.

After its fight for independence, Haiti became only the second independent republic in the western hemisphere. The other was the United States which was founded shortly before Haiti.

You would think that the newly formed, so-called personal freedom loving United States republic would have supported the Haitian march to freedom from tyranny and help it form a democracy that paralleled the United States. But we know better than that.

The triplets used against Haiti

Instead of applauding the Haitian march to freedom, Thomas Jefferson and the U.S. leadership denounced the hard fought freedom won by the Haitian slaves. Not only that, they shamefully worked to economically suffocate the newly formed Republic of Haiti. What the French could not do militarily, their European allies, including the United States set out to do economically.

Part of the reason why the Haitian slaves were successful against the French is because of the House of Esau's internal power struggles as a result of the characteristic corruption and greed that is the hallmark of the House of Esau.

The French, English, and Spanish were all fighting for the right to steal the most resources out of the "New World". The struggle against these corrupt forces is deceptively given as the reason that the United States was founded. But just a few decades into its founding, the United States was already engaged in using the giant triplets to help the House of Esau retain power.

Once France came to the realization that it was overextended in its quest for power and could not win a war against its slaves, it moved to another tactic. That new tactic was to put forth the outrageous idea that France should receive monetary reparations from its former slaves. This bizarre idea was supported by the United States and others. In a well worn tactic that the members of the House of Esau have used many times since to extort countries, the U.S. and France threatened to put a blockade around Haiti that would effectively shut off Haiti's trade activity with the rest of the world.

After its hard fought war to become free of slavery, Haiti agreed to pay an outrageous yearly ransom to France in order to be a recognized nation by the controllers of Europe. This agreement effectively began an era of Haitian debt slavery to France and the House of Esau.

Around the time of Marcus Garvey's Movement (1918), the United States invaded both Haiti and its island mate, the Dominican Republic, to "protect U.S. interest". This was really a military campaign to protect the right of U.S. corporations to steal resources and re-enslave the people of the island through starvation and debt.

By the 1940's the millions of dollars that Haiti was paying to France finally bankrupted the country. The United States then installed and backed a series of corrupt leaders to ensure that Haiti could never be economically independent.

Even before the devastation of the recent earthquake, Haiti had become a country that did not produce much of anything. The United States under Bill Clinton, basically took away Haiti's ability to produce even its own food by dumping subsidized rice into its markets.

Haiti, once one of the highest producing countries in the world now does not even produce its own rice in quantities enough to feed its own citizens.

Instead of being one of the riches countries in the world, Haiti is now the poorest country in the Western Hemisphere.

The Haitian slaves used spirituality in order to gather the courage to go to physical war with their masters. The problem is that this "spirituality" is not tied to their true identity.

Once the country was taken, the newly free slaves had no way to govern outside of what they saw from their European masters. They thought that they had to join the corporate world system of the House of Esau. This was true to a point since the United States was always waiting to strike militarily.

False ending of the war

Most people do not see how these global realities affect their day to day lives. This is a mistake. Economics deals with how the resources of the entire world are divided. This division affects each person's ability to survive and live a life free of stress and worry.

As long as the mindset that produces the triplets of racism, materialism, and militarism is in control of the world's resources, every person on the planet is in danger of war, famine, disease, strife, and other man-made disasters.

The giant triplets define the sometimes hidden intangible threat that hangs over the people of color – The House of Jacob. Racism, materialism and militarism can be and have been deceptively hidden in order to place the victims in a state of confusion and unconsciousness as to whom and where the economic attack is coming from.

Many people believe that events like the end of slavery, voting rights, or limited inclusion in the middle class ended the economic war against the people of color.

The tendency of the House of Esau to deploy the giant triplets creates a constant threat that can sometimes be hidden and overlooked. But even in their invisible intangible form the giant triplets create a liability that threatens the whole world with war, poverty, and chaos at any moment.

We tried to help the House of Esau

> **If the wicked restore the pledge, give again that he had robbed**, walk in the statutes of life, without committing iniquity; he shall surely live, he shall not die. - Ezekiel 33:15

Whatever the reason that the United States honors Martin Luther King, it really should be for his effort in trying save the children of the House of Esau from total spiritual destruction. Whether this was right or wrong, this is what he did.

Dr. King was willing to give his life for this cause.

The children of the House of Esau have to understand that it is futile to seek to save a way of life that is destined to collapse under its own injustice.

The spirit bears witness

Empire building has mixed up the natural order. It has also spread people across the earth. This makes identification purely by skin color difficult. The only way to truly know who is who is by the spirit, by the definitions that you will accept. In the end, the choices that you make and the consequences of your actions will bear witness to who you are.

The belief system that you will or will not accept is the final indicator of what group you belong to and what race will mean as we move into new forms of society.

Take away from this chapter:

1. Esau is the progenitor of the so-called European Caucasian race.

2. Racism is about obscuring the origins and true nationality of all people.

3. The Bible speaks against the House of Esau for the violence and oppression that it continues to commit against the House of Jacob.

For they have consulted together with one consent: **they are confederate against thee**: The tabernacles of Edom, and the Ishmaelites; of Moab, and the Hagarenes; Gebal, and Ammon, and Amalek; the Philistines with the inhabitants of Tyre; Assur also is joined with them: they have holpen the children of Lot. - Psalm 83:5-8

5 Racism Reset

The brainwashing dilemma

> Envy thou not the oppressor, and **choose none of his ways**.
> - Proverbs 3:31

1. Why does race matter?
2. What is the number one source of racial confusion?
3. How do we end racism?

For the sake of understanding we will use race and nationality interchangeably because they both reference your bloodline.

Race is just a set of definitions. Pride in one's family and one's race is the first love and first concern of all people. This is the natural order. Racism means that you move from dignity and pride in your own race into injuring other races.

This includes creating confusion as to how you define the races. So-called "Jewish" people have done this by successfully conflating a religion into a race of people. The same thing has happened with the homosexual agenda. By defining themselves by their own false definitions, homosexuals have sought to make sexuality equal with a race. They have successfully high jacked the Civil Rights Movement that was meant to bring justice to the victims of the white supremacy system. All of this has been done by simply making up false definitions and labels that go against the natural order. Both of these are examples of subtle but devastating racist practices. The core evil of racism is that it distorts definitions and causes confusion.

How do we end racism? We have given the main answer already in this book. We have to revert back to the correct definitions. We have to move away from the definitions that have been created by the white supremacy system. We have to put everything back under proper classifications. We must reject the false classifications given by the white supremacy system and turn back to the truth.

We have to redefine success, we have to redefine failure, we have to redefine the white race, we have to redefine the black race, and we have to redefine justice. When we do this, we redefine race relations.

Undefined notions of right and wrong, justice and injustice, and success and failure are the legacy of the white supremacy system. Believing that politics will solve the problems caused by white supremacy is a mistake. Politics under the white supremacy system is used to create a forum for endless opinions and unlearned debates instead of clear definitions.

When things are classified properly, choices become clear. Once we are dealing with proper classifications, we are forced to make public decisions about our own morality.

When given a choice, a sane person will choose success, justice and what is right; no sane person will choose failure or something that is not in his best interest. When these things are misclassified or not clearly defined, you cannot make sound decisions because you cannot tell the difference between these things. These blurred lines create confusion and turmoil.

Trying to keep things blurred is the last tactic of the white supremacy system. Ironically, the Civil Rights Movement aided in developing this tactic. Under the idea of "diversity" and "personal freedom" we are being led into making choices that are against our own best interest. Returning to the practice of clearly delineating things and recognizing clear boundaries is what will finally end the white supremacy system.

Many people of color resist this truth because their whole idea of self concept results from their relationship with white people. As the lies of white supremacy are destroyed, they may feel lost and betrayed and are not sure how to identify themselves. We are going to show you exactly where this confusion comes from.

The #1 source of racial confusion

Were you told that this is a picture of your God? Is this your savior? Is this what you have been praying to? Has this image made you not believe in God or the Bible?

For if he that cometh **preacheth another Jesus**, whom we have not preached, or if ye receive **another spirit**, which ye have not received, or another gospel, which ye have not accepted, ye might well bear with him. - 2 Corinthians 11:4

NOWHERE in the Bible does it say that Jesus was an effeminate looking white man.

For there shall arise false Christs, and false prophets, and shall shew great signs and wonders; insomuch that, if it were possible, **they shall deceive the very elect.**
- Matthew 24:24

THIS IMAGE OF WHITE CHRIST IS A BLATANT LIE.

And the great dragon was cast out, that old serpent, called the Devil, and Satan, **which deceiveth the whole world:** he was cast out into the earth, and his angels were cast out with him. - Revelation 12:9

The false image of Christ is of the Devil not of God. I know it may be difficult for you to hear this but that is the way of the Devil. He can convince you that an obvious lie is the truth and when he is found out, he then tries to convince you that the truth doesn't matter, or that there is no right and wrong, that Jesus was a spirit and not a man, or that he looks different to everybody, and all matter of ridiculous false logic. If you believe any of these things, you are in complete rebellion against God and are under the control of Satan himself. There is no in between in this matter. Either you follow the truth, or you are under the power of Satan. You must return to the truth. This is what it means to repent.

The House of Esau's biggest distortion

And laid open the book of the law, wherein **the heathen had sought to paint the likeness of their images.**
- 1 Maccabees 3:48

White Jesus is blasphemy on the highest level. Believing in white Jesus leads to a corrupted and confused spirit in both white and black people.

Watching elders in our community bowing and pleading to white Jesus automatically makes the children believe that white people are the standard of excellence and have authority over them.

Christ is undoubtedly the most influential world figure of the last two thousand years. We are going to show that his image and teaching has been distorted by church doctrine and propaganda. This can be found out by simply opening up a King James 1611 Bible and reading what it actually says. You will find that other recent white supremacy created translations of the Bible will aid in the deception but they still cannot cover up the truth that we are presenting here.

False church doctrine and white supremacy

The earth is given into the hand of the wicked: he covereth the faces of the judges thereof; if not, where, and who is he? - Job 9:24

The false image of Christ should be the obvious tip off that you are being fed a false doctrine in the churches that promote this obviously false image.

Did Jesus come in the flesh? What color was that flesh? Many Christians when confronted with these questions say it doesn't matter. Does the truth matter? Of course it does. Christ told us that it is the truth that will make us free. How can you get free if you believe in falsehoods?

Changing the truth of Christ through propaganda is the key to pulling off the illusion of white supremacy. To hide the identity of the House of Jacob, Christ's image had to be distorted.

Ye shall make you no idols nor graven image, neither rear you up a standing image, neither shall ye set up any image of stone in your land, **to bow down unto it**: for I am the Lord your God. - Leviticus 26:1

To accomplish its deception, white supremacy religion had to turn Christ into an idol of white supremacy. Once people associate white people with the Savior and the chosen people, they are more likely to conflate all of the actions of white people into that of gods, no matter how sinister and evil their history and current behavior may be.

The false image of Christ is the reason why the world is confused as to the true bloodline of Israel. This confusion can be directly attributed to the false teachings of the Roman Church.

Ask yourself these questions:

1. Does your love for the false image of a white Jesus enhance your love for yourself or does it project an image of the goodness on those who are trying to deceive you?

2. Does the false image subliminally make you believe that people who look like him are gods to be worshipped and feared?

3. Do you worry about offending God or this white Jesus and those who look like him?

4. Does the man in this image have any rules or does he just allow you to do anything and will still accept you?

5. Do the court systems that have you swear on the Bible take the same stance of not judging and live and let live?

This is nothing more than psychological warfare. The controllers of white supremacy have not only lied about the image of Christ but they continue to lie about his teachings and his doctrine eventhough you can read it for yourself in the Bible.

The only god that allows you to do whatever you want and has no rules is Satan. Period.

When you follow the so-called Christian religion, you are really professing your love for white Jesus and submitting yourself to the false white supremacy doctrine, neither of which is found in the Bible. You are submitting yourself to Satan worship.

Who was Christ?

For it is evident that **our Lord sprang out of Juda**; of which tribe Moses spake nothing concerning priesthood.
- Hebrews 7:14

The truth is that the Bible describes Christ as a black man who was an Israelite from the tribe of Judah (a Jew). The Old and New Testament gives his name as Immanuel, meaning God among us (Isaiah 7:14 and Mathew 1:23).

We already know that history and the Bible shows the tribe of Judah as a dark skinned people, not Caucasians.

The Bible continuously warns about attaching meaning to images and objects because they can become idols that confuse the mind. Idolatry short circuits your understanding. This is exactly how the false image of a white Jesus has been used in white supremacy propaganda.

Before you can properly understand God, the Bible, history, or anything else, you have to cancel the false image of white Jesus out of your mind. It may be difficult but it must be done.

Where did the false image come from?

> 11 And for this cause **God shall send them strong delusion,
> that they should believe a lie**: 12 That they all might be
> damned who believed not the truth, but had pleasure in
> unrighteousness. - 2 Thessalonians 2:11-12

During the 1400s, paintings and sculptures were produced to reinvent major world events and ancient history to include the white race. The images of Jesus, all the prophets of the Bible, the kings and queens of Europe, and any remnants of rule by the dark races were remade by white artist such as Michael Angelo and Leonardo da Vinci to make it appear that all of these people and events of history were the work of the white race.

The picture of Jesus that we have all come to accept without one shred of proof is an Italian man named Cesar Borgia the son of Pope Alexander VI. The same Pope that authorized the Discovery Doctrine that allowed the murder, land theft, and slavery of the Israelite nation. Pope Alexander's son Caesar Borgia was the model used by Leonardo da Vinci when he was commissioned by the Roman Church to make a false white image of Christ. Michelangelo, da Vinci's contemporary took the model and made paintings and sculptures of his own.

The model for the false image of Jesus, Caesar Borgia, is described as one of the most ruthless, power hungry and vile men in history. Obviously the people who promote this image of Christ do not fear God if they believe in God at all.

The Black Messiah

What did Christ look like? Most Christians will probably tell you that "no one knows" or "it doesn't matter". But if it didn't matter, why does the Bible tell you what Christ looked like?

The only place where a physical description of Jesus is given is in the Bible. The skin color of Christ is directly referenced in both the Old Testament and the New Testament.

The Bible says that anybody confessing to be of God that does not confess that Christ came in the FLESH is NOT of God. This is how you test the spirit of those professing to be of God. If Jesus came in the flesh, what did his flesh look like?

> 2 Hereby know ye the Spirit of God: **Every spirit that
> confesseth that Jesus Christ is come in the flesh is of**

> **God**: 3 And every spirit that confesseth not that Jesus Christ
> is come in the flesh is not of God: and this is that spirit of
> antichrist, whereof ye have heard that it should come; and
> even now already is it in the world. - 1 John 4:2-3

Why would an obvious lie be put into place by people who claim to
represent God? The Bible gives us the simple answer: BECAUSE THEY
DON'T REPRESENT GOD AND ARE NOT OF GOD.

But if they don't represent God, who do they represent? God is not the
author of confusion. God does not put forth lies. This image of Jesus
is the work of Satan, the deceiver.

According to the Bible, If you believe that Jesus "was a spirit" you have
been fooled by the antichrist.

Jesus was a flesh and blood man. He was a black man according to the
Bible. This is plain and simple and cannot be refuted.

14 His head and his hairs were white **like wool,** as white as snow; and
his eyes were as a flame of fire; 15 And **his feet like unto fine brass,
as if they burned in a furnace**; and his voice as the sound of many
waters. - Revelation 1:14-15

The same reference is made in the Old Testament:

> His body also was like the beryl, and his face as the
> appearance of lightning, and his eyes as lamps of fire, and
> **his arms and his feet like in <u>colour</u> to polished brass**, and
> the voice of his words like the voice of a multitude.
> - Daniel 10:6

Again, the Bible tells us that Jesus was an Israelite from the tribe of
Judah.

> For it is evident that **our Lord sprang out of Judah**; of which
> tribe Moses spoke nothing concerning priesthood.
> - Hebrews 7:14

We have already shown the many references to Israelites having black
skin throughout the Bible. This description of the Israelites also
matches archeology and written history outside of the Bible.

Finally, the prophet Isaiah prophesied in the Old Testament 700 years before Christ was born on how the real Christ would be ignored and that he would be considered physically unattractive, undesirable, rejected, and despised.

> For he shall grow up before him as a tender plant, and as a root out of a dry ground: he hath **no form nor comeliness; and when we shall see him, there is no beauty that we should desire him**. - Isaiah 53:2

Does this sound like the rock star hippy that is worshipped as Christ? No. This describes someone who comes from among the people who are today told that their skin color is unattractive and their facial features are beautiful only if they are in line with the standard set by white people and white Jesus. Today even the true Israelite women hate their own beauty and prefer to try themselves, to look like this false image of white Jesus down to the skin color, facial features, hair texture, and hair color.

Bible prophesy is fulfilled as we continue to ignore the truth and focus on upholding an obvious lie of white supremacy. You must learn to despise this blasphemous image that has created so much death and destruction across the earth. Only a people with a slave mind would continue to believe in slave teachings when they can clearly see for themselves what is going on.

Why does race matter?

Race only matters because the enemies of the truth and the enemies of God made it matter. As long as you believe the picture of white Jesus, you will never be able to see the truth. White Jesus is, by far, the most wicked false image of the Renaissance Period.

> The Lord is nigh unto all them that call upon him, to all that **call upon him in truth**. - Psalms 145:18

You cannot serve God under the pretence of a lie. The truth is what makes you free. As long as you believe in lies you are a slave to sin and a slave to sinners.

We have already shown you that the Israelites are black and brown people. Jesus was an Israelite from the tribe of Judah, a black man.

The spiritual problem in the world starts with white Jesus. Lie after lie builds on itself from there to create total confusion and chaos among the people of the world.

Those who believe in the religions given to us by our slavers are being fed a steady diet of a white man as their lord and savior. Is there a wonder why we don't see Christ in each other? You hear our people constantly proclaiming that Jesus is a spirit and nobody knows what he looks like, or his race is not important.

Never mind the fact that the Bible explicitly says not to make images of things that are supposed to be Holy. If the race of Jesus was not important, why would white supremacist deliberately remake his race in their own image?

> For there shall arise **false Christs**, and false prophets, and shall show great signs and wonders; so that, if it were possible, **they shall deceive the very elect.** - Mathew:24:24

The false white image of Jesus has both run people away from the Bible and seduced those who try to follow religion into total agreement with the idea of white supremacy. This has placed them in total agreement with Satan. This is why our community is in the low state that it is in eventhough there are five and six churches in one city block.

Confused belief system

> But he answered and said, **I am not sent but unto the lost sheep of the house of Israel.** - Mathew 15:24

White Jesus equals white supremacy. White Jesus is a lie and white supremacy is a lie. Both lies are meant to create a confused, corrupted belief system.

Make no mistake, no matter what religion you follow, if you believe that there was a white Jesus you have been indoctrinated into the white supremacy belief system. Common sense should tell you that if someone would tell blatant lies about who they proclaim to be their God, you have been indoctrinated into something that is very, very sinister.

If you believe in and confess your love for white Jesus you are openly professing your love for white supremacy and professing your hatred of the truth of God.

The cross and white Jesus have been front and center at some of the most heinous crimes against humanity in the history of the world. From slavery, colonization and racial terrorism, to child molestation, to sanctioning war, to the overthrow of governments, to economic extortion, nothing has been too illicit for the churches of white supremacy to be involved in.

> **The words of his mouth were smoother than butter, but war was in his heart**: his words were softer than oil, yet were they drawn swords. - Psalm 55:21

Through it all, the meek, pious looking, white Jesus is still worshipped as god by billions of people. This false image is still able to recruit new victims who shun the words of the Bible because they are emotionally mesmerized by the imagery and spectacle of religious rituals and icons. The top icon and spectacle by far is white Jesus.

The white Jesus lie is so insidious that even after you know the truth, when you close your eyes and hear the word Jesus the false image still may come into your mind.

Undoing the brainwashing

> Study to shew thyself approved unto God, a workman that needeth not to be ashamed, **rightly dividing the word of truth**. - 2 Timothy 2:15

White supremacy brainwashing seeks to influence victims by blurring definitions or by substituting one definition for another in a deceptive manner. Again, these are the ways of Satan, not God. The most basic form of this propaganda is to repeat a lie over and over until it becomes perceived as the truth. This kind of propaganda can be detected when the words do not match the imagery or actions. If the propaganda is truly effective however, even obvious inconsistencies will not change the minds of the indoctrinated.

The repeated lie is what passes for history, news, entertainment, information, and religion under the white supremacy system.

It starts with the educational and religious systems. We are taught to regurgitate instead of evaluate and question. The main thing that is taught is obedience to authority. But whose authority?

In this kind of illusionary alternative reality society, how do you know what is real and what is propaganda?

Martin Luther King was killed because he asked and answered the question: Do the words, imagery, and actions of this narrative match?

We all must ask this question in order to wake up from the illusion. The words always show the true spirit. Matching words and actions is more reliable than focusing on symbols and idols.

In his speech Beyond Vietnam, Dr. King gave us the objective way to evaluate our situation. By looking at the giant triplets of racism, materialism, and militarism we can overcome the propaganda tricks and see things for what they really are.

The truth is that all Dr. King did was try to objectively apply the wisdom of the Scriptures to describe the current situation.

If Dr. King erred in any way, it is that his own indoctrination in the America system of white supremacy blinded him to the fact that, according to Biblical definitions, a country that has committed the evil that America has committed is eventually going to collapse under the weight of its own evil. Biblical teaching tells us that wicked nations always reap what they have sown.

> **And therefore be thou not curious how the ungodly shall be punished, and when**: but enquire how the righteous shall be saved, whose the world is, and for whom the world is created. -2 Edras 9:13

It was not the Bible but the white supremacy religious and educational indoctrination that caused Dr. King to feel that he should attempt to save America from its fate. His Beyond Vietnam speech demonstrated that Dr. King had come to grips with the fact that the words of the Bible showed the truth that the country that he was taught to love was not a nation of God but a nation of evil that operates under the power of Satan and not God.

Had he lived a few more years, Dr. King would have most likely come to the truth that he himself was an actual Israelite -- that he himself was most likely descended from the tribe of Judah, the same tribe as Christ.

Starting over

> And said, Verily I say unto you, **Except ye be converted, and become as little children**, ye shall not enter into the kingdom of heaven. - Matthew 18:3

To be born again is to start over. To come back to wisdom of the truth from whatever you have been taught or believed in the past. This is how you end the hold that white supremacy programming has over your perception of the world. You must be willing to admit that you have been the target of deception and negative mental programming. You must understand how imagery can cloud your perception of the truth.

Icons are specifically spoke against in the Bible because they lead to confusion and idolatry. Religious spectacle and illusions eventually will confuse your emotions. That is what they are meant to do.

As we have shown the most damaging lie created by white supremacy is that Christ and the prophets of the Bible were white. This can be called the founding lie of white supremacy that starts most of the confusion that we all live under now. This lie has caused many of us to dismiss the Bible altogether. Dismissing the Bible is just as damaging as accepting the lie of a white Jesus.

People always ask for evidence that the Bible is real. This is because they cannot believe that the Bible is not about white people as they have been taught to believe. The Bible seems inconsistent and unreal because it is inconsistent with the false history that is told by the white supremacy system. When you look at the history that could not be white washed by racism, you see that the Bible and true history match up perfectly because the Bible itself is a part of the history that could not be changed by the white supremacy fabricated narrative of past events.

Real icons and images

Where are the real images? Are there any left? There are images in the Roman Catacombs that can't be explained away. The Catacombs are early Christian underground burial tombs that clearly show that the early Christians were black. Christianity was started by Israelites (The House of Jacob, tribe of Judah and Benjamin) who started promoting the teachings of Christ (also and Israelite, tribe of Judah).

These early Christians were the ones who were made to fight to the death in the Roman Coliseums. The movie Gladiator depicts this era.

The movie of course fails to show you that the gladiators were black people.

The Catacomb burial caves under Rome contain artwork done by these early Israelite Christians. The art work clearly shows that these Israelites who the Romans began calling "Christians" were "Negro" people.

Eastern Europe is full of original artwork showing the black Popes, saints, kings, queens, knights, and noble men. Of course "historians" will try to tell you that these were African rulers who came to Europe as slaves or some other far fetched analysis.

The pyramids and ruins of Egypt also could not easily be destroyed. There is not a white face to be found on any ancient wall or hieroglyph. These ancient renderings prove that there was no such thing as a white Israelite. The House of Jacob was always and still is comprised of black and brown skinned people.

The Bible is the best ancient evidence that we have. It was written originally in Hebrew and could not be easily understood or destroyed by the creators of religions. The text of the Old Testament was around thousands of years before Christ. Christ himself read and quoted scripture from this ancient text. The Bible survived because it was very difficult to exterminate writings that had already reached far reaching parts of the world. Instead of trying to destroy the Bible, the white supremacists simply created contradictory church doctrine in hopes that people would never understand what was actually written in the Bible.

King James destroyed the strategy of false church doctrine when he had the Bible translated from the original Hebrew and Greek in 1611 by bypassing the Latin translations. No more could the controllers of the church use the limited understanding of Latin to deceive the masses of people about what is in the Scriptures.

Finally, you can look at the current people themselves who are known to be the oldest inhabitants of India, China, Malaysia, Cambodia, Pakistan, Mexico, the Middle East and other places that still have very dark skin and stand out from the rest of the lighter skin more recent populations.

Below are some examples of paintings of the early Christians. As you can see, these icons are black people. These are the true founders of Christianity, the Saints. Just like Christ himself, they are Israelites,

The House of Jacob. The Catholic Church turned these Saints into idols.

These are the real Christians.

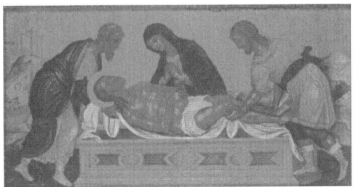

You still find these images in Orthodox Churches and museums in Eastern European countries.

When you think of the Bible, you need to think of these images. When you do that the words of the Bible will seem to jump off the page and a light bulb will go off. It will all start to make sense.

There is no doubt that spectacle and illusions are very effective ways to play on and confuse your emotions but we are going to show that the ancient words of the Bible give the history that cuts through the illusion to reveal the truth.

Here are the words of the Apostles that give the complete understanding of who Christ was and what he came to do:

> Then Peter and the other apostles answered and said, **we ought to obey God rather than men. The God of our fathers raised up Jesus**, whom ye slew and hanged on a tree. Him hath God exalted with his right hand **to be a Prince and a Saviour, for to give repentance to Israel, and forgiveness of sins.** - Acts 5:29-31

Christ was not some tree hugging hippy walking around handing out hugs to the entire world. That is the myth of white Jesus not the true Messiah as written of in the Bible. Christ did not come to bring all people together. And he did not come to accept everyone no matter what they do. He came to show Israelites how to properly use the laws of God to rightly divide things and people into clean and unclean, into good and evil, into righteous and unrighteous. That is the purpose of the law and the purpose of the Bible.

Here is what Christ the Israelite black man from the tribe of Judah actually said out of his own mouth:

> Suppose ye that I am come to give peace on earth? I tell you, **Nay; but rather division**: 52 For from henceforth there shall be five in one house **divided**, three against two, and two against three.
>
> 53 The father shall be **divided** against the son, and the son against the father; the mother against the daughter, and the daughter against the mother; the mother in law against her daughter in law, and the daughter in law against her mother in law. - Luke 12:51-53

Those who will not hear the truth will be divided from those who do. These two groups are not equal and Christ has nothing whatsoever to do with those who continue in following the traditions of wicked men instead of the word of God. The Bible is crystal clear:

To be saved means to be rescued. How can someone who does not want to separate from his capturers be rescued?

Anyone who chooses to be blinded by racism and ignore the truth about the lie of white Jesus and the false teachings that go along with him is not a follower of Christ; they are a follower of Satan and are an enemy of God. Period.

Take away from this chapter:

1. The false depiction of Christ as a white man is the number one source of racial confusion across the earth.

2. The false image of Christ is accompanied by a white supremacy doctrine that is not found in the Bible.

3. The truth of the Bible destroys the false ideas put forth by the white supremacy system.

O Lord God of Abraham, Isaac, and of Israel, our fathers,
keep this for ever in the imagination of the thoughts of the
heart of thy people, and prepare their heart unto thee:
- 1 Chronicles 29:18

6 Heritage Reset

The misinformation dilemma

> The thing that hath been, it is that which shall be; and that which is done is that which shall be done: and **there is no new thing under the sun.** - Ecclesiastes 1:9

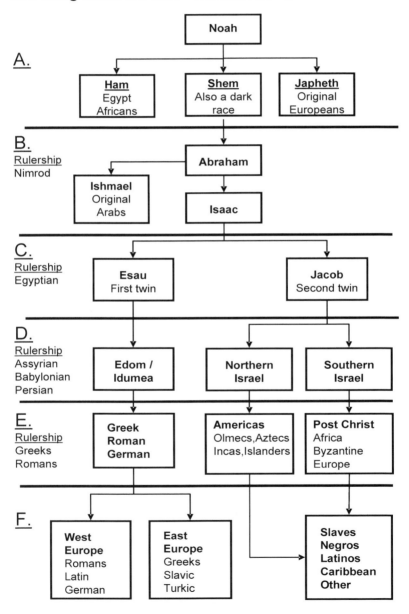

1. How do we know the truth about the past?
2. What is the difference between history, myths and parables?
3. How does history relate to your current reality?
4. How does history give instructions about the future?

The heritage chart shows the basic outline of world history as it relates to the House of Esau and the House of Jacob.

To reset your understanding of history and see the real nature of the current situation, you must study the history of racism, materialism and militarism. To properly understand history you must follow the history of war, empire, and rulership. This can be problematic because the victor of a war writes and rewrites history to his own benefit.

Useful history

The point here is not so much to give a detailed history lesson but to point out that the history that you have gotten is false; to show you glaring holes in what you believe to be true and the actual facts. Once you realize the inconsistencies, you can approach new information with a more critical eye.

> Neither give heed to **fables and endless genealogies**, which minister questions, rather than godly edifying which is in faith: - 1Timothy 1:4

This information may be too detailed for some and not detailed enough for others. The aim is to put forth the building blocks that give us a common understanding of historical facts.

Also, the scholars in our community need to focus on building on a foundation of common truth instead of building theories based on the false assumptions put forth by white supremacy. The reason why our true nationhood has been hidden is because all world history has been falsified by the white supremacy system.

The heritage diagram traces six different periods of history.

Historical behavior patterns

The purpose of understanding history is to provide a basis for predicting the future. When you study history you find that it is a series of repeating patterns. For this reason all useful history can be reduced to a parable. When you approach history with this understanding history becomes the foundation of building mental models that show you the proper thing to do in the current time period. Myth, parable, and history all serve the same purpose; to influence your current behavior.

The Bible contains elements of both fact and mythology. It doesn't matter if things actually happened exactly as it is written or whether things have been translated into multiple languages over thousands of years , what matters is who believes it and how they are incorporating this history into their belief systems and how societies are formed around various belief systems.

If enough people believe something to be true, they can have massive influence over other people who don't even have to be aware of the actual belief system or its causes. The handing down of narratives and myths is an undisputed historical fact.

The heritage chart breakdown

The Bible gives the physical and the spiritual beginnings of all races on the planet today. The Book of Genesis gives the history of how the world began. Chapter 10 of the Book of Genesis gives the table of nations that shows the lineage of all people.

> When the Most High **divided** to the nations their inheritance,
> when he **separated** the sons of Adam, he set the bounds of
> the people according to the number of the children of Israel.
> - Deuteronomy 32:8

Prehistory

> And the Lord God formed man of the **dust of the ground**,
> and breathed into his nostrils the breath of life; and man
> became a living soul. - Genesis 2:7

Before the story of Noah and the formation of the nations, the Bible gives the spiritual understanding of how evil entered into the world through the story of Adam and Eve.

The Bible tells us the Eve actually birthed two bloodlines (Genesis 3:15). The Scriptures tell us that Noah is a direct descendent of Adam.

The first split in humanity came when Eve bore two sons, Cain and Able. One found favor with the Lord (Able) and one did not (Cain). This is a repetitive theme throughout the Bible. Repeatedly we see the first born losing favor just as Cain did not find favor with God. Cain eventually killed Able.

Adam and Eve eventually had another son Seth who is the progenitor of Noah.

The story of Noah tells us that Noah, his three sons and his sons' wives were responsible for repopulating the earth after a great flood that caused the regeneration of the earth.

Noah's sons Ham, Shem, and Japheth were all dark skinned people. The original people of ALL physical nations were dark skinned people because they were originally populated by these three dark skinned men. This should be common sense, since there is no way for two so-called white people to produce a dark skinned child.

All the original bloodlines were separated through their progenitors even though they all had dark skin. This is a very important point that cannot be denied.

Only eight people: Noah, his wife, his three sons, and their three wives where spared. Noah's three sons form the original bloodlines of the earth today.

These three bloodlines are Ham, Japheth, Shem. These three are the basic classifications of all the bloodlines of the world that exist today. At this point in history, there were NO white skinned people.

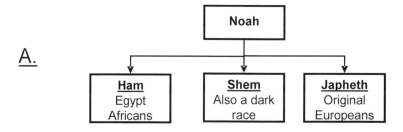

A. All the progenitors of the races had to be dark skinned people because there is no genetic way that two white skinned people could have produced the dark skinned people of Africa. Two dark skinned people can genetically produce light skinned people and all other human features. Noah, Ham, Shem, and Japheth were all dark skinned men.

Each bloodline eventually branched off into the various bloodline nations that we have today. Although all of these nations were initially connected, The Bible tells us that God separated them into their own nations for there own purposes.

When the Most High divided to the nations their inheritance, when he separated the sons of Adam, he set the bounds of the people according to the number of the children of Israel. - Deuteronomy 32:8

The map below shows the original locations of all the original bloodlines on the earth. Notice that they all originated around the so-called Middle East. Also notice that this is why the Middle East is not its own continent or attached to any of the other 7 continents according to the rulers of the earth today.

All the bloodlines on the earth today come out of the so-called Middle East. You can go to the Appendix for a larger version of this chart.

The House of Ham

These are the sons of Ham, after their families, after their tongues, in their countries, and in their nations.
- Genesis 10:20

Africa is the land of the children of Ham.

One of the biggest myths told about so-called African Americans is that they are Africans that originated from the bloodline of Ham. This is not true. Here is the correct definition of Ham from the Bible Dictionary.

Zondervan's Compact Bible Dictionary: Ham - The youngest son of Noah, born probably about 96 years before the Flood; and one of eight persons to live through the Flood. He became the progenitor of the dark races; **not the Negroes**, but the Egyptians, Ethiopians, Libyans and Canaanites.

1. Cush (The Ethiopians) settled in Ethiopia south of Egypt, also early in their history some of them migrated to an area north of the Persian Gulf (Gen. 10:8-10)

2. Mizraim (The Egyptians) the Bible name for Egypt, settled in northeastern Africa.

3. Phut (The Libyans) sometimes translated Libya, settled in northern Africa.

4. Canaan (The Canaanites) settled above Africa east of the Mediterranean (Later was given to the Hebrews).

Colonial white supremacy historians tried to convince the world that the victims of American slavery were from the nation of Ham. They concocted an easily debunked lie that black skin was the curse of Ham according to the Bible. But the Bible clearly shows that the curse was on Ham's son Canaan and that he would serve the other nations. The curse actually shows that Canaanites were cursed with leprosy that turned their skin and hair WHITE.

The nations of Ham included some of the most fierce enemies of the Israelite nation and the land of the Canaanites was eventually conquered to create Israel in the time of Moses.

Ham proves that Noah was a black man. There is no way that Ham could have come from a white man.

The House of Japheth
Japheth is the father of the original dark skinned Europeans and East Asians and East Indians.

1. Gomer (The Cimmerians) settled north of the Black Sea, but afterwards his descendants probably occupied Germany, France, Spain and the British Isles.

2. Magog (The Scythians) lived north of the Caspian Sea.

3. <u>Madai</u> (The Medes) settled south of the Caspian Sea.

4. <u>Javan</u> (The Ionians or Greeks) Javan is the Hebrew name for Greeks, they settled in Greece.

5. <u>Tubal</u> (The Turks) lived south of the Black Sea.

6. <u>Meshech</u> (The Slavs) lived between the Black and Caspian Seas,

7. <u>Tiras</u> (The Etruscans) located west of the Black Sea.

Japheth is not the focus of the Bible. This nation was the original founders of what is now known as Europe and they were a dark skinned people.

The House of Shem

These are the sons of Shem, after their families, after their tongues, in their lands, after their nations. -Genesis 10:31

Shem is the forefather of the nation of Israel, also the original black Arabs, and the Edomites.

1. <u>Elam</u> (The Persians) settled northeast of the Persian Gulf.

2. <u>Asshur</u> (The Assyrians) the Biblical name for Assyria, settled between the Euphrates and Tigris Rivers.

3. <u>Arphaxad</u> (Abraham's forefather) settled in Chaldea.

4. <u>Lud</u> (The Lydians) settled in Asia Minor, but some of them sailed across the Mediterranean and settled in northern Africa.

5. <u>Aram</u> (The Syrians) the Biblical name for Syria, located north and east of Israel.

Shem's bloodline is where Abraham, Isaac, and Jacob and Esau come from (through Arphaxad #3 on the list). This common lineage is shared by the Israelite nation and the Edomite nation. Esau is the twin brother of Jacob. Their father is Isaac.

B.

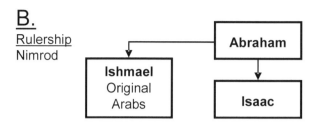

Rulership
Nimrod

B. The Bible is written from the standpoint of the lineage of Abraham. Abraham is the father of many nations. Ishmael was the first born of Abraham's sons. Ishmael and Isaac had two different mothers. Ishmael was born to one of Abraham's wife's servants with the permission of his wife. Ishmael is the father of the Arabs. Islam was created by the descendants of Ishmael.

Isaac is the father of the Israelites; he is also the father of the Edomites. Isaac actually receives the inheritance of Abraham because, although he was the second son, he was born to Abraham's natural wife.

Ishmael was the first born of Abraham but did not receive Abraham's inheritance. Ishmael is the father of the Arabs. Many people of color are following the religion created by the Ishmaelites, Islam. This is not the religion of Isaac the progenitor of the Israelites.

Nimrod was the ruler during the time of Abraham. Nimrod was the first to try to build a global empire. The Bible tells us that this rulership was destroyed by God because God never meant for all nations to come together.

The story of the tower of Babel in the Bible is the story of Nimrod trying to build a tower into the sky to fight against God himself. The story goes that when God saw this he destroyed the tower and so this would not happen again He confounded the speech of the people (created different languages) so that the different bloodlines could not easily communicate with each other.

> And the Lord said, Behold, the people is one, and they have all one language; and this they begin to do: and now nothing will be restrained from them, which they have imagined to do. - Genesis 11:6

This story clearly expresses the folly in trying to undo the natural boundaries that exist among humanity. This has been a rule that has constantly been broken since the time of Nimrod.

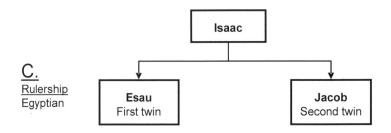

C.
Rulership
Egyptian

C. Jacob and Esau were twin brothers. Esau was born with a different skin color than Jacob. Esau is described as being born "red and hairy". This notation is given to show how the Caucasian race began. Esau is the progenitor of the majority of Caucasians. Because Esau was the first born twin, he was supposed to get the birthright of his father Isaac. When he was a teenager, Esau sold his birthright to Jacob for basically nothing, a bowl of soup. Later on when Esau realized what he had done he hated Jacob. Esau vowed to kill Jacob when their father died. He didn't kill Jacob but their descendants became bitter enemies. The Egyptians ruled during this time. The Israelites eventually became ruled over and went into slavery under the Egyptians.

Jacob and Esau
The following scripture describes the beginning of the real war that is going on in the earth today. It describes how the House of Jacob and its ongoing enemy, the House of Esau were born. Jacob and Esau are the great grandsons of Abraham. They were twins born of the same father, Isaac.

21 And **Isaac** intreated the LORD for his wife, because she was barren: and the LORD was intreated of him, and Rebekah his wife conceived.

22 And the **children struggled together within her**; and she said, If it be so, why am I thus? And she went to enquire of the LORD.

23 And the LORD said unto her, **Two nations are in thy womb, and two manner of people shall be separated from thy bowels**; and the one people shall be stronger than the other people; **and the elder shall serve the younger**. 24And

when her days to be delivered were fulfilled, behold, there were twins in her womb.

25 And **the first came out red**, all over like an hairy garment; and they called his name **Esau**. 26 And after that came his brother out, and his hand took hold on Esau's heel; and his name was called **Jacob**: and Isaac was threescore years old when she bare them. - Genesis 22:21-26

What is this passage telling us?

Esau looks different than his brother and his parents. He was born red and hairy. His color is highlighted denoting that he looks different from his twin brother and his parents. This is what so called science is now confirming, that white people came out of the black race. They try to say that "we all came out of Africa". This again is a deception meant to obscure the true heritage of Edomites.

Jacob's sons

Jacob's 12 sons became the twelve tribes of Israel. One tribe, the tribe of Dan was basically disowned when the tribes split. Dan is believed to be the Ethiopian Jews. The tribe of Dan was replaced by the tribe of one of Joseph's sons, Manasseh. This gave Joseph representation in two tribes.

Esau's sons

When we begin to trace the House of Esau we must start with his sons. We find the information on Esau's lineage in Genesis chapter 36. Esau's sons formed the nation of Edom (also called Idumea).

The Edomites became Greeks, Edomite Jewish, Roman, Germans, Slavs, and Edomite Arabs. They left Edom to eventually create the global empire that we see today.

Skin color

Scientific evidence and common sense tells us that melanin, which is responsible for skin color, is the most dominant trait that a human can possess. So called white skin is a melanin deficiency. So called white skin is pinkish in color because the lack of melanin causes the blood to show through. This skin condition denotes a defect, an abnormal condition, not superiority. Since melanin is a dominate trait, so-called white skin had to have come from dark skinned people. ALL of the original people of the earth had to have dark skin. There are probably not many people who will dispute this at this point. But there is a bigger point to this.

This arrives us at the inescapable fact that **every continent in the world was originally inhabited by dark skinned people** who we would now characterize as "Black" or the African type.

The table of nations in the Bible (Genesis chapter 10) shows us that all of these dark skinned people are NOT all from the same exact bloodline, even though white supremacy desperately tries to cover up this fact. White supremacy scientists and historians have falsely tried to formulate that the "African type" is one race of people. This is definitely not the case and is the source of much confusion especially when so-called Negroes try to find their original place in the world.

The European continent remained a mostly dark dominated continent until the Greek and Roman eras. In the 1400s "Renaissance Period" the white race gained control of the entire European continent. At the time of Pope Nicolas V's decree of war, the Edomites finally conquered Europe, only a short time before they began trying to conquer the Americas.

How white skin came into the world

Science now tries to confirm what was written in the Bible for thousands of years; that the white race came out of a black race. Even this admission comes with a deceitful motive.

To straighten out your understanding, you must accept the truth that every single civilization on the planet was originally founded and inhabited by people who had dark skin. Dark skin is still the most prevalent and dominate trait on the planet today.

As we have stated, the original Europeans, Greeks, Egyptians, Asians, Chinese, Persians, Indians, Arabs, etc., were all very dark people. Every human feature --straight hair, slanted eyes, blond hair, red hair, various eye colors, various facial features, and body types -- can be found within what we would call the black race. The bottom line is that the white race developed out of the black race. Science bears this out.

So where did white skin come from? For the explanation we can turn to both The Bible and modern science. They do not disagree.

The Bible describes white skin and blond hair as leprosy. Today's scientists call this phenomenon Albinoism.

The Book of Leviticus chapter 13 in the Bible is devoted to dealing with leprosy, which is a form of albinoism that turns the skin and the hair white.

> 12 And if a leprosy break out abroad in the skin, and the leprosy cover all the skin of him that hath the plague from his head even to his foot, wheresoever the priest looketh;
>
> 13 Then the priest shall consider: and, behold, if the leprosy have covered all his flesh, he shall pronounce him clean that hath the plague: it is all turned white: he is clean.
> -Leviticus 13:12-13

Mixed races

To consider a person to be of mixed race requires repeated isolated contact. One relative does not change that mixture.

The Bible deals with this by generally stating, you are what your father is. However the children of a mixture of the races can enter into the congregation after a few generations. This would seem to point out the fact that the majority of a gene pool cannot be cancelled out by limited contact with another race.

It would take multiple generations of mixed race females breeding outside of their race to effectively breed out the previous majority characteristics. This is how the white race grew into a separate race on the earth.

Physical proximity was the initial way that nations were identified because it said something about the genetic make up of the people. The fathers of the nations may have initially taken various wives of other nations but the offspring tended to breed in isolated areas which created a nation both in the sense of location and genetic make up.

This basic understanding is essential in dealing with the race and identity problems that exist on the earth today.

The Mount of Esau

The Mount of Esau is the ruling class of the House of Esau. They are the Edomites who have kept their bloodlines relatively pure throughout the various empires and evolutions of the Edomites.

They are sometimes referred to as "Blue Bloods", "Nobles", or other terms to denote their elevated status above the other members of their race.

The Mount is the top of the class system within the House of Esau. They have less outside blood mixture than the rest of the Edomites. The Mount of Esau are the controllers of the global corporate empire. They are ultimately the beneficiaries of the House of Esau's corporate empire.

Edom becomes despised by God

Since Esau had no regard for his birthright, God turned his back on Esau and his descendants. This is why you have churches that are set up by the House of Esau that work in direct opposition to the word of God.

> 16 Lest there be any fornicator, or profane person, as **Esau**, who for one morsel of meat sold his birthright.
>
> 17 For ye know how that afterward, when he would have inherited the blessing, he was rejected: **for he found no place of repentance**, though he sought it carefully with tears. - Hebrews 12:16-17

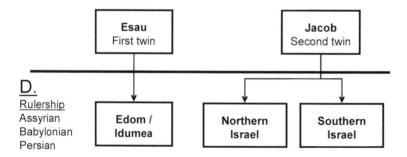

D. Ancient times 1200 B.C. 700 B.C.

Moses led the Israelites out of the captivity of Egypt, he is credited with writing down the Laws of God and the history contained in the first 5 Books of the Bible. He also created a mysterious power source that linked the Israelites to God. The power source was called The Ark of the Covenant. It contained the stones that the Commandments were written on. The Ark was carried into battle and according to the Bible had the power to burn men alive if touched.

The Israelites conquered the land of Canaan to form the land of Israel. King David and then his son King Solomon were the only unified rulers of Israel. David made plans to build a temple that would house the Ark. His son Solomon carried out the plans. The temple was called Solomon's temple.

Solomon took 700 wives, many of which came from other nations. At the end of his life, his wives convinced him to erect temples to other gods. The Bible tells us that Solomon broke the covenant with God by following the gods of his wives. The Scripture says that Solomon affectively activated the curses contained in the Law of Moses by enticing the Israelites to follow strange gods.

After the death of Solomon (930 B.C.), just as the Law of Moses predicted, the tribes became split when the Northern Tribes began worshiping these other gods.

The tribes went to war with each other over the worship of these idols and strange gods. The nation became split with the Southern tribes of Judah, Benjamin, and part of Levi becoming the Southern Kingdom now known as Judea. These tribes are together known as Jews. The other ten tribes plus part of Levi became the Northern Kingdom. These tribes are referred to after the split as the tribes of Israel.

One tribe, the tribe of Dan, refused to join either side. Dan most likely ended up in Ethiopia. Dan was replaced in the hierarchy of tribes by the tribes of Ephraim and Manasseh (Ephraim and Manasseh are Jacob's grandsons; they were the sons of Jacob's son Joseph). So Joseph is represented by two tribes while the other eleven sons of Jacob are represented by one tribe each.

During the in fighting, Ramses III of Egypt (950 B.C.) raided Solomon's temple and the Ark of the Covenant disappears.

During this period, Esau's descendants, the Edomites, became mercenaries who sided with the various rulers against the Israelites. The Edomites had their own land, Idumea, that was set up by the ruling powers and given favor by the Babylonians and latter the Assyrians. This favored position allowed the Edomites to begin to rule over the Israelites which further created Israelite bitterness towards the Edomites.

The Assyrians went to war with the Northern Kingdom. The Assyrians eventually destroyed the Northern Kingdom and placed other people in their lands (720 B.C.). The Northern tribes eventually escaped to the Americas.

Later in 586 B.C., the Babylonians conquered the Southern tribes and took most of the people into slavery. Many of the main prophets of the Bible come from the Babylonian captivity period. Fifty years later in 536 B.C. the Persians conquered the Babylonians. The Persians allowed the Southern Kingdom to be rebuilt.

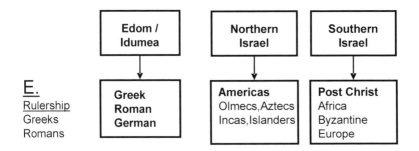

E. Hellenistic Period 536 B.C. – 142 B.C.

During the rule of the Persians, certain tribes of Edomites took over the land of the original Greeks. These Edomites began calling themselves Greeks. The Edomite Greeks then fought against the Persians for rulership.

In 334 B.C. the Edomite Greeks under Alexandra finally defeated the Persians and began the total take over of Europe and other lands controlled by the Persians.

During this time, the Israelites became assimilated into Greek culture and were considered "Hellenized" Greeks. The Greeks wanted one unified culture and sought to end all Israelite customs and practices. After the death of Alexander, the Greek Empire fell apart and was split up among his generals.

Around 166 B.C., the Israelites rebelled against the split Greek Empire and won independence for a time. This fight for independence is chronicled in the Books of the Apocrypha that has been removed from most Bibles. During this time the Israelites converted many Greeks into becoming followers of Israelite customs.

A faction of the split Greek Empire became the Romans.

In 27 B.C. the Romans sought control of the entire Greek empire and came against the rest of the Greek territories. The Romans finally gained control of the empire and became rulers over Israel. This was the time of Christ.

At this time the only tribes that were left were the Southern Kingdom, the Jews. The Romans finally destroyed Jerusalem in 70 AD. The Israelites of the Southern Kingdom fled into Africa and went on to found the Empire of Ghana with the capital being Timbuktu.

In 332 A.D., the Romans installed Christianity as its state religion eventhough the actual Christians were Israelites (the Saints) who believed that Christ was the Messiah. The Romans incorporated all of the pagan customs that they were already following into the state religion of Christianity. They adopted the Bible but created their own theology that most times contradicts the Scriptures, which were all originally written by the Israelites.

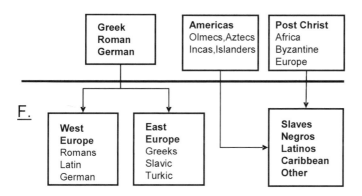

F. Splitting of the Roman Empire 476 - 1452

Around 476 A.D. another faction of the Edomites who were mercenaries under the Assyrian Kingdom (700 BC), now known as the Germans, came out of Western Europe to split the Roman Empire into two empires. The Germans were able to control the Western Roman Empire, The Holy Roman Empire. The Greeks were able to retain control over the Eastern Roman Empire, The Byzantine Empire. The Christian church was also split into two different churches: The Roman Catholic Church and the Greek Orthodox Church. The Byzantine Empire was ruled in large part by Israelites.

113

The Greek Orthodox Church for the most part kept the historical accuracy of the dark skinned Israelites while the Roman Catholic Church changed the images of the Israelite Saints to that of Edomites. The Turks were an Edomite faction of the Greek Empire who adopted Islam as their religion.

The Turks under the Ottoman Empire rose up against the Byzantine Empire and finally defeated it in 1453. Eventually the Edomites were able to control all of Europe, North Africa, and what we now call the Middle East. Along with the Arabs, they enslaved and subdued Israelite controlled kingdoms and eventually went on to enslave the Northern tribes of the Israelites that had fled to the America and the Southern tribes that fled into Africa centuries earlier.

Roman Empire – present day

The various bloodlines of Esau became apparent with the rise and fall of the unified Roman Empire.

Rome seemed to come out of nowhere to fill the power vacuum left by the death of Alexander the Great around 200 BC. After his death, Alexander's Greek Kingdom was split up among his top generals. It became a splintered and over extended empire.

The Romans came in and absorbed the Greek territories and expanded it even further.

When Rome finally fell it was at the hands of the Germanic tribes. This split the Roman Empire into two kingdoms, The Holy Roman Empire of the west and the Byzantine Empire of the Greek east.

The empire was basically split along Roman and Greek culture.

The Greeks

The rise of the Greeks is the most well documented history that we can bring out in our analysis. The Bible cross references with other historical accounts concerning this lineage.

Zepho, Esau's grandson became the ruler of Greece. He is the grandfather of Alexander "the Great". Alexander accomplished the conquest of Europe that was started by his father Phillip of Macedonia.

The original people of Greece were of the bloodline of Japheth. These people would later be run out of Europe or exterminated by the "new" Greek Edomites.

The account of Alexander shows that the Edomites became mercenaries and found their way into societies that they would later overthrow. This is a pattern that they would continue throughout history.

The Germans

The Germans would seem to have gotten to Germany by way of being mercenaries for the Assyrians. They are probably descended from Esau's grandson Gatam and became the Goths.

The now Germanic countries are: Great Britain, Netherlands, Germany, Austria, Switzerland, Belgium, France, Spain, Portugal, Scandinavians (Denmark, Sweden, Finland, Norway, Iceland, Faroe Islanders, not Sami)

The Turks

The Turkish people would appear to be descended from Esau's grandson Teman. They came to power under the Ottoman Empire. Ottoman seems to be a corruption of "Teman".

The now Turkic countries are: Turkey, Egypt, Iran, Libya, Iraq, Jordan, Kuwait, Lebanon, Oman, Qatar, Saudi Arabia, Syria, United Arab Emirates, Yemen, Bahrain.

The people in these countries today are not Arabs or Muslims as they like to generically call themselves. These are not nationalities. The original Arabs are Ishmaelites who are dark people and cousins to the Israelites. Ishmael was the first son of Abraham. The pale "Arabs" that control what we now call the Middle East are a mixture of Greek Edomites and Turkish Edomites.

The Slavic people

The Slavic people would seem to have descended from Esau's grandson Kenaz. Ashkenaz is the ancient term for the areas of central Europe. Ashkenza is also the Biblical name of the Japhetic peoples that originally inhabited the land. It seems more than just a coincidence that Slavic Jewish people call themselves Ashkenazi Jews after this region. The Slavic people that inhabit Europe today are not the original Japhetic people of Europe. Japhetic people did not have white skin.

Slavic Jews would seem to be descended from Esau's grandson Amalek. Amalekites are in the most close contact with the children of Israel throughout the Bible and are the arch enemy that seeks to trip up Israel at every turn.

115

Slavic countries are: Russia, Ukraine, Poland, Greece, Hungary, Macedonia, Albania, Azerbaijan, Belarus, Bosnia and Herzegovina, Bulgaria, Croatia, Czech Republic, Hungary, Georgia, Kosovo, Moldova, Montenegro, Romania, Serbia, Slovakia, Slovenia, Estonia, Latvia, Lithuania.

The Romans

Although Rome is still ruling the earth through the Catholic Church, no one seems to know the origins of Rome. But it is widely established that Romans are Edomites. In the Bible, Edom is used synonymously with Rome. The Roman word for Edom is Idumea.

Everybody else

The table of nations from Genesis chapter 10 also contains the origins of the rest of the peoples of the world. The bottom line is that at this point in history, the House of Jacob and the House of Esau are the two spiritual systems that we ALL must choose between. Everyone will be forced to pick a side no matter what your racial background may be.

Those who are of the House of Jacob will gravitate back to their belief system and those who are of Esau will press forward with their tactics. The point is that you can make a choice. We are trying to show you that the choice is clear.

The white supremacy empire of injustice that was created under the House of Esau will collapse, the only question is when.

Esau's World Wars

The world wars have been fought among the House of Esau. The various tribes and factions that came out of the Roman Empire split, are still split today. The Edomites still have an Eastern Block European, Western Block European, Ottoman Turk split. This is the same split that the Edomites had when they came out of the Roman Empire.

This may not be apparent because the Ottoman Turks now call themselves Arabs and inhabit the so-called Middle East and North African countries. Just as the European Edomites have assumed the religions and customs of other people, the Turks have assumed the religion of Islam and the identity of Arabs.

Just as Germany ended the unified Roman Empire, Germany also sought to control the entire House of Esau through the World Wars. It should be noted that the ruling monarchy of Great Britain are also Germans.

116

Modern slavery of the Israelites 1453 - present

> The Lord shall bring a nation against thee from far, from the end of the earth, as swift as **the eagle** flieth; a nation whose tongue thou shalt not understand; - Deuteronomy 28:49

Coinciding with the fall of the Byzantine Empire (Eastern Roman) in 1453 to the Edomite Turks was the colonization of the "New World" and the Trans Atlantic slave trade by the Western Roman Empire.

The slave trade and colonial land theft was first authorized by the Catholic Church when in 1452 Pope Nicholas V issued the papal order "Dum Diversas". This pronouncement allowed Portugal to enslave what the Church considered "pagans" in West Africa. It also allowed Portugal to steal any lands it could conquer in the "New World" and enslave the natives.

What the church really did was allow Portugal to declare war on Israelites. The Catholic Church declared perpetual war and enslavement of the offspring who the Bible says were to inherit the promises of God.

In probably the most sinister piece of white supremacy war propaganda ever devised, the Pope --himself a heathen according to the Bible--as a justification for war against the tribes of Israel came up with the outrageous scheme to redefine God's chosen people as heathens and tell heathens that they were God's chosen people as long as they followed the church. This was carried out despite the fact that the Bible shows the direct opposite.

This Church declaration is the founding law of all so-called property rights claims of the white supremacy global Edomite Empire. The United States has upheld this church doctrine as the basis of all property rights under U.S. law.

The "Discovery Doctrine" has been used as a basis for white supremacy all over the globe but no other nation besides the House of Jacob has been so completely dismantled by it in terms of losing its entire national identity as well as its land and property.

A whole other people is now claiming the identity of the House of Jacob and the world is made to sympathize with their plight as Gods chosen while the true children of Israel continue to suffer at the bottom of every society.

The church law that calls for perpetual slavery of the House of Jacob has never been rescinded.

The Jacobean Era

King James was the last black ruler in Europe. He had the Bible translated from Hebrew and Greek into English so that the masses of people would have a true record of history and an understanding of who are the true Israelites. This is the 1611 King James Bible. By 1619 King James was dead. The colonies that he authorized in America had begun enslaving Israelites; history was obscured and falsified by white washed images and phony facts and the prophecy of the Bible continued to come to pass. The Bible remains to tell the record.

The ancient race problem

As you can see the "race problem" goes back to Ancient times but it is not about skin color. Remember this is spiritual warfare. The race problem is just a diversion that keeps us from understanding the real problem which is spiritual.

Take away from this chapter:

1. Understanding history is absolutely necessary in understanding current reality.

2. People who do not know history are doomed to repeat the mistakes of the past.

3. The struggles going on in the earth are ancient and Biblical.

And they that are left of you shall pine away in their iniquity in your enemies ' lands; and also in the iniquities of their fathers shall they pine away with them. - Leviticus 26:39

7 Economic Warfare Reset

The social arrangement dilemma
The materialism dilemma

> **Therefore my people are gone into captivity**, because they
> have no knowledge: and their honourable men are famished,
> and their multitude dried up with thirst. - Isaiah 5:13

1. What is economic warfare?
2. What are the roadblocks to economic freedom?
3. How do you win an economic war?

Nature is a closed system that provides for everything that exists in it,
including man. So why then should mankind struggle and toil to get
what is basic to its survival? Why do other animals seem to know what
to do to survive while man attempts to create ever changing systems to
solve the same problems that have existed since the beginning of time?

The answer is that our own imagination and emotions, our perception,
can create stumbling blocks to our own physical survival.

What is economics?

Wealth = <u>real value</u> + perceived value

Economics deals with the substance of the physical world, real value.
Specifically, it is the distribution of resources among the members of
society. To practice proper economics you must be able to rightly
divide physical things into assets and liabilities. You then use this
information to divide activity into productive versus unproductive
activity.

There are two basic opposing mental approaches to dealing with
economics: The abundance mindset and the scarcity mindset. The
abundance mindset recognizes that nature is naturally productive and
provides enough to sustain all life forms, including man. The scarcity
mindset believes just the opposite, that there is not enough to go
around, so man must compete for his survival against other men,
animals, and nature itself.

The current economic system created by the House of Esau is set up under the scarcity mindset. This mindset creates the perception that one person's gain must mean another person's loss. It is the mindset that creates competition, greed, and envy. The main emotion involved in the scarcity mindset is fear. Fear creates the perception that mankind must struggle against each other and also struggle against nature.

This is the mentality that produces materialism. Materialism is a fear based mindset. It is driven by fear. It is fear that produces the greed, envy, and hording behavior that are the indicators of a materialistic mentality.

Economics under the current system of white supremacy is the same as physical warfare because of the adversarial inverse relationships that it creates between the races and classes. The liabilities of people of color (food, water and shelter) are assets for the House of Esau under the white supremacy system.

In this type of environment, economic war is a game of access and keep away. <u>Groups that have similar interests and a similar perspective form an economic class whether they like it or not.</u>

Economic duality (freedom versus servitude)

> **Therefore shalt thou serve thine enemies** which the Lord shall send against thee, **in hunger, and in thirst, and in nakedness, and in want of all things**: and he shall put a yoke of iron upon thy neck, until he have destroyed thee.
> - Deuteronomy 28:48

Many of us refuse to admit that our community, The House of Jacob, has economic enemies. Too many of us refuse to admit that we are not one with, have never been one with, and will never be one with Caucasians, the House of Esau. When you are in this state of confusion, you become an agent for the white supremacy system and the enemy of your own people. You become an enemy of truth and an enemy of justice.

The above verse clearly shows that the Israelites have enemies and they would economically serve these enemies. Who are the Israelites enemies? How does this fit with the accepted narrative of so-called integration and assimilation? How does the failure to recognize your economic enemies impact your economic decision making and your economic prosperity?

120

According to the above verse, servitude is indicated by depending on your enemies for food, water, clothing, and all other things that are needed for basic survival. This verse clearly describes what has happened and is still happening to so-called people of color. The Israelites are still in economic servitude in the Western Hemisphere because they do not control the basic resources needed for survival. The House of Jacob is in servitude under the House of Esau because it must rely on the House of Esau for all things related to basic survival.

Economic justice

When you realize that justice is on the side of the oppressed, you see that the House of Jacob has the most potential power in the history of the world. The House of Jacob and those who side with it will recapture all of the energy that is being lost to the spiritual and economic blockage caused by the rulership of the House of Esau. To get this understanding you must understand the power of hidden intangible assets and liabilities.

You can call it karma, you can call it reaping and sowing, you can call it cause and effect. But whatever you call it, all evidence points to the fact that the House of Esau has built a massive intangible liability because of the negative emotion, destruction, and lies that it continues to propagate across the earth.

> **He that leadeth into captivity shall go into captivity**: he that killeth with the sword must be killed with the sword.
> Here is the patience and the faith of the saints.
> - Revelation 13:10

To believe in white supremacy economics is to believe that justice will never be done. This is really the belief that God does not exist and the belief that the vain customs of the white supremacy system are superior to the truth of cause and effect. This is a monumental mistake for those who are the historical victims of white supremacy injustice. When you believe in the white supremacy economic system, you give away your competitive advantage and the competitive advantage of your nation – economic justice.

On-going servitude

What was once deemed as slavery and economic tyranny has now been accepted as our normal everyday lifestyle.

We are still in economic captivity because we are basically a one product nation. Most of the income of our nation comes from selling one resource, our labor. This does not create wealth because all productive activity must be measured by time.

When you sell your time, the net result is that someone else is able to use that time to artificially produce more time and energy for themselves. This is how the controllers of capitalism gain their power over our community. They are able to control the energy of our nation by controlling our time because we sell our labor to enterprises that we do not own. Because we have no ownership in these institutions and enterprises, we do not receive the true benefit of our labor.

> **Is Israel a servant?** is he a homeborn slave? why is he spoiled? - Jeremiah 2:14

We must decide that were not made to be a servant class for the economic schemes of other races. It takes courage and vision to see the alternative to the unjust economic system that has gripped the whole world. To gain this vision you must understand the true nature of the system and understand how it historically came about. You must understand the hidden costs of siding with injustice just because you are made to feel that you have no other choice. You must understand the unforeseen consequences of being willing to turn your back on the truth in hopes of receiving a so-called comfortable lifestyle.

Resistance

Having money or a comfortable economic status does not necessarily do anything to solve the problems that are created by the giant triplets of racism, materialism, and militarism.

> Even so faith, if it hath not works, is dead, being alone. Yea, a man may say, Thou hast faith, and I have works: shew me thy faith without thy works, and **I will shew thee my faith by my works**. - James 2:17-18

Resisting unjust economic schemes and developing economic activity based on the truth requires faith. Your willingness to resist these economic schemes demonstrates your faith. If you believe that it can't be done, this proves your lack of faith in the ability of God to defeat these systems that have been built by men to go against God.

To resist these schemes we must consider the condition of our people a crisis and we must focus exclusively on productive activity. We must stay focused on the true indicators of success and failure. We must rightly divide the word of truth.

Discretion and economics - cash up for grabs

> Wherefore do ye spend money for that which is not bread? and **your labour for that which satisfieth not?** hearken diligently unto me, and eat ye that which is good, and let your soul delight itself in fatness. - Isaiah 55:2

As technology moves forward, there is very little of the world's basic needs that cannot be solved by applying some kind of tool or technology. There is absolutely no reason for anyone to go without adequate food or shelter. It has been that way since the beginning of time. The poverty situation on the earth is a creation of very sick human minds.

> **The earth is given into the hand of the wicked**: he covereth the faces of the judges thereof; if not, where, and who is he? - Job 9:24

When you talk about economics under the white supremacy system you are most likely dealing with money that is completely up for grabs because most of the economic activity of the House of Esau deals purely in perceived value. This is a major weakness that can be exploited to gain power over the system. If you can change perception, you can quickly create value. When you create value, you create wealth. When you create wealth for yourself, you remove wealth from some aspect of the competing system.

Most of us have probably herd the reoccurring press reports about the buying power of the so-called black community. The reports like to throw around the fact that the so-called black community has a trillion dollars in buying power. This is done to pretend like this is a measure of progress.

The truth is that through unnecessary and reckless consumer behavior, most of this trillion dollars is constantly up for grabs and 99% of the time it is turned back over to the white supremacy system from where it came from in the first place.

Even more disturbing is that most of this so-called buying power only comes from providing labor to the white supremacy system and not from business or entrepreneurial pursuits. What really is up for grabs is not money, but the time and energy of our people. When your time

123

and energy is turned over to another nation, your nation is a captive of that nation and your people are slaves.

The way to recapture all of the money that is up for grabs is to employ the spiritual technology that we will be discussing in this book. How physical technology is implemented is a matter of spiritual values. It takes innovators and entrepreneurs who are using the right definitions to recapture this lost energy and get us out of economic captivity.

Anything that does not defend our community against the giant triplets of racism, materialism, or militarism cannot be considered productive activity. Anything that is considered unproductive activity should be analyzed to see if it can be converted into productive activity. If it cannot, it needs to be avoided at all costs.

Time and capital

The power of capitalism is that embedded in capital is generations of time. Providing or denying access to this time is the idea behind institutional lending. Access to capital provides instant leverage because the person receiving the capital instantly has access to more time and energy than his own. He is receiving the past labor that is embedded in the capital. This allows him to control the time and energy of people in the current time by offering to use the capital to pay wages for their labor.

Of course the majority of the labor embedded in capitalism came from the free labor of people of color during the slave trade.

Under the corporate capitalistic system, the average CEO of a large corporation earns more than 400 times the pay of the average worker. The CEO of Walmart earns somewhere in the neighborhood of $11,000 per hour. What could he possibly offer society that is that much more valuable than the millions of other workers that keep Walmart going? After the third or forth day of any year, he has earned more than the yearly pay of 98% of the people in the entire world. What does he do with the excess money after all of his basic needs for the year are covered after only a few hours of work?

Companies like Walmart refuse to pay a decent wage out of its massive profit but will overpay executives who will never share the money with anyone outside of their own class. What they are really doing is stealing the time and energy of low paid workers and giving it to higher paid workers. They are creating instant leverage for one person while draining the time and energy of millions of people to do it.

Time and luxury

Leisure time is the ultimate luxury. Physical luxuries mean nothing if you have no time to enjoy them.

Luxury is the idea of additional convenience that can far exceed basic necessities. In technologically advance societies most desires are in fact luxuries. Luxury is that which is over and above what is needed to survive in the physical world.

In economic terms luxury is expressed as profit and loss. Anything that is left over from the resources that you began with is a profit. Anything that takes away from what you had originally is considered a loss. This is a situation where your assets exceed your ongoing liabilities.

Time and income mobility

If you trade your time for money, you are always working on a fixed income. If you are on the bottom of the economic scale and you engage in luxury purchases you are passing your wealth up to those who are already in a better position than yourself. This only accelerates the problem.

It may be true that our economic enemies control the basics of physical survival such as food, water, and shelter. But we are also letting them unnecessarily control our leisure time and our idea of luxury.

When dealing with wealth and the social classes, the idea of luxury is used to pass wealth sideways or to siphon wealth from the lower classes into the upper classes. Those who are rich tend to buy overpriced unnecessary things from other rich people. This is really a deceptive game of keep away. This type of economic activity insures that the profit stays within the social class where it began. The economic boundary is preserved.

The only way to neutralize this is to put a check on unnecessary spending outside your own community or to engage in the selling end of providing luxury to your own community as well as people outside your community.

The economic dilemma

The basic trade off in economics is between the wants and needs of the individual and the wants and needs of the group. Peace is achieved when the two are in sync.

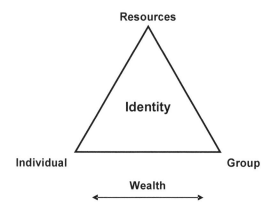

The above diagram shows that wealth comes from the interaction between the individual and the group. In modern economics, resources are allocated to the individual by some sort of interaction with a group of people. Wealth involves a specific group arrangement that determines how resources are allocated to individuals.

Basic needs have always been and always will be supplied by nature, not man. We are living in a time where this natural process is being altered and modified through the social structure of mankind.

Modern wealth is a function of personal desires and the social arrangement of society. Theoretically wealth comes from each person's usefulness to society. Clearly this is not the current reality that we are living under. There is no conceivable way that the CEO of Walmart is more useful than thousands of other employees combined, as his salary would seem to suggest.

The scarcity mindset problem

A recent economic study reported that 85 people control the same amount of wealth as half of the people in the entire world. This means that just 85 people control the wealth of 3.5 billion people.

How can something this outrageous go on? Why can't 3 billion people put a stop to the 85 people who are impoverishing half the world? How do these 85 people accomplish this super human feat? How can 85 people be that much more powerful than half of humanity combined?

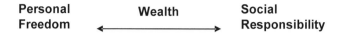

Personal Freedom ⟷ **Wealth** ⟶ **Social Responsibility**

The history of economic warfare

Despite what the United States promotes, capitalism is just another scheme in a long line of class-based feudal schemes that create a system of nobles, peasants, and slaves.

Through the use of propaganda and deception, capitalism has developed into a highly disguised system of top down control by a few over the many. The key to the disguise is that it only works because the controllers of capital actively seek to fool the participants by means of false information.

White supremacy is fueled by capitalism and capitalism only exists to serve the false ideology of white supremacy. These two concepts are linked and inseparable.

White supremacy/capitalism is a class system based around money. The white supremacy class system can not be overcome without changing the economic formulas that you are using to deal with it. These formulas are mental constructs. Mental constructs are the ideas, assumptions, and social arrangements that are embedded in the system. These mental formulas must be exposed, examined, and altered if you want to overcome the negative effects of the system.

The House of Esau's global corporate empire

Behind economic domination there is always a spiritual attack. Spiritual attacks are subtle often involving deceptive changes in the definitions of what things mean which can make the root causes of economic problems very difficult to detect. This is where we are today. Many of the victims of economic attacks are told that their difficulties are their own fault and that they are making up their own problems and "playing the victim". But what is indisputable is the fact that capitalism and white supremacy are built on murder, theft, and enslavement. These destructive activities are what have created the modern idea of wealth.

What can we do about the wealth problem and the on-going economic attack against our people and our community?

The astounding wealth and income gap is the direct result of the fact that the world's wealth is being dominated and mismanaged through a corporate global empire that is currently under the control of the House of Esau.

The House of Esau's global empire consists of a matrix of large multinational corporations that interconnect to form a sometimes difficult to identify power structure that has engulfed the entire world. This obscure corporate configuration is used to create the illusion of personal freedom even as it creates destruction across the earth and reigns misery on most of the world's population.

Under the rulership of the House of Esau, the world has become a global plantation because the corporate structure cannot survive without introducing some form of slavery.

Like all empires throughout history, the global corporate empire acts under the illusion of solving the problems of humanity. And like all other empires, the corporate empire has grown to be a cancer that threatens to kill its human hosts.

Empire building has long ago been discredited as a way of solving the age old tug of war between the individual and the group. This new empire like all the rest will end in miserable collapse.

Just as both Dr. King and Marcus Garvey warned, it is not only black and brown people who are being harmed by the system of white supremacy. The masses of white people are themselves being victimized by this system of uncompetitive unearned wealth accumulation and distribution.

Today we can clearly see that is not just a few unfortunate "minorities" that are being oppressed under the white supremacy system. The majority of the people in the world, black and white, rich and poor are being manipulated under the madness of this sick system.

The whole world has been enslaved under this new global plantation, and it is poised to devour even those who believe that they are benefiting from it.

The beginning of Esau's corporate empire
The beginning of the current corporate empire can be traced back to the creation of the first global corporations. These were called the East India companies.

In 1602, the Dutch were the first to use a stock issuing corporate structure as a means to dominate international trade. The British soon followed the same path. These were the first companies to trade with and then conquer India and China. These companies are labeled "Dutch" and "British" but they were really owned by private individuals in these countries. The French also created an East India Company to compete with the Dutch and the British. All of these companies were controlled by the Edomites, the House of Esau.

The Dutch East India Trading Company and the British East India Trading Company were the superpowers of the colonial times. They had their own private militaries that were not controlled by the governments of their respective nations. They invaded countries, fought wars against each other and acted in a manner that would lead you to believe that they were their own nations.

Another Dutch controlled company, The Dutch West Indian Company (1621), supplied slaves to the Spanish colonies. The Dutch slave trade was mainly controlled by "Jewish" Dutch citizens.

The profit centers of the India companies were spices, slaves, drugs, and guns. They used the giant triplets to become the rulers of the entire world. These first global corporations are at the root of the crushing wealth disparity that exists on the earth today.

The East India companies first came to India as traders but shortly after seeing the wealth and abundance of India attempted to take the whole country by force. This is a repeating pattern of the House of Esau.

In the mid 1600s, the Dutch and British East India companies went to war with each other for the control of India. These Anglo-Dutch Wars were fought over a hundred year period from 1652 to 1789. The British East India Company ultimately prevailed over the Dutch East India Company in these wars.

The fall of King James and the rise of corporations

It was the rise of the British East India Company that finally ended the rule of King James' bloodline (Israelites) in England and Scotland and ushered in white rule over the entire continent of Europe. King James's rule was ended by the rise of the East India companies as super powers that were almost completely independent and detached from the countries where they originated from.

Once the British East India Company gained control of India, they set their sights on China. It is because of the British East India Company that the British people gained their cultural taste for tea, silk and other Chinese made goods.

The colonist of the United States were not actually fighting against England, they were fighting against the British East India Company and their strangle hold on North American commerce, especially tea. This dispute against the British East India Company culminated in the "Boston Tea Party".

Drugs and spices and war

As the British taste for tea and silk grew, Britain was spending more and more money with China. This left a huge trade deficit owed by Britain to China. Since Britain had no products that China desired, Britain, using the British East India Company, forced heroin from India onto the Chinese people in order to recapture the British gold and silver that was being transferred to China through the tea and silk trade.

When the Chinese government objected, Britain declared war on China to protect the heroin trade that was being conducted by the East India Company. These were called the Opium Wars. This is another repeating pattern of the House of Esau. When nations refuse to trade with them, they declare war and take what they want.

The British East India Company's conquer and theft of India's land and resources; and the government backed heroin dealing in China catapulted Britain into superpower status.

Today, multinational corporations like British Petroleum and Royal Dutch Shell still dominate governments and world trade, ferment wars, and create economic disparity in the same fashion as their East India Company predecessors.

Corporate fiction

The artificial lifestyle created by the corporate structure blocks the natural order. It creates a corporate beast that is a cancer on mankind. This corporate beast and the artificial lifestyle needed to sustain it is the cause of the massive economic injustice that exists across the globe today.

Dr. King warned about the corporate beast in his Beyond Vietnam speech when he stated:

"We must rapidly begin the shift from a thing-oriented society to a person-oriented society."

He went on to describe the corporate beast in relation to the giant triplets:

"When <u>machines and computers, profit motives and property rights</u>, are considered more important than people, the giant triplets of racism, extreme materialism, and militarism are incapable of being conquered."

Corporations are a conglomeration of machines, computers, and physical property held together by human fear and greed that is deceptively mislabeled as the "profit motive".

The very make up of large corporations facilitates racism, materialism, and militarism. They are a continuation of the white entitlement system (racism) that got its resources by theft of ideas and resources (materialism), and are the driving force behind the war machine that targets certain populations for land theft and servitude through physical force and murder (militarism).

Today multinational corporations combine to form one corporate beast that is the embodiment of the three giant triplets. These global corporate fictions have been given life through the false belief system of white entitlement and its "thing oriented" laws, customs, and traditions.

The only law or morality that the corporate beast recognizes is profit and loss. Material gain is the only value system practiced under the white entitlement corporate system. It lives in a totally thing oriented world.

Consumer capitalism cult

Consumerism links the giant triplets together under one powerful cult-like ideology. Consumerism is a belief system that promotes the idea that buying things means freedom. It works on the false idea that unnecessary luxury is freedom. Consumerism convinces people to buy things that they do not actually need with money that they do not actually have. It produces slavery through illusions, debt, and unnecessary desire.

Most people do not realize that they have been indoctrinated into this belief system. Those who are indoctrinated are made to believe that the choice of what to buy gives purpose to life and is the greatest expression of human freedom. It is the ultimate "thing based" belief system.

Consumerism is the preferred method of control by the controllers of the global empire. The controllers have found that through consumerism they can get people to submit to their own enslavement. The East India Companies proved that as "things" become the most important measure in people's lives, they can be made to submit their own humanity to the corporate beast.

The term consumerism is never used as a part of politics and public policy. The idea of consumerism is usually disguised under the term "middle class".

What is the middle class?

The answer lies in those 12 million white immigrants that were allowed into the United States between The Garvey Movement (1900s) and Dr. King's movement (1960s). The so-called middle class is these 12 million "new Americans" and their descendants. The original white "old Americans" eventually became the 10% that still controls most everything under the new corporate mask.

Enter the first triplet; racism.

Middle class and racism

The so-called middle class was created to act as a buffer between the existing white Americans and the other "new Americans"-- the newly freed slave population.

Had white immigrants not been recruited into the United States, the slave population of the South could have instantly shifted the power structure of the United States and possibly the wealth structure of the entire earth.

This significant turning point was one of the reasons why the Garvey Movement was met with such a heavy handed attack by the United States government.

The same white immigration strategy was employed in South America and the Caribbean. If Garvey's nationalistic movement would have been successful he could have linked the economies of countries like Haiti, the Dominican Republic, and Brazil all of which still to this day have 80 to 90% black populations. This was a direct threat to the domination of the global corporate empire.

The "middle class" was to become the new worker class that would replace slave labor in the new machine-based industrial society.

Government sponsored racism allowed the new subservient middle class to feel as though they had instant status and a chance of "moving up" through the system because they were given better opportunities than the black population that had been laboring in America for hundreds of years before their arrival.

In reality, this new white worker class was used to redistribute wealth that rightfully belonged to the newly freed slaves and their descendants. This redistribution of unearned wealth, and the privileges that came along with it, is what the Justice Movements of the 20th century were really fighting against. Racism was a key strategy in this wealth redistribution process.

The new white middle class and the existing former black slave population were thrown into a competition for the small amount of token wealth that was being redistributed by the corporate beast. This is where the top 10% broke away from the rest of the population--both black and middle class whites.

False ideas about race were used as a method of confusion. At the heart of racism is an attempt to take away the humanity of non white people. It is a way of turning other people into things instead of people. But as blacks and whites came into greater contact with each other and were allowed to compete against one another, even under uneven circumstances, it became apparent that the racial superiority hoax was doomed to fail.

As Garvey and others proved, if blacks were left to their own devices, even under heavy handed racist government policies, they could easily compete with the new middle class. So it was on to the other main tool used to keep people under control? Corruption. Enter the next triplet, materialism.

Debt and the middle class

If people could be made to value things more than even their own humanity, they would be more willing to sacrifice the majority of their lives for the promise of material things. Under consumerism, things are the measuring stick of success. This is the way artificial superiority could be implemented as white citizens were given more access to things than black citizens.

A financial racket was formed around financing things that the middle class could never afford without borrowing from the rich. This desire, debt, and promise of upward mobility negative loop traps the middle class into carrying out the bidding of the ruling class just as any slave would have done in early America.

The drive for self interest created a middle class that became both the oppressed and the oppressor of others at the same time, as their value system became corrupted by the cult of consumerism.

The believers in consumerism delude themselves into voluntarily participating in oppressive schemes as long as they feel that their own self interest is being served. The key word here is "feel". Like racism, consumerism is driven by irrational emotionalism instead of sound logic.

In an even sicker twist on colonial slavery, the consumer slave will go out and murder and allow himself to be murdered in wars created purely to steal resources for his corporate master. Under the influence of their corrupt consumer value system the indoctrinated will kill and hurt themselves or others if the possibility for material gain appears to be involved.

Like racism, consumerism is in reality a cult of fear, greed, emotional manipulation, and false logic that is fueled by propaganda and misinformation.

The middle class enablers of the corporate beast themselves eventually become prey as technology makes it possible to use less and less humans to control the machines of production.

Like all cults, the cult of consumerism eventually leads its victims to spiritual destruction.

Corporate plantation

How does the global plantation operate? It begins with the giant triplets of racism, materialism, and militarism.

The product of the triplets is mass delusion. Delusions are false theories about reality. How does this happen? The overall strategy is to implant confusion and corruption amongst the masses of people. This mass delusion is how 3 billion people are being dominated by 85 people. The 3 billion are living in a world of illusion.

As we have discussed, corporate capitalism cannot exist without some form of slavery. Consumerism it is just a new form of slavery that has ensnared poor white people into servitude with blacks.

Debt slavery

As the modern era of black slavery ended, new schemes were put in place by the controllers of the white entitlement system in an attempt to hold on to the resources accumulated through colonial land theft and slavery.

In an attempt to retain white entitlement, the corporate empire has extended the slave plantation across the whole earth. This global plantation is real and is being accomplished through a matrix of global corporations.

This exported slavery is accomplished by a financing racket that works by first trying to corrupt leaders of resource rich countries into selling out their nations. If the leader cannot be corrupted, the United States finds a reason to invade the country, kill the leader, and steal the resources directly. They do this by either direct military action or by hiring local thugs to create a "revolution".

Most of the world leaders that the average American has been convinced are "evil", are really those leaders who would not be corrupted by money or are those who gained the courage to try to put an end to the financial shake down. Most Latin American leaders of the last 100 years that have died in office have met this fate. Saddam Hussein met this fate. Moammar Gadhafi met this fate. The list is long and shameful.

The way that the financial scheme works is that the global corporate bank (the World Bank) makes unnecessary loans through a corrupt leader that they know can never be paid back. These loans are like a massive credit card that is then spent on worthless projects that are contracted out to white supremacy controlled corporations. The global bank is in effect paying itself and forcing the people of the country to pay the money back with interest.

So now you have whole countries that are caught up in the consumer debt spiral eventhough the money never actually reaches the people of those countries.

When the loans default, the bank comes in and forecloses on (steals) the natural resources of the country. They take over the water, electricity, food, and any other valuable resource that the country may have.

Corporate propaganda uses terms like "privatization", "globalization", and "free trade" to mask what is really an extortion, racketeering, and slavery scheme. It is no surprise that the United States is the biggest promoter of this scheme.

The banking corporation then "sells" the country's assets to white supremacy linked corporations that will literally starve the people and make them so desperate that they are forced to work in corporate sweat shops that supply cheap goods to the white supremacy societies. The United States is the chief consumer of these goods. This is the secret of the so-called American good life.

Corrupting the people

Murder, violence, and fear through the threat of military force is always the bottom line of the white supremacy system. But who is actually carrying out the policies? Can a few ultra rich people, even if they possessed all the weapons available, actually physically subdue the entire world? Who would plant their food? Who would sew their suits? Who would fly their private planes?

The system actually survives by corrupting the masses of people into believing that what they are doing is in their best interest.

The corporate plantation detaches you from your connection to the past, implants you with a vague value system through deception and fear so that you will lack the courage or conviction to resist physical and mental attack.

You can then be made to believe that illusions are real. Once fully indoctrinated into this mindset, you begin to look to illusions for security. In this condition, you can easily be manipulated through your emotions into accepting the illusions as the only solutions.

Once you turn away from the truth and accept illusions as real, you become completely under the control of the corporate controllers, you become an economic slave.

This all comes down to a matter of the definitions that you use. To break this spell you must return to the truth.

Take away from this chapter:

1. Economics is a form of warfare.

2. The economics of the white supremacy system works almost exclusively off of perception and perceived value.

3. False perception is used to spiritually corrupt the masses of people into working against their own self interest.

For the wisdom of this world is foolishness with God. For it is written, He taketh the wise in their own craftiness.
-1 Corinthians 3:19

8 Spiritual Warfare Reset

The militarism dilemma

> **And fear not them which kill the body**, but are not able to
> kill the soul: but rather fear him which is able to destroy
> both **soul and body** in hell. - Matthew 10:28

1. How do you win a spiritual war?
2. How do you avoid spiritual corruption?
3. What is spiritual death?

Spiritual warfare deals with perceived value.

Wealth = real value + <u>perceived value</u>

Just as physical history predicts today's current physical
circumstances, spiritual history predicts today's current spiritual
circumstances. The difference is that the spirit is eternal meaning
spiritual things never change.

> The thing that hath been, it is that which shall be; and that
> which is done is that which shall be done: and **there is no
> new thing under the sun.** - Ecclesiastes 1:9

The reason why there is never really any new thing under the sun in
the physical world is because the spirit behind things never changes. It
is only our perception that changes, but the truth never changes. It is
only our understanding of the truth that can change. The change is
really only a change in our own minds.

Studying spiritual things automatically puts you in control of the
physical world that seems to change arbitrarily by the minute. All real
change actually happens in the perception of the human mind. This
mental change can either take you further from the truth or bring you
closer to the truth. Your thoughts will either move towards the truth or
move away from the truth. It is just that simple.

What is the spirit?

> While we look not at the things which are seen, but at the things which are not seen: for the things which are seen are temporal; but **the things which are not seen are eternal**.
> - 2 Corinthians 4:18

The spirit is the core that defines what something is. It is the originating force that gives shape, creates form, and controls action. It is the essence of what something is. Everything that exists takes the form of the spirit from which it originates. This spiritual energy governs the relationship between things and sets the boundaries of things and actions.

When you destroy the boundaries of a person, place, or thing it ceases being what it was, and becomes something else.

Personhood is defined by the spirit. The spirit is the driving force behind our actions. Our thinking manifests various spirits that can either create or destroy. We get feedback through our emotions. The emotions prompt us to direct and intensify our thoughts which in turn call on various spiritual forces.

Humans have the ability to become aware of the rules that govern our environment. This consciousness is what separates us from other living things.

Spirituality and wealth

Spirituality deals with perception and the perceived value portion of the wealth formula.

Most of the so-called developed economies in the world today operate mostly on perceived value. So at its core, economic warfare is a war of spiritual values. These values are definitions and rules that translate into actions, methods, and behaviors.

The intangible is everlasting, it is permanent, and the tangible physical world is the opposite of this which is temporary. The concept of time separates the two. Because of the concept of time we are faced with a dilemma. How do you prioritize immediate needs and desires with future and unseen needs and desires? The drive to survive can be directed in either direction.

The spiritual war

The following Scripture shows how you win or lose at spiritual warfare.

> **He that justifieth the wicked, and he that condemneth the just**, even they both are abomination to the Lord.
> - Proverbs 17:15

If you justify the wicked you lose. If you condemn the wicked and side with the just you win. It is as simple as that.

Notice the Scripture does not actually say he that justifies "wickedness", which would mean an act or behavior. It says "the wicked" meaning a person or people who practice wickedness.

> The wicked are estranged from the womb: **they go astray as soon as they be born, speaking lies**. - Psalm 58:3

There is a separate and distinct difference between a just and a wicked person or group of people. Many of us are seduced into justifying wicked people because we have no real spiritual compass or understanding by which to gauge situations or people. Through false philosophies and religions many of us have been taught that there is no objective right and wrong and we should "live and let live" and that "we are not supposed to judge".

The reason why people go along with wickedness and evil is because they are not able to rightly divide things into their proper place. They are fooled by their own perception which has been manipulated through emotion.

> For we know that **the law is spiritual**: but I am carnal, sold under sin. - Romans 7:14

The Bible was given to us as a book of laws and definitions that make up what it is to be spiritual. Anyone who tries to convince you that "the law was done away with" does not know the Bible or is purposely trying to manipulate you into spiritual and economic slavery under a sinful wicked lifestyle.

All of the problems in the world today exist because the wicked are in rulership and the majority of the people of the world justify the wicked and condemn those who resist what is popular. Under the rulership of the House of Esau wickedness has become the standard lifestyle.

Under the lifestyle of the House of Esau, anyone who tries to oppose the standard becomes viciously attacked by those who want to justify the wicked.

> **The earth is given into the hand of the wicked**: he
> covereth the faces of the judges thereof; if not, where, and
> who is he? - Job 9:24

The wicked describes a person or a group of people who have a false perception of reality. Wicked people erroneously place a higher priority on the carnal rather than the spiritual. The laws and definitions of the Bible show the difference.

People who have been seduced by a wicked lifestyle falsely believe that the temporary physical world is more important than the permanent spiritual world. This causes them to create confusion and chaos as they operate from false definitions. They use deception, unnecessary violence, and all manner of destructive behavior as they attempt to influence and control the physical world. All of this upsets the natural order. The spiritual world controls the physical world. That's the way that it is. That is the natural order. That is what makes sense. That's the way the Creator ordered things.

When you identify with and justify those who are wicked, you become wicked yourself. When you identify with and side with those who are just, you become just yourself. The key is that you must be able to tell the difference.

Spiritual warfare is difficult because by definition the wicked are deceitful and crafty people who are able to disguise the difference between wickedness and justice.

> **And that ye may put difference** between holy and unholy,
> and between unclean and clean; - Leviticus 10:10

Spirituality means that you know how to tell the difference between the just and the unjust, the clean and the unclean. The spiritual person never justifies the wicked and never condemns the just. And if he does make a mistake, he quickly reverses to shun the wicked and get back on the side of the just. The just and the wicked are not equal. The spiritual person never seeks equality, only justice.

The Civil Rights Movement and other so called truth and justice movements have had limited effectiveness because they have convinced us that equality should be the main goal when equality and justice are not the same thing. Again, the wicked and the just are not equals. There should be no equal treatment afforded to the wicked and the just. The wicked are condemned and the just are to be exalted and lifted up. They are not equals, they are opposites and deserve opposite treatment.

The devastating equality error has put us into a lifestyle of total spiritual breakdown since we are constantly trying to gain and equal footing with the wicked. We are encouraged to live our lives justifying the wicked and attacking those who refuse to agree that equality with the wicked should never be our goal.

When you seek justice, you automatically condemn the wicked. When you speak equality, you blur the lines between the wicked and the just. The only equality is that the wicked have a choice to change, if they do not, they are to be condemned, not justified.

When you are spiritually in tune you are able to properly prioritize things and are able to put things into their proper perspective. You know the difference between the wicked and the just, the clean and the unclean, the holy and the unholy.

The spiritual dilemma - things versus people

> For the flesh lusteth against the Spirit, and the Spirit against the flesh: and **these are contrary** the one to the other: so that ye cannot do the things that ye would. - Galatians 5:17.

To further understand spirituality we can go back to Dr. King's analysis of the giant triplets.

"We must rapidly begin the shift from a "thing-oriented" society to a "person-oriented" society. When machines and computers, profit motives and property rights are considered more important than people, the giant triplets of racism, materialism, and militarism are incapable of being conquered."

The boundary between a thing and a person is the key to understanding spirituality. These two opposite views of the world produce very different behaviors and results.

The goal of the corporate system that was created by the House of Esau is to create a thing oriented society that can be controlled and dominated by just a few misguided people. The corporation itself is a thing. Things can only have dominion over other things. Corporations are designed to use the triplets to reduce people into objects--things.

Under the spell of the corporate value system, people become objects that can be controlled by corporate fictions with a total disregard for their humanity, or human rights.

Denying the humanity of the victim has always been the justification for slavery and exploitation. Denying the humanity of the victim creates an illusionary world that is made real in the mind of the participants. But illusions are only temporary. When reality corrects these illusions, much human suffering occurs.

The whole idea of racism is to reduce people into things. Racist ideology attempts to give the illusion that people are objects that can be exploited for another person's gain.

Likewise, extreme materialism turns people into thing oriented, object-defined beings. As you become more and more attached to material things, you begin to lose your focus on the human issues that really matter.

And of course, the chief aim of militarism is the physical destruction of human beings. Military training is geared around getting people to deny the humanity of the person on the other side of the barrel. It also reduces the person doing the shooting to that of a tool that can be used to carry out murder and destruction.

> While we look not at the things which are seen, but at the things which are not seen: **for the things which are seen are temporal**; but **the things which are not seen are eternal**. - 2 Corinthians 4:18

The choice is between the physical life which is temporary and the spiritual life which is everlasting. This is really the choice between the wicked and the just. The choice seems obvious but because the unseen deals in uncertainty, faith is required as the evidence that the unseen even exists. This is the spiritual dilemma.

The factor of time and whether something will materialize in a certain time period is what really causes the dilemma. The unknown of time and our physical liabilities combine to force choices between these opposing forces.

Wisdom is the measure of how successful you are at solving this dilemma. Success itself is difficult to measure because intangibles are unseen, unknown, or may occur far off into the future.

Your spiritual body

> It is sown a natural body; it is raised a spiritual body. **There is a natural body, and there is a spiritual body.**
> - 1 Corinthians 15:44

We are living in two worlds at once. The physical world interacts with our physical body and the spiritual world which interacts with our spiritual body. The physical body is only temporary but the spiritual body is meant to be everlasting. Because this is the opposite of what we perceive, many of us believe that the physical world is all that there is.

The spirit is made up of the rules that define the characteristics of a person, place, or thing. The spirit governs a person, place, or thing and sets the boundaries that define what a person, place, or thing is, and what it is capable of.

> **It is the spirit that quickeneth; the flesh profiteth nothing**: the words that I speak unto you, they are spirit, and they are life. - John 6:63

The Scriptures tell us that the natural body is temporary but the spiritual body is permanent. It is our ability to think that connects us with our spiritual body. The spiritual body can be altered or corrupted by the thoughts and actions of the natural body.

This spiritual essence is what defines personhood. When you lose touch with this essence, you reduce yourself to being an object with no connection to your spiritual body.

Everlasting spiritual life

The Scriptures tell us that everlasting life is the natural state of mankind. Because man continually chooses to go against the natural laws of nature, he corrupts himself into believing that the physical world is the only thing that is real. By ignoring the spiritual nature of the world, man is shut off to the truth that physical death does not end spiritual life. This concept ties into the idea of justice. Judgment must transcend physical life or there could be no justice.

> For he that soweth to his flesh shall of the flesh reap corruption; **but he that soweth to the Spirit shall of the Spirit reap life everlasting.** - Galatians 6:8

The white supremacy system is so spiritually dangerous because it distorts the idea of justice. Its victims falsely believe that the practitioners of crimes against humanity have gotten away with their heinous crimes because they died without being brought to justice. It even seems like these criminals have done a great thing for their heirs and the nations that they have created. This is not the truth. What they have really done is doom their heirs and their nations to spiritual death if they do not wake up and repent.

The Scriptures foretell that most people will follow corrupted nations, refuse to see the truth of everlasting life, and will be punished or destroyed in accordance with justice.

Spiritual death

> Know ye not that ye are the temple of God, and that **the Spirit of God dwelleth in you**? If any man defile the temple of God, **him shall God destroy**; for the temple of God is holy, which temple ye are. - 1 Corinthians 3:16-17

According to the Scriptures there is only one real death and that is spiritual death. Under a blurred perception you are led to believe that there is no difference between the tangible and the intangible. You are led to believe that what you see is all that there is. Under this perception you are only looking at half of the picture. The other half is what is hidden from you when you ignore truth and justice. Spiritual death is where the blurred lines lead you.

When human consciousness is lowered, a man or a woman can be made to take on the characteristics of an object. This is called spiritual death. The main lifestyle "choices" in the white supremacy system creates this state and eventually turns people into objects and idols. They become "things" that can be easily controlled by the system.

The Bible tells us that because we are spiritual beings we can experience two deaths. There is a death that is inevitable and one that does not have to happen. Physical death of the temporary body is inevitable but spiritual death is the death of the permanent part of us - the soul. Upon the death of the soul we cease being human. This is where the concept of living in heaven or hell comes from.

> But the fearful, and unbelieving, and the abominable, and murderers, and whoremongers, and sorcerers, and idolaters, and all liars, shall have their part in the lake which burneth with fire and brimstone: **which is the second death**.
> - Revelation 21:8

If you refuse to believe that there is another death, you can be easily manipulated and controlled by the illusions of the physical world. The Bible's chief aim is to help us avoid this second spiritual death by showing the order of importance.

The belief in the second death is the major difference between the House of Esau and the House of Jacob. Esau never considered the impact of his actions on his future generations. Esau was supposed to inherit the blessings of his father and the covenant with God. He did not value the blessings so he gave them away to his brother Jacob for a few pieces of meat. The key point of understanding is that eventhough Esau himself prospered he spiritually doomed his descendants.

> And **the world passeth away**, and the lust thereof: but he that doeth the will of God abideth for ever. - 1 John 2:17

The focus on the temporary is how you know the House of Esau. You can see this short sightedness built into the nature of the societies that are ruled over by Esau's descendants. For example, George Washington and the so-called founding fathers of America, through their crimes against humanity, have set in motion a major judgment that will befall their generations further down the line. This is where we are today. The Frankenstein that their ancestors unleashed has spun out of their control and has set up a scenario where the descendants of Esau will cause their own physical and spiritual destruction.

Jacob on the other hand, was thinking about his generations and sought blessings not for himself but for his lineage. His lineage has therefore received an everlasting covenant that transcends the physical death of his forefathers and his descendants. The faith of the bloodline of the covenant, from Jacob's forefathers to his bloodline descendent Christ, is in the truth of everlasting life. This faith automatically means that you understand the possibility of spiritual death. The wisdom written in the Scriptures shows how to avoid this spiritual death.

Dr. King explained the concept of spiritual death as applied to a nation.

146

"A nation that continues year after year to spend more money on military defense than on programs of social uplift is approaching spiritual death."

Regeneration of the spiritual body

The idea of justice demands the regeneration of the spiritual body. Think about it. Did George Washington receive justice for his participation in slavery and other crimes against humanity? No. He is exalted as a hero whose name is spoken daily in one way or another. This is the very definition of justifying the wicked. How then can there be any justice if a man can get away with horrific crimes and never directly be punished for what he has done?

To understand reincarnation of the spirit, there are a few Scriptures that you must understand. The Book of Ecclesiastics deals with the understanding of regeneration of the physical and the spiritual.

There is no new thing under the sun.

> The thing that hath been, it is that which shall be; and that which is done is that which shall be done: **and there is no new thing under the sun.** - Ecclesiastic 1:9

The world moves in cycles.

> **One generation passeth away, and another generation cometh**: but the earth abideth for ever. - Ecclesiastic 1:4

Man cycles and recycles through the earth like everything else.

> **That which hath been is named already, and it is known that it is man**: neither may he contend with him that is mightier than he. - Ecclesiastics 6:10

When the spirit returns, there is no remembrance of what happened before.

> **There is no remembrance of former things**; neither shall there be any remembrance of things that are to come with those that shall come after. - Ecclesiastes 1:11

This is the main reason that we MUST understand history. History ALWAYS repeats itself.

The reason why we MUST understand the Scriptures is because we do not come back with the memory of the former things, so without the scriptures, we have no compass and we are doomed to repeat the mistakes of the past.

The two spiritual extremes

The two basic spiritual opposites are the creative spirit and the destructive spirit. These two spirits are the two extremes of spirituality. They both serve a purpose in life, death, and the regeneration of life. These two extremes coincide with positive and negative emotions.

The Bible shows that spiritual elements reincarnate from generation to generation. They repeat through the thought patterns, behaviors, and social interactions of humans.

What we call evil, stems from thoughts that are rooted in negative emotions. They are the spirits that destroy, the death spirits. These are sometimes called demons.

What we call good, stems from thoughts that are rooted in positive emotions. They are the spirits that create, the life spirits. These are sometimes called angels.

The interaction between these two spirits creates the human experience and the human social environment. Your spiritual body is a compilation of these interacting spirits as manifested through your thoughts.

Spirit of rebellion, corrupted definitions, and spiritual death

How does your spiritual body become corrupt?

As we have shown, we are always operating in two worlds at once: One that is temporary and one that is permanent. You should immediately recognize that the permanent is more valuable than the temporary.

The temporary will eventually give way to the permanent. You must stay spiritually connected to the permanent while you operate in the temporary.

The illusions created by a corrupt society may cause you to mix up the order of these two opposites or even dismiss the fact that they are two separate things.

Extreme stress caused by traumatic events can cause us to call on the negative emotions of fear, greed, hatred, etc as a way to try to relieve the stress. The problem with this is that the negative emotions are meant to serve a temporary survival function. They are meant to give us the energy to get us out of life threatening situations. They are not meant to be a way of life.

Using negative emotions beyond their natural functions will cause spiritual corruption. They may give you great power for a temporary period of time, but prolonged use of these emotions will bring about death and destruction, including your own spiritual death.

The spirit of false authority – Jezebel spirit

The spirit of false authority is the spirit behind the giant triplets of racism, materialism, and militarism.

Dr. King described this spirit as the Drum Major Instinct. It is the overwhelming desire to control, to be out front, to be number one, to get your way at any cost. The Bible calls this the Jezebel spirit.

The Biblical account of Jezebel in the Book of Kings is where this spirit gets its name. Jezebel became the queen wife of the worst king of Israel, King Ahab. Ahab took Jezebel as his queen even though she was from another nation and worshiped another god. Jezebel influenced Ahab to worship the pagan god Baal. Baal is a false god that is spoke of harshly throughout the Bible for requiring the worship of idols and human sacrifices.

Because Ahab was influenced by Jezebel and her false god, the whole nation of Israel fell under the spell of a false pagan belief system.

> But there was none like unto Ahab, **which did sell himself to work wickedness in the sight of the Lord**, whom Jezebel his wife stirred up. - 1 Kings 21:25

Jezebel used cunning, deception, and murder to direct people into doing her bidding eventhough she had no real authority. She obtained all of her power by manipulating people into doing her bidding. She is the personification of the destructive spirit that takes control of the rulership of godless people.

The story of Jezebel shows how power can be co-opted by a wicked spirit. A wicked spirit is one that attempts to go against the natural order.

The Jezebel spirit is wicked because it is a spirit of false authority. It is the same spirit of the serpent that is told of in the Adam and Eve story.

It was this spirit that told Eve that she could do whatever she wanted and that told Adam that he should listen to his wife instead of God.

Eventhough it is named after a woman, the Jezebel spirit has both male and female characteristics. It can afflict an individual or a whole nation of people.

In men the Jezebel spirit can appear as an effeminate spirit that uses deception and cunning instead of open warfare. In females it can come off as an overly aggressive spirit that appears as the need to gain power and control over men.

In exhibiting both male and female characteristics the Jezebel spirit can morph between extreme seduction and extreme aggressiveness. Using false flattery, false promises, and deceit, it will draw you in, then start to attack you, then try to tear you to pieces. It is the death spirit.

We can easily spot the presence of this spirit in addictive habits like drugs, alcohol, and smoking. These things have been proven to destroy most if not all of its victims in one way or another, yet people are somehow still drawn to these things.

The Jezebel spirit shows itself in prideful, rebellious behavior, and the refusal to apologize or repent.

Corrupted lifestyles

> **There is a way which seemeth right unto a man**, but the end thereof are the ways of death. - Proverbs 14:12

The Jezebel spirit is much more difficult to detect when it becomes socialized as a "normal lifestyle". This is the aim of the constant propaganda put out by the controllers of the white supremacy system. The controllers themselves are under this spirit. The Jezebel spirit leads them to find more and more victims. This spirit makes the controllers believe that they themselves will somehow be immune to the poison that is being spread. This is the same thing that Satan convinced Eve in the Garden of Eden.

The Jezebel spirit is actually a death spirit that is triggered through fear and rejection. It seeks to intimidate or eliminate perceived threats. It disguises itself by appearing to offer "freedom" or "free will". But it does just the opposite. It enslaves and destroys. It is a corrupting spirit that moves you to defile and destroy yourself.

This is the death spirit that the white supremacy system has unleashed across the whole earth. Like a deadly virus, this spirit would destroy all of humanity if it is left unchecked.

The Jezebel spirit is the spirit that gives the corporate Frankenstein its life. As people are sucked in by it, they surrender their humanity and become objects that can be used to support the false authority of the white supremacy corporate empire. Corrupted human life is the food that this beast feeds on. It cannot live without the support of corrupted weak leaders that help it create illusions and unsuspecting followers who cannot discern what is happening.

White supremacy is the extreme case of the Jezebel spirit that tries to usurp the authority of God. White supremacy philosophy tries to convince the world that the so-called intellect of man and man-made creations can replace the natural law that existed before man was even created.

The spirit of false submission - Ahab spirit

There can be no Jezebel spirit without a corresponding Ahab spirit from which it can draw power. The Ahab spirit induces you to give up your authority over your own mind and your own affairs. It is the spirit of submission to false authority. This spirit is triggered by greed, fear, doubt or any number of negative emotions.

Because a person acting under an Ahab spirit is confused and spiritually weak, they are easily controlled by the aggressive and controlling Jezebel spirit of false authority.

If a person under the Ahab spirit turns back to the truth and resists false authority, the Jezebel spirit must move on and seek out some other host.

By refusing to confront and resist the Jezebel spirit, the person under the Ahab spirit will lose everything and become completely enslaved. This is the spirit that must be present for the system of white supremacy to exist.

This submissive posture is also born out of spiritual rebellion against the truth of the natural order. When you rebel against the truth, you become subject to false boundaries and false authority.

This lack of compass causes unwanted results as you try to manifest things but are using destructive spirits that are not meant for that purpose.

This is where the spiritual war is fought. The Jezebel spirit does not want to come under the control of legitimate authority and the Ahab spirit calls on the Jezebel spirit by relinquishing personal responsibility and authority. People under these spirits can be emotionally manipulated into blindly following false authority. They will defend this false authority over the legitimate order and boundaries that appear to them to be distasteful and controlling. The fact is that they are willingly allowing themselves to be totally controlled by some other person or institution that is also operating under the Jezebel spirit at a more cunning and effective level.

Eventually both Ahab and Jezebel were destroyed by the death spirits that they called on. They were both killed because they refused to follow the natural order.

Correction, definitions, and authority

It is the spirit that quickeneth; the flesh profiteth nothing: **the words that I speak unto you, they are spirit, and they are life**. - John 6:63

You can never be ruled by a person or a group of people; rulership comes through your belief system, the definitions that you use. The set of definitions that you are following is your belief system. A person can become the focal point of that belief system but no person or few people can rule over the masses without using the power of a belief system. Your belief system is comprised of a set of definitions that govern your behavior.

The key to overcoming spiritual corruption is to submit to the definitions of real authority and resist the false definitions put forth by false authorities.

The question is then: How do you know what the real authority is?

Take away from this chapter:

1. The war going on across the earth is spiritual.

2. There are two kinds of death, physical death and spiritual death.

3. Not recognizing spiritual death and real authority leads to the spiritual corruption that has taken over the whole earth.

For what shall it profit a man, if he shall **gain the whole world, and lose his own soul**? Or what shall a man give in exchange for his soul? - Mark 8:36-37

9 God Reset
The authority dilemma

The fear of the Lord is the beginning of wisdom: and the
knowledge of the holy is understanding. - Proverbs 9:10

1. What is real authority?
2. How do you know that God exists?
3. What is the will of God?

The Creator-creation relationship is the first definition that defines
every other thing in existence.

The above diagram shows that God is the unchanging link between
actions and consequences.   This link provides the true definition of
what something is. How something acts, and reacts, tells us what the
purpose of that thing is.

The diagram also shows that your idea of god is linked to your
community identity. Community identity is tied to the definitions that
are shared among a group of people.

Your understanding of the Creator-creation relationship will determine
where you seek to gain power.

God is a Spirit: and they that worship him must worship him
in spirit and in **truth**. - John 4:24

The U.S dollar has written on the top of it "In God We Trust". The question is what God is it speaking of? If it is speaking of the God of the Bible, why do the symbols on the dollar bill directly contradict the God of the Bible?

Both symbols found on the back of the dollar bill, the eagle and the pyramid, are symbols from nations that the God of the Bible condemns. The eagle is the symbol of Edom, the House of Esau and the pyramid is the symbol of Egypt the nation that enslaved God's chosen people according to the Bible.

The Scriptures concerning these nations are crystal clear:

> **Though thou exalt thyself as the eagle**, and though thou set thy nest among the stars, thence will I bring thee down, saith the LORD. - Obadiah 1:4

The whole Book of Obadiah is the prophecy of the condemnation that will come upon the House of Esau whose symbol is the eagle.

The following verse is an example of the extreme adversarial nature of the Bible towards Egypt.

> **For I will pass through the land of Egypt this night**, and will smite all the firstborn in the land of Egypt, both man and beast; **and against all the gods of Egypt I will execute judgment: I am the Lord**. - Exodus 12:12

So what God is the U.S. dollar referencing and where do we find this God written of? Why are the presidents of the United States, congress, military personnel, and other officials sworn in on a Bible when they obviously set out to create their own changing laws that are more often than not in direct contradiction to the Bible?

Ultimately the will of God is expressed in definitions and rules. Your understanding of God is expressed in the definitions that you use and the rules that you follow. In this context, the dollar bill really reads "In this certain set of definitions We Trust". What is that set of definitions and where do they come from? Is there a way to vote out the definitions, rules, and consequences of God? Does man even have such authority? Has this ever worked?

> **And the Lord shall bring thee into Egypt** again with ships,
> by the way whereof I spake unto thee, Thou shalt see it no
> more again: and there **ye shall be sold unto your enemies
> for bondmen and bondwomen**, and no man shall buy you.
> - Deuteronomy 28:68

The Bible prophesized the enslavement of the children of Israel in a new
Egypt where no one from their nation will be able to redeem them from
bondage. Has this happened? Yes it has.

This is why you have so many Egyptian symbols incorporated in to
America. The pyramid on the dollar and the Washington Monument
being the most prominent examples of these symbols that appear to
have nothing to do with the nations that colonized the Americas. The
reason for the use of these symbols is that America, just like Egypt, has
enslaved the children of Israel.

> And thou shalt become an astonishment, **a proverb, and a
> byword**, among all nations whither the LORD shall lead thee.
> - Deuteronomy 28:37

And just as the Bible prophesied, the children of Israel would lose their
identity and be called by other names. And just like Egypt, the Bible
says that America will rise to spectacular heights only to be destroyed
as proof of the power of God.

It should be obvious that the god expressed on the dollar bill is not the
God of the Bible. So where does the United States seek to get its power,
authority, and justice? How does the U.S. define itself as a just society
given its horrific history of murder, theft, slavery, and oppression?

Which god are you following?

> **Now for a long season Israel has been without the true
> God**, and without a teaching priest, **and without law**.
> - 2 Chronicles 15:3

Nationality is important when we are dealing with the concept of God
because, historically, every nationality had its own gods. The Bible
shows that the gods of the other nations are idols. We know this is the
truth because of the various assortment of symbols or images that are
being worshiped in connection with these false gods. The true House of
Jacob is under the captivity of these symbols and idols because it has
lost its nationality and therefore has lost the knowledge of its God.

Without our nationality, so-called people of color have been conditioned to fear the white man more than our God. We are captive under the unnatural definitions that are created by man and not the natural definitions given by God.

White supremacy is the highest form of idolatry that the world has ever seen because it has engulfed all other pagan belief systems that came before it and morphed them into one system.

The Scriptures accurately tell us that we are still being ruled by wicked Godless nations because we are serving their inferior gods, not the Most High God of the House of Jacob.

Because we have forgotten our own God, we have made the lies of white supremacy our refuge. Believing lies and false doctrines is what makes us powerless to end our oppression. Because we have no understanding of our God, we have no sense of justice and no way to understand the nature of the enemy that has spiritually enslaved us.

Because we have lost the ability to connect with our God, the world is in a state of imbalance. The Scriptures tell us that the House of Jacob will restore peace and balance once they remember who they are and bring the light of their God back into the world. This is a hard pill to swallow for those who believe in white supremacy, which is exactly why the House of Esau and the House of Jacob will become locked into a final spiritual battle. The House of Esau will never want to relinquish its false authority and repent from its system of false definitions, unjust laws, and oppressive social arrangements.

Thus saith which Lord?

> **Every one that is proud in heart is an abomination to the LORD**: though hand join in hand, he shall not be unpunished. - Proverbs 16:5

The God of the House of Jacob is the Most High God. This title leaves no doubt as to what definitions that you are following and where you are drawing your strength from. The God of Abraham, Isaac and Jacob is the God of the Bible – The Most High.

The Most High God is the single point of reference that provides consistency in thought and action.

Without the single point of reference of the Most High there is no truth or knowledge.

Submission to real authority

> Talk no more so exceeding proudly; let not arrogancy come out of your mouth: for **the Lord is a God of knowledge, and by him actions are weighed.** - 1 Samuel 2:3

You must have a concept of something that is greater than yourself in order to be able to objectively evaluate things.

> So that we may boldly say, **The Lord is my helper, and I will not fear what man shall do unto me**. - Hebrews 13:6

Everything is classified according to and in relation to God. From God, all of the natural borders, lines, and divisions between things are drawn. These boundaries make wisdom possible.

When you lack the understanding of proper divisions, functions, and classifications you are vulnerable to rulership by false authority. God sets the boundaries and classifications and functions. Without an understanding of the Creator, you are unable to define anything else. There is no way to define the purpose of existence itself.

There is no personal freedom or free will without boundaries. How can there be freedom if there is no difference between freedom and slavery? How would you know the difference?

You must submit to the real authority of the Most High God or you will find yourself submitting to the false authority that comes from either your own negative emotions or the negative emotions of someone else.

Under God, everything has a proper time, place, and function. Everything has a proper relationship to everything else. Knowing the difference between things and the separate function of things is wisdom.

All true knowledge, wisdom, and understanding leads you back to the one Creator of all.

The most intelligent idea

> For my thoughts are not your thoughts, neither are your
> ways my ways, saith the Lord.9 For as the heavens are
> higher than the earth, so are **my ways higher than your
> ways, and my thoughts than your thoughts.**
> - Isaiah 55:8-9

To believe in the unseen God is the most logical position that you can take because The Most High God is the highest intelligence.

The intelligence of God is far beyond man's capacity and does not adjust to the understanding of man. God does not adjust to man just as the truth does not adjust to man. Man must adjust to God or be destroyed by truth. This simple fact undermines the idea of man made authority.

White supremacy attempts to distort your understanding of the Most High God and replace God with human understanding, intellect, emotions, methods, and authority. In the name of being "logical", humans have developed an ignorance of God that leads them to make devastatingly illogical decisions. These decisions of false logic lead to man causing his own suffering and destruction.

The belief in the unseen is the beginning of ALL logic. Consider these logical statements:

1. If I can declare that I see something, then I am also simultaneously acknowledging that there must be something that is unseen to me. The unseen creates the seen.

2. If there is something that I know, then there must be something that I don't know and can't know. If this were not true, knowledge would mean nothing.

3. For time to exist, something must exist outside of time.

4. If I am a creation, then I MUST have a Creator; this is the first and most important relationship of existence.

Man's so-called scientific discoveries only prove his ignorance to the physical world around him. Just like scientific discoveries, God is only revealed to man when man changes himself to see the truth.

The identity of the Most High

The Most High God is the life force that everything exists in subjugation to. God is a living force, not a thing.

Here is what Moses was told concerning the Most High God of Abraham, Isaac, and Jacob – The God of Israel.

> 13 And Moses said unto God, Behold, when I come unto the children of Israel, and shall say unto them, The God of your fathers hath sent me unto you; and they shall say to me, <u>What is his name?</u> what shall I say unto them?
>
> 14 And God said unto Moses, **I Am That I Am**: and he said, Thus shalt thou say unto the children of Israel, **I Am** hath sent me unto you. - Exodus 3:13-14

What does the name I AM mean?

It means that everything has a beginning and an end except God. God is the living force that acts on everything in creation. All other power is subservient to the power of God. All other forces, both positive and negative, exist under the force of the Most High God – I AM.

All creations must have a Creator. God is the Creator of all. Everything that is not God, the Creator, is a creation. God is the compass by which all creations are aligned and judged.

Above everything else I AM means that God is consistent. God is the one truth and does not change.

Labels, names and confusion

> **O house of Jacob**, come ye, and let us walk in the light of the Lord. - Isaiah 2:5

Various religious doctrines have created confusion as to the name of the God of the Bible. Just as images of God are forbidden in the Scriptures so is using God's name in vain. This is because placing man made labels on God is a form of idolatry. Creating names and translating names into new languages created by men leads to vanity. The Scriptures call people by their function not vain labels that can be interpreted in multiple ways.

When the Scriptures say call on a name, they are saying call on the function of that name. These are spiritual titles not physical titles.

What we know for sure is that God is not the author of confusion. Any confusion as to the name or function of God is caused by the vain ideas of men. To end the confusion we need to look no further than the teachings of Christ himself.

Christ, the Israelite from the tribe of Judah, who the Scriptures say is the Son of God, himself never called his Father by a proper name. Out of respect, most people do not call their earthly fathers by their first names. Why then would we call the Father of heaven and earth by a proper familiar name, especially if it causes confusion on the earth?

The God of the Bible is the God of Abraham, Isaac, and Jacob. The insistence by some religions on reducing the Most High to a proper name and worshiping that name is a form of idol worship.

If you get caught up in names that steer you away from a single point of reference, you are not following the Most High God. Any religion that claims the Bible as its base must also acknowledge that the Bible is the worship of the God of Abraham, Isaac, and Jacob. The only book that contains this God is the Bible.

All names, all other gods, all other philosophies, and everything in existence must exist under the Most High God that was worshipped by Abraham, Isaac, and Jacob. This is the defining characteristic of the Most High God and why identifying the children of Israel is vital and is the purpose of the Bible itself.

> And God said moreover unto Moses, Thus shalt thou say
> unto the children of Israel, **the Lord God of your fathers**,
> the God of Abraham, the God of Isaac, and the God of Jacob,
> hath sent me unto you: **this is my name for ever**, and this
> is my memorial **unto all generations**. - Exodus 3:15

The first line of the Lords Prayer given by Christ should clear up how we should call on the Most High God. Christ said that these words should be said exactly as he recited them, and in private:

> After this manner therefore pray ye: **Our Father** which art in
> heaven, Hallowed be thy name. - Mathew 6:9

Our Father is a clear reference to Exodus 3:15, the God of Abraham, Isaac, and Jacob. This is the God of our Fathers.

Hallowed means holy or set apart from all other gods called on by the pagan nations. There can be only one Supreme God and that is the God of heaven that can not be represented accurately by any earthly name or label.

When Israelites call on the Most High, it is clear that they are calling on the Father that is in heaven and not any other representation or name, or anything else that can lead you away from the power that showed Himself to Abraham, Isaac, and Jacob. The Bible tells us that the insistence on calling on pagan gods and falling into the vain philosophies of men is what sent the Israelites into multiple captivities up until this day.

Finally, the Bible prophesizes that the name of God will cause confusion until the last days when everyone on earth will know His name and speak it in one tongue.

> **For then will I turn to the people a pure language**, that they may all call upon the name of the Lord, to serve him with one consent. - Zephaniah 3:9

Cause and effect and God

> **The Lord killeth**, and maketh alive: he bringeth down to the grave, and bringeth up. - 1 Samuel 2:6

Under the force of God, everything has a definite purpose. Man is the only creature that can attempt to change the purpose set by God. When man goes against the order set by God, he creates destruction. Invoking this destructive force will ultimately result in man's own destruction. There are no two ways about it, either you are following the purpose of the Creator or you are not. The question is how do you know that you are following the purpose of the Creator?

How many truths are there? One. Everything that is not the truth is an illusion, falsehood, or lie. How many illusions, falsehoods, and lies are there? Unlimited. Either something is the truth or it is not true. Without a compass, man has no real way of knowing the difference between truth and illusions. God is that compass.

God is that force that creates the effect for every cause. Every action that man takes causes some reaction to come into existence. The compensating force in this equation is God.

Thére is not your truth or my truth, there is only The Truth. The truth is The Most High God. The Most High God represents the power behind everything in the universe. Everything else is a creation and has its own particular place. Everything has a creator except the Creator of All which is the only unchanging truth that does not change based on our perceptions or opinions.

What we do know is that illusions, falsehoods, and lies are the creations of man, not God. All falsehood comes out of the imagination of man.

God is the truth and the truth is God. You have to adjust to the truth of God. By definition, the truth of God will not adjust to your will. We can bend and twist falsehoods all day long but all this does is make different lies and falsehoods. Sooner or later you will run up against the truth that will not budge. That truth is God.

Divine opposites of the Most High

> I form the light, and create darkness: **I make peace, and create evil**: I the Lord do all these things. - Isaiah 45:7

We live in a world of opposites. God set the boundaries of the world using pairs of opposites. One thing must be used to define another. God is the only self-defining force.

True and false are the basic distinctions that are created by God. The truth demands order, requires structure, and is clearly defined. Falsehoods require no rules, structure, or order.

God created both the negative and positive opposing forces that make all existence possible. God is known through the consistent patterns that exist throughout all of existence.

God is the one link to ALL creations. The failure to understand God means that you cannot properly define anything else.

The diagram shows that there is a right hand and a left hand power of God. The right hand power is the creative force. The left hand power is the destructive force. God is the compass that sets the boundaries and keeps straight which power is which.

Wisdom is the ability to recognize and properly categorize these opposing forces.

All opposites cancel each other out. This means that the presence of one means the absence of the other. If one thing is likely to happen, its opposite is less likely to occur. God is the compensating force that holds these relationships in place.

The right hand power of the Most High

> Which he wrought in Christ, when he raised him from the dead, **and set him at his own right hand in the heavenly places**,
> - Ephesians 1:20

The right hand is the spirit of creative power. The right hand denotes a preferred position. The right hand power of God is the force of justice. It is activated by positive emotions.

Positive emotions summon the life spirit. This is the creative spirit that neutralizes the stress caused by the destructive negative emotions.

Positive and negative emotions cannot exist at the same time.

Right Hand
• Messiah
• Angels
• Creative Force
• Life Spirit
• Human Based
• Truth
• Positive Emotions
• Faith
• Permanent
• Spiritual World

Faith in the unseen creative force is the natural defense to becoming prey to the death force. Faith that provisions have been made to deal with man's basic survival needs protects us from unnecessary negative emotions.

Using the right hand power of God to relieve stress of other people is what we call doing good.

The Bible shows that Christ was sent into the world to relieve the stress of the House of Jacob and by extension, the stress of the world. The Scriptures tell us that Christ is the first creative force created by God.

The left hand power of the Most High

> Now there was a day when the sons of God came to present themselves before the Lord, and **Satan came also among them**. - Job 1:6

The Book of Job shows us that Satan is under the direct supervision of God. He sits on the left hand of God and is given the power over the physical realm.

Left Hand

• Satan

• Demons

• Destructive Force

• Death Spirit

• Thing Based

• Deception

• Negative Emotions

• Stress

• Temporary

• Physical World

The left hand power of God is activated by negative emotions. The result of these negative emotions is stress.

Stress is the only natural predator of mankind. Stress activates the death spirit in man. Stress is embedded in our daily lives because we are constantly in need of the basic provisions of survival. The need for water, food, and physical safety causes at least temporary stress in all human beings.

Understanding how to deal with stress is what makes you wise. Dealing with stress with only negative emotions causes even more stress in the long run. This stress may be transferred onto other people.

The transference of stress onto other people is what we call evil. The Bible attributes this behavior to Satan.

The Book of Job highlights how Satan attaches to worry and doubt. It describes Satan as roaming the earth under God's direction.

> And the Lord said unto Satan, Whence comest thou? **Then Satan answered the Lord**, and said, From going to and fro in the earth, and from walking up and down in it. - Job 1:7

Satan is the only natural predator of man. Negative emotions activate this death instinct.

Be sober, be vigilant; because your adversary **the devil, as a roaring lion, walketh about**, seeking whom he may devour: -1 Peter 5:8

Satan is the god of the triplets of racism, materialism, and militarism. He is the god of those who are overly focused on the physical world. He is the god of white supremacy.

Man calls this force into existence by attempting to solve problems through the over use of negative emotions.

He that committeth sin is of the devil; for the devil sinneth from the beginning. For this purpose the Son of God was manifested, that he might destroy the works of the devil. - 1 John 3:8

This may be tough to hear, but Satan is the god of the earth and is the god that is being called on to power the United States and all of the House of Esau.

Christ like all other fleshly men was himself tempted by Satan:

5 And the devil, taking him up into an high mountain, shewed unto him all the kingdoms of the world in a moment of time.

6 **And the devil said unto him, All this power will I give thee, and the glory of them: for that is delivered unto me; and to whomsoever I will I give it.**

7 If thou therefore wilt worship me, all shall be thine.

8 And Jesus answered and said unto him, Get thee behind me, Satan: for it is written, Thou shalt worship the Lord thy God, and him only shalt thou serve. - Luke 4:5-8

The chosen people of the God of the Bible

Contrary to the teachings of white supremacy created religions, the Bible does not say that the will of God is equality. It says that the will of God is justice. Everything is balanced under its own purpose. This does not mean that everything is equal and that every person or nation is the same under The Most High God.

> For thou art an holy people unto the Lord thy God: the Lord thy God hath chosen thee to be a special people unto himself, **above all people that are upon the face of the earth.**
> - Deuteronomy 7:6

Does this Scripture say that "all men were created equal" as the American Constitution so proudly states?

> He that leadeth into captivity **shall go into captivity**: he that killeth with the sword **must be killed with the sword**. Here is the patience and the faith of the saints. - Revelation 13:10

Does this Scripture sound like those who led people into captivity are now equal with those who went into the captivity? What sense would that make? How would that be justice?

> Yet now hear, O **Jacob** my servant; and Israel, whom **I have chosen**: - Isaiah 44:1-8

What does being the chosen people of God mean? It is both a blessing and a curse. The House of Jacob, the Israelites are the chosen people of God according to the Bible.

The chosen nation was given the laws of God and therefore is the one that is punished under the law. The laws of the Bible are the Spirit of God. The definitions of the Bible show you how to deal with the left hand and right hand power of God.

> 19 **He sheweth his word unto Jacob**, his statutes and his judgments unto Israel. 20 **He hath not dealt so with any nation**: and as for his judgments, they have not known them. Praise ye the Lord. - Psalms 147:19-20

White supremacy religions desperately try to convince you that the laws of the Bible are done away with. Then what are the rules? How can you make any decisions if you have no rules to follow? White supremacy tries to replace the laws of the Bible with its own laws. All you have to do is look at the track record of the white supremacy so-called justice system to see the folly in trying to usurp Biblical wisdom.

> They which are the children of the flesh, **these are not the children of God**: but the children of the promise are counted for the seed. - Romans 9:8

The laws of the Bible have not and will not change while the laws of white supremacy change daily. This inconsistency is the evidence that white supremacy laws are not of God. The truth of God does not change by the whims of man.

Why would you submit to white supremacy's clearly unjust laws but believe that the rules of God can be done away with? This kind of false logic is proof positive evidence of spiritual enslavement.

This is why it is absolutely necessary to understand the history and customs of the Israelites before you try to understand the New Testament in the Bible. White supremacy theology uses the New Testament as a prop to propagate its pagan ideologies and religions.

> For finding fault with them, he saith, Behold, the days come, saith the Lord, when **I will make a new covenant with the house of Israel and with the house of Judah**:
> - Hebrews 8:8

The truth is that The New Testament is in total agreement with the Old Testament concerning the laws of God. The only thing that changed is how you are to sacrifice for breaking the law—the judgment under the law. We will go into this further in the chapters on religion and the Bible but you must understand that the laws that you follow are an expression of the God that you follow. God is the law and the law is God. The law is holy. The law is spiritual. The law is knowledge. The law is truth. The law is justice.

> For I could wish that myself were accursed from Christ for my brethren, my kinsmen according to the flesh: 4 **Who are Israelites; to whom pertaineth the adoption, and the glory, and the covenants, and the giving of the law**, and the service of God, and the promises; - Romans 9:3-4

The chosen people are bound by the definitions given by God. The law is what defines their God versus the pagan gods on the other nations.

> **And ye shall be holy** unto me: for I the Lord am holy, and
> **have severed you from other people**, that ye should be
> mine. - Leviticus 20:26

What is sin?

> **Now we know that God heareth not sinners**: but if any
> man be a worshipper of God, and doeth his will, him he
> heareth. - John 9:31

To sin is to work against the natural boundaries set by God. Sin is the
transgression (breaking) of the law.

The problem with the "law is done away with" doctrine that is promoted
by the Christian Church is that it promotes sin. What is sin? Sin is
the transgression of the law. This is a disruption of the natural
boundaries. By attempting to usurp the natural order and boundaries,
white supremacy religions have attempted to usurp the power of God.
Through the giant triplets of racism, materialism, and militarism it has
convinced the world to turn away from the Most High God. It has tried
to replace God's definitions and laws with the definitions and laws of
white supremacy.

> Whosoever committeth sin transgresseth also the law: for **sin
> is the transgression of the law**. - 1 John 3:4

This Scripture is from the New Testament proving that the idea that the
Old Testament laws are done away with is ridiculous. If the rules of
God are done away with, how would you even know what sin is? How
could you correct yourself if you cannot even identify what is correct or
incorrect? This is a totally illogical concept. Why would you believe
that the laws and customs of white supremacy are correct but question
the laws of the Bible?

Free will

Man was given freewill meaning that we can temporarily break the
boundaries set by God. By temporarily breaking boundaries, we prove
where the boundaries are. These temporary breaks show that man is
bound by a higher law than his own. We call these temporary breaks
miracles.

> **The fool hath said in his heart, There is no God**. They are
> corrupt, they have done abominable works, there is none that
> doeth good. - Psalm 14:1

Man is free to delude himself and attempt to redraw the boundaries set by God. The ultimate collapse of these unnatural methods shows that there is a Higher Power and that His boundaries are real. Man's attempt to break these boundaries are just temporary illusions of his own mind.

Man is free to attempt what ever he wants, but once he violates the natural order, he must suffer the consequences of his so-called free will. In this respect, man's ignorance and the continual collapse of his vain pursuits proves the existence of a higher authority.

Accepting the correction of God

> If ye love me, keep my commandments. - John 14:15

To love God is to submit yourself to correction by the definitions of God. Sin causes a disconnect in your understanding of cause and effect relationships and a disconnect from these definitions.

There is no way to escape the correction of God. There is no greater pain that can be inflicted on humanity than the correction of God.

The House of Jacob has gone through multiple captivities because they were given the law. Because they were given the law, they have suffered the correction under the law. This is the whole point of the Bible. The House of Jacob is a living example that the laws and definitions of God are true and everlasting.

Corruption through sin is the reason why the House of Jacob is unable to free itself from the oppression of white supremacy.

Rebellion against God

The Bible teaches that to love God is to keep his commandments, his definitions. This is how you know what God you are worshiping.

Through captivity in other nations, The House of Jacob has been taught to go against our own God. We are still captive and oppressed because we are following the laws customs and traditions of other nations. These nations practice pagan religion not the laws of the Most High God of the House of Israel.

And it shall come to pass, when ye shall say, Wherefore doeth the Lord our God all these things unto us? then shalt thou answer them, **Like as ye have forsaken me, and served strange gods in your land, so shall ye serve strangers in a land that is not your's.** - Jeremiah 5:19

The Bible clearly shows that the people get the leaders that they deserve. Godless people wind up with Godless leaders and Godless rulers over them. In the end the Godless rulers will be destroyed along with those who follow them. That is justice.

God is on the side of justice. God is always on the side of humanity. When you lose your humanity you lose God. When you have no God or when you are following false gods, there is no justice. Justice is a return to the natural boundaries set by God.

Idolatry and other gods

Therefore say unto the house of Israel, Thus saith the Lord God; **Repent, and turn yourselves from your idols**; and turn away your faces from all your abominations.
- Ezekiel 14:6

The worst sin possible is idolatry because idolatry creates false gods. These false gods come along with their own rules and laws that contradict the definitions, rules, and laws of the Most High God.

For all the gods of the nations are idols: but the Lord made the heavens. - Psalms 96:5

Contrary to what most people are made to believe, the Bible talks about many different gods. Historically, every kingdom and empire has invoked its own pagan gods in order to gain power over people.

And the high places that were before Jerusalem, which were on the right hand of the mount of corruption, which Solomon the king of Israel had builded for **Ashtoreth** the abomination of the Zidonians, and for **Chemosh** the abomination of the Moabites, and for **Milcom** the abomination of the children of Ammon, did the king defile. - 2 Kings 23:13

Here is more proof.

> And the children of Israel did evil again in the sight of the
> Lord, and served **Baalim**, and **Ashtaroth**, and the gods of
> Syria, and the gods of Zidon, and the gods of Moab, and the
> gods of the children of Ammon, and the gods of the
> Philistines, and forsook the Lord, and served not him.
> - Judges 10:6

The Bible shows that the children of Israel fell under the spell of these
other pagan gods. Because they followed the pagan traditions of these
other gods, the nations that created these gods were able to dominate
Israel.

The history of idolatry is simply this: Where idolatry is practiced,
insanity takes over. The insane notions of world wars, the insane
notion that a few thousand people can rule over hundreds of millions of
people, the insanity of trusting man's changing perceptions as wisdom.

Idols disconnect your reference point from the truth of God.

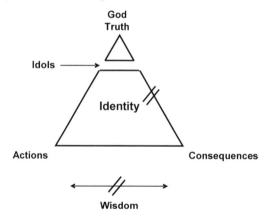

The diagram shows that when you worship a creation instead of God
there is no single point of reference. There is a break that creates room
for many different reference points. This creates confusion and
instability. This diagram should look familiar since it looks very similar
to the representation of the pyramid on the back of the dollar bill. It
shows you that you are being cut off from the truth by worshiping false
images and believing in false doctrines.

Idols can be money, material objects, people, or any number of false
reference points. Idols involve worshiping the creations instead of the
Creator.

For the worshipping of idols not to be named is **the beginning, the cause, and the end, of all evil**.
- Wisdom of Solomon 14:27

Idolatry is the worship of the creations of God or the creations of man, but not the Creator Himself. Although idols are not a real single point of reference, they can create an artificial one that can fool the human mind. Idols can become powerful in social settings if many people believe in the same idol, but this is only illusionary power created out of the imagination of humans. They are not and can never be the highest power. The real power, God, cannot be reduced to things that decay or pass away.

We are all bound by and must serve the spirit under which we are operating. In this sense we are all slaves. The question is what will you serve? Will you serve life or will you serve death? How do you know which is which?

Repentance

Contrary to propaganda about the Israeli "Jewish" state that was created in 1948 by the white supremacy system, the true House of Jacob is still dwelling in the lands of their captivity and still do not fully realize who they really are. They continue to be oppressed under unjust schemes because they are ignoring the God of their fathers and therefore do not know justice from injustice or reality from illusion. They can only use "being equal" with the foolish lifestyles and customs and philosophies of white supremacy as an indication of what is fair and just.

The Scriptures tell us that when the true children of Israel realize who they are and recognize why they are at the bottom of all of these societies, they will then return to the only help that they are going to receive, the Most High God.

> 40 **If they shall confess their iniquity, and the iniquity of their fathers**, with their trespass which they trespassed against me, and that also they have walked contrary unto me;

> 41 And that I also have walked contrary unto them, **and have brought them into the land of their enemies**; if then their uncircumcised hearts be humbled, and they then accept of the punishment of their iniquity:

42 **Then will I remember my covenant with Jacob**, and
also my covenant with Isaac, and also my covenant with
Abraham will I remember; and I will remember the land.
- Leviticus 26:40-42

Take away from this chapter:

1. God is a generic term that denotes the definitions that you are
   following.

2. God separated things into their own purpose and functions.

3. People are being led by the false authority of men instead of the
   real authority of the Most High God of Abraham, Isaac, and
   Jacob.

4. Recognizing God is the beginning of all wisdom and intelligence.

But I say, that the things which the Gentiles sacrifice, **they
sacrifice to devils, and not to God**: and I would not that ye
should have fellowship with devils. - 1 Corinthians 10:20

10 Bible Reset
The doctrine dilemma

> Cry aloud, spare not, lift up thy voice like a trumpet, and
> **shew my people their transgression, and <u>the house of
> Jacob</u> their sins.** - Isaiah 58:1

1. What is the Bible?
2. How do we know that the Bible is the truth?
3. What is the difference between the Bible and religion?

The Bible is the scientific observation of thousands of years of study. It deals with both physical history and spiritual history.

Anyone who believes that their one lifetime of memories and understanding is more powerful than thousands of years of applied wisdom, outcomes, and consequences is deluding themselves. Yet this is what you are going to find, when you try to show people the truth about the Bible. Our people have been so destroyed by false information that they believe that their emotions and gut feelings can be substituted for facts, logic, and reasoning.

> All scripture is given by inspiration of God, and is **profitable
> for doctrine, for reproof, for correction, for instruction in
> righteousness:** - 2 Timothy 3:16

Real scholarship
Education is really the story of cause and effect relationships, the story of history. The story of history is the story of wars, empires, and rulership. No book tells this story more vividly than the Bible. The Scriptures show how God, His ways, His House, and His people are separate from other gods, their ways, their houses, and their people.

The Bible explains some key things for so-called people of color:

1. Our true national identity
2. Why we were taken into slavery
3. The reason for our current condition
4. The nature of the enemy that we are up against
5. What we need to do to change our condition

Biblical wisdom trumps all other scholarship. This is a bold statement but it is true. The beginning of all wisdom is the understanding of the single source that all knowledge disseminates from.

> Thus speaketh the Lord God of Israel, saying, **Write thee all the words that I have spoken unto thee in a book**.
> - Jeremiah 30:2

It is useless to attempt to impose European so-called scholarship on the Bible because the Bible is a spiritual Book written by and for spiritual people. If you can not understand the Bible, it is probably because you are not meant to understand it.

Having said that, when you study the so-called knowledge put forth by the white supremacy system, you find that the knowledge contained in the Bible is the basic book used in nearly every discipline.

The Bible covers law, economics, leadership, psychology, science, sociology, business, accounting, and any other discipline that is taught in the white supremacy educational system. Beyond all of that, the Bible is the original book of definitions. It clearly shows the difference between the definitions of The Most High God, the single point of reference, and the definitions of false gods that cannot serve this purpose.

The Bible gives the rules and definitions that bring about truth, peace, and justice. This is the reason why the Bible is said to be the word of God.

The Book of the House of Jacob

Ultimately, the Bible was written to be the tool that would awaken the House of Jacob from their mental and spiritual sleep in the land of their captivity. The Bible provides the record that reawakens our memory of the past which gives us knowledge of the future.

> Now go, write it before them in a table, and **note it in a book**, that it may be **for the time to come for ever and ever**: - Isaiah 30:8

How did the ancestors of the House of Jacob create the book that is said to be the word of God? Through suffering and affliction, they were able to understand the truth and understand that the truth never changes. The Holy men of the House of Jacob brought the understanding of the belief in One God into the world. An understanding of the truth inspired them to produce what we now call signs, wonders, miracles, and prophesy.

> **Hear ye the word of the Lord, O house of Jacob**, and all
> the families of the house of Israel: - Jeremiah 2:4

Every other nation in the world follows a belief in idols and multiple gods. The Bible spells out in no uncertain terms that the men of our nation become powerless and under the control of these nations when we follow these inferior belief systems and their inferior gods. Our contrary belief system is our greatest gift to the world, but it has also caused us to be a much hated and despised people.

> **Now all these things happened unto them for examples**:
> and they are written for our admonition, upon whom the
> ends of the world are come. - 1 Corinthians 10:11

White supremacy has caused us to try to contort ourselves into the Bible covenant and promises when all we have to do is read it as it is written.

> **Who are Israelites**; to whom pertaineth the adoption, and
> the glory, and the covenants, and the giving of the law, and
> the service of God, and the promises; - Romans 9:4

Our lack of faith in the doctrine which was specifically given to our nation has allowed inferior systems to take control over the earth. The world is now totally off course and out of order because our ancestors turned away from this doctrine. But as the Bible itself has prophesied, if we turned away from our doctrine, it would eventually be brought to us by the enemies of our people in strange lands where we would slowly remember who we are.

Indeed, our doctrine has been brought to every corner of the world through the Bible. All religions have used our doctrine for their own purposes and have created their own books and philosophies based on our doctrine.

How does the Bible accomplish its purpose?

The law of the Lord is perfect, converting the soul: the testimony of the Lord is sure, making wise the simple.
- Psalm 19:7

Here is a short list of what The Bible shows you when you have a proper understanding:

- Gives the understanding of the Most High God
- Shows the true nature of man (spiritual versus physical)
- Shows the relationship between people places and things (table of nations)
- Shows how to tell the difference between the profane and the righteous (to avoid personal corruption)
- Shows how to order society (avoid corruption of society)
- Helps predict the future (prophecy)
- Gives the power of discernment (wisdom)

White supremacy revisions

There are multiple versions of English translated Bibles. Why? When you look at the differences you see that they mostly have to do with watering down the true doctrine of the Israelites in order to make it suitable for the false teachings of white supremacy.

The King James 1611 Bible is the best available translation from the original ancient text into English. King James VI, son of Mary Queen of Scots was himself a <u>black man</u> from the House of Jacob who sat on the throne of England, Scotland, and Ireland at the same time. His rule over England was called the "<u>Jacobean</u> period".

Any Bible that contains the words "new" or "revised" or "standard" must be checked against the King James 1611. What you will find is that contrary to what is commonly promoted, these new and revised Bibles were not made to translate Old English into New English. They were actually made in a vain attempt to revise the word of God itself. These so-called revisions are white supremacy Bibles that attempt to distort the identity and importance of the children of Israel. As we discussed in previous chapters, some of these Bibles have multiple missing verses when compared with the King James 1611.

To prove this to yourself go to the Book of Revelations and check these verses:

Revelation 13:10 and Revelation 22:14.

You can go to the website biblehub.com to see the various translations of the same verse.

These important verses show the blatant distortion that these so-called new and revised Bibles try to introduce into the world. These Bibles are meant to compliment the false image of white Jesus and the false narrative of white supremacy and the delusion that the white race will not be held accountable for the atrocities that it continues to perpetuate across the earth. These false "translations" are meant to turn you away from the laws of God and into the laws of blasphemous men who are the enemy of God and God's people, the Israelites, the House of Jacob.

The Apocrypha – the missing Books

When people regurgitate the myth that the Bible has been corrupted because books have been removed, most don't know that they are really talking about the Apocrypha. You can find these Books easily because they were originally included with the King James 1611 Bible.

If you remember the account that we discussed of how William Penn, the so-called founder of Pennsylvania referenced the Book of Esdras when explaining the native peoples of America. The Book of Esdras is not found in most Bibles because it is one of the Books that has been removed in recent times.

The Apocrypha are 14 Books that were included in the original King James 1611 translation. They are still found in the Catholic versions but removed from the Protestant versions of the Bible.

These Books include further prophecy and books of wisdom and understanding written during the time of the Persian and Greek captivity of the Israelites. They add historical continuity and deeper understanding to the Old Testament.

White Protestants removed the Books of the Apocrypha in the 1700s because they provide more clarity as to the true identity of the Israelites and expose the Caucasian converts to Judaism who are now claiming to be Jews. The white supremacy protestant church removed the Apocrypha, told the real Jews that they are Gentiles and the laws were done away with, then said that white Jesus loves everybody even while they committed some of the worst atrocities in the history of mankind.

Without the Books of the Apocrypha you do not have a full Bible.

How to read the Bible

> Knowing this first, that **no prophecy of the scripture is of any private interpretation.** 21 For the prophecy came not in old time by the will of man: but holy men of God spake as they were moved by the Holy Ghost. - 2 Peter 1:20-21

Contrary to what most of us may believe, the Bible cannot be interpreted in multiple ways. To get any real understanding the Bible must be read as it is written. Understanding the structure can end a lot of the confusion and debate as to what the Bible is and who wrote it.

The structure of the Bible can be broken down into seven parts:

1. **Genealogy** - the Book of Genesis - The genealogy, bloodline, and nationhood aspects of the Bible are the most overlooked. This is what causes most of the problems with understanding the Bible. Without the understanding of nationhood, the Bible cannot be fully understood. It was written by one nation of people, the Israelites, and is their continuing history. Israelites are the so-called people of color in the western hemisphere and other scattered places around the world.

2. **The Law** - Genesis to Numbers - The Law is the purpose of the Bible. The Law is a system of living and governance that leads to peace and prosperity. Saying that the Law is done away with has opened the door for the further enslavement of the Israelites under the unjust laws of men.

3. **History of the Kingdom** - Joshua to 2 Chronicles - These books give the history of how the Israelites used the Law to form the physical kingdom of Israel after their enslavement in Egypt. These books show the Laws in practice.

4. **The proof of the power of the Law** - Ezra to Malachi plus the Books of the Apocrypha - The books of the prophets of the Old Testament tell the story of what happens when the Israelites stop following the Law. They prove that the Law is the word of God. The Books from Job to Song of Solomon are books that show the wisdom of the Law. These Books of wisdom are where most people read from in the Old Testament because they contain concepts that can be said to be universal wisdom. These books show that men of wisdom are those who know and follow the truth of the Law. The rest of the books of the prophets of the Old Testament show that the Israelites become

enslaved by the other nations because they refuse to follow the Law. This is the repeating pattern of the Bible and how you know that the Bible is the truth. The prophets were warning the Israelites, the Israelites did not listen and went into multiple slaveries including the current slavery in the Americas as prophesized by Moses.

5. **Christ** - Mathew to John - These books are the witness that Christ walked the earth. Mathew, Mark, Luke, and John are different accounts of the same events surrounding the life of Christ. These accounts are given as multiple witnesses that these things actually happened as is required under the Law. Christ is the Law made into flesh (the word made flesh). He is the final proof that the Law is real and that it is the word of God. The Old Testament prophets going back to Moses prophesized about the coming of the Messiah that would come to save the Israelites from their enemies if they would repent and turn back to the Law.

6. **The building of seven Churches in Greece and Asia Minor** - Acts to Jude - The letters to the churches provide the final clarity to the Law with the understanding of Christ and how to organize the House of Jacob and the other nations under Christ. But the letters to the churches cannot be understood if you do not understand who the Israelites are, the Law, and the structure of the Bible. The letters written by Paul and the Apostles completely reconcile to the teachings of Christ, the Law of the Old Testament, and the writings of the prophets. Obscuring the meaning of these letters is the key to deceiving the masses of people about what the Bible is. It is also the reason why the Bible has survived and is still inadvertently promoted by the very people that it condemns.

7. **Revelation** - The Book of Revelation - Revelation is the final book and final prophecy in the Bible. It builds on all the other prophets including Christ. Revelation prophesizes that a country like the United States (Babylon the great) would rise out of the ashes of the Roman Empire and encompass all the wickedness of all previous empires that were all under the rule of Satan. The Revelation prophecy shows that the children of Israel would be enslaved by this new wicked empire and need a Savior to break the hold of wickedness not only over the House of Jacob but over the entire world.

When you recognize the structure, everything in the Bible is consistent. The New Testament and the Old Testament are in complete agreement. The Old Testament shows the penalties and punishments under the Law. The New Testament in Christ shows the benefit of following the Law which is rulership of the earth and everlasting spiritual life.

How has the Bible been misused?

> But if our gospel be hid, **it is hid to them that are lost**: In whom the god of **this world hath blinded the minds** of them which believe not, lest the light of the glorious gospel of Christ, who is the image of God, should shine unto them.
> - 2 Corinthians 4:3-4

Although the Bible has been read by all other cultures, all of them have chosen to create their own law, which most times, is in direct opposition to the doctrine of the Bible.

The reason why most churches skip over the real history of the Old Testament is because they cannot make the Old Testament apply to the narrative of the superiority of the white race. By skipping the Old Testament and removing the Apocrypha, people can be misled into taking the New Testament out of context. The New Testament and the Old Testament apply to the same people. Christ continued dealing with the same Scriptures as his forefathers and spoke to the same people. These people are the Israelites. Christ spoke these words:

> For had ye believed Moses, ye would have believed me; **for he wrote of me**. But if ye believe not his writings, how shall ye believe my words? - John 5:46-47

The whole world needs to understand the law of the House of Jacob but they cannot if they do not understand who the people are. You must match the law to the history in order to get the full understanding that the law is real. What the prophets said would happen has happened and is still happening. Failing to understand this puts you into total spiritual rebellion against God.

The children of the House of Jacob have gone into captivity under a system that has corrupted the entire planet. The collapse of this system is inevitable. When it does collapse the system of the House of Jacob will fill the void. Those who refuse to return to the truth will suffer as the Scriptures have foretold.

The system of the House of Jacob was given to the children of Israel and everybody on earth can benefit, but not if the other nations continue to overlook the actual situation of the true House of Jacob. This is why identity is so important.

Clearing up Biblical misunderstandings

But let your communication be, Yea, yea; Nay, nay: **for whatsoever is more than these cometh of evil.**
- Matthew 5:37

The Bible is a self defining book. Any confusion that you may have about a particular subject or meaning can be cleared up through another verse in the Scriptures. This is called using precepts. Precept upon precept is how you must read the Bible. Following precepts is the only way to verify that your understanding is correct. When you read the Bible this way you see that there is no inconsistencies and no confusion in the Scriptures.

Because the Bible is a Book of definitions, it is nearly impossible to insert your own meanings into the Scriptures. What you can do is get people to ignore the fact that the Bible builds on itself and repeats its concepts throughout each period in history that it covers.

Many of us who actually read the Bible have been deceived into powerless action by Roman religious doctrine that actually has nothing to do with the principles that are written of in the Book.

Through thy precepts I get understanding: therefore I hate every false way. - Psalms 119:104

Any interpretation or misunderstanding that you find in your reading of the Bible can be cleared up by other scriptures in the Bible itself. Take for instance when people read "love thy neighbor" in the Ten Commandments. One may then ask the question, what is meant by my neighbor? You would then look for other Bible verses that deal with the idea of "neighbor" to get a clearer understanding.

This is surprisingly easy in the age of the internet and smart phones. Much of the confusion with interpreting the meanings of Bible verses has been that it was much more difficult to search out the precepts that would give you the correct understanding of an unclear verse.

How the words remained pure

> **Seek ye out of the book of the Lord**, and read: no one of these shall fail, none shall want her mate: for my mouth it hath commanded, and his spirit it hath gathered them.
> - Isaiah 34:16

The precept phenomenon is what allows the Bible to retain its significance and purity through thousands of years.

Those who sought to tamper with the scriptures would have to find and eliminate all of the precepts that would make their changes valid. Adding or taking away from the Scriptures without removing all the precepts that go along with that scripture is nearly impossible.

Every correct interpretation of an unclear Bible verse must therefore be proven with another Bible verse. If not, the interpretation or translation cannot be said to be the truth.

Any religious book, religious doctrine, or philosophy that deals with the Bible must be able to stand up to this same scrutiny.

Prophecy

> **For the prophecy came not in old time by the will of man**: but holy men of God spake as they were moved by the Holy Ghost. - 2 Peter 1:21

The difference between the Bible and religious writings is that the Bible is a prophetic book. It is through prophecy that the Bible authenticates itself. The Bible is not theory or the philosophy of man. It is to be read as it is written.

The church promotes religious theory, but the Bible is prophecy. Prophecy is the manifestation of cause and effect which is the basis for all science.

Prophecy means "to say before". The prophets who physically wrote the Bible were able to predict events that would befall their nation and other nations because they understood the truth.

If you understand the Bible, you can see that NONE of the Bible prophesies has ever failed to come into existence. The Bible does NOT ask the reader to believe in things that have not happened.

184

Bible prophecy is a warning, an explanation, and a solution. This is difficult to understand if you do not correctly identify the children of Israel.

The prophecy of the Bible is evident throughout history and in the current times in which we live. The Bible prophesizes the condition of the earth today.

Even the people who the Bible speaks against can not resist taking it to the four corners of the world as the Book itself prophesizes

Parables

> 11 And he said unto them, Unto you it is given to know the mystery of the kingdom of God: **but unto them that are without, all these things are done in parables:**
>
> 12 That seeing they may see, and not perceive; and hearing they may hear, and not understand; lest at any time they should be converted, and their sins should be forgiven them.
> - Mark 4:11-12

The reason why the Bible has not been destroyed is because it is written in a way that confuses the unlearned. This is also why it can be abused by thousands of different religions. This is why you have 1,400 different denominations of Christianity all claiming that they are following the same book. There is no way to get any understanding of the Bible if you cannot identify the children of Israel, it is their Book and written to solve their particular problem.

Theology versus the Bible

> Jesus answered and said unto them, **Ye do err, not knowing the scriptures**, nor the power of God.
> - Matthew 22:29

By studying precepts you can see the glaring difference in what the Bible teaches and what the religions that claim to follow the Bible are teaching. By following religions, and not the Bible, the House of Jacob remains powerless and at the mercy of the laws and false definitions of their enemies.

Theology is "thus said the white man". It is nothing more than religious theory, most of which directly contradicts the Bible.

185

There are so many falsehoods that religions have perpetrated against the Bible that we can't list them all here. We will just give you an idea how blatant and outrageously obvious that these contradictions are. We do this not to bash religion but to show that if your intent is to follow the wisdom of the Bible you must completely divorce white supremacy religion from your Biblical understanding. To put it bluntly, for the House of Jacob, either religion has to be reformed to conform to the Bible or abolished all together. We must have a consistent set of beliefs.

Common religious practices that are not found in the Bible:

Sunday worship, Christmas, Easter, Virgin Birth, worship of Mary, rosary beads, crosses, white Jesus, Popes, unmarried Priests, Mass, ashes on foreheads, praying to walls and stones, praying with closed hands, praying in public, tithing to priest and pastors that are not from the tribe of Levi.

Common cultural practices spoken against in the Bible:

Charging interest on debt, eating unclean animals: pork, shrimp, crab, lobster, shell fish, Christmas trees, homosexuality, melting pot nations, abortion, taking oaths and pledges of allegiance, creating debts longer than 7 years, convicting a person of a crime with only one witness or no witness; all of these things are directly spoken against in the Bible but have become our lifestyle under the House of Esau.

These practices show that we are slaves under the laws of wicked men and not following the Laws of God. The Bible tells us when this happens, the world would be in turmoil and God would not hear our prayers and pleas for help in our captivity.

> **Now we know that God heareth not sinners**: but if any man be a worshipper of God, and doeth his will, him he heareth. - John 9:31

The following chart will help you dispel some of the misconceptions that many people have concerning the teachings of the Bible. In the first column we list what is commonly taught in theology. In the second column we list what the Bible actually says. In the third column we list the multiple verses (the precepts) from the Old and New Testament that prove the truth.

There is no need to fight against the Bible as it is written. No matter what you have been taught, you have to humble yourself to the truth. Again, this proof comes from both the Old Testament and New Testament, proving that there is no contradiction in the Bible. The contradiction comes from theology, not the Bible. The Bible defines itself and validates itself.

	Theology The church says	**Bible** The Bible says	**Precepts** Verses /Proof
1.	All men are created equal	God has a chosen bloodline of people, the Israelites	Deuteronomy 7:6 & 32:8 Proverbs 147:19 Isaiah 45:7 Joel 3:19 Mark 12:29 John 4:22 Romans 9:4 Revelation 7:4
2.	The Church is the chosen	The Israelites are the chosen because they were given the law	Deuteronomy 6:4 & 7:6 Exodus 2:25 Psalms 135:4 & 147:19-20 Isaiah 43:15 Amos 3:1 Mark 12:29 Luke 1:68 Hebrews 8:8 James 1:1 1 Peter 2:9
3.	The Law of Moses is done away with	The Laws stand forever. The Law is the Holy Spirit of God. The Law is the only way you know what god you are following	Leviticus 26:46 Proverbs 3:1 & 119:21 Isaiah 59:21 Mathew 7:12 John 3:14 & 5:46-47 & 9:31 Romans 3:31 & 7:7 1 John 2:4 & 2:7 &3:4& 5:3 Revelation 14:12 & 22:14

	Theology The church says	Bible The Bible says	Precepts Verses /Proof
4.	Christ is God	Christ is the Son of God	Mark 1:1 John 5:30 & 7:16 & 8:18 & 8:28 & 8:42 &14:9-10 Hebrews 5:8 1 John 3:8 & 4:15
5.	God is all love	God loves and hates. Good and evil work at the hands of God.	Leviticus 20:23 Psalms 110:6 Romans 9:13 & 9:15 1 John 2:15 Revelations 13:10
6.	God is only about peace	God is about war and peace	Exodus 15:3 Deuteronomy 32:39 1 Samuel 2:6 Isaiah 45:7 Mathew 10:34 Luke 12:51
7.	God forgets about the past	God always remembers the past or there could be no justice	Leviticus 26:45 Ecclesiastes 3:15 Psalms 109:4 Jeremiah 6:16 Isaiah 46:10

	Theology The church says	**Bible** The Bible says	**Precepts** Verses /Proof
8.	Jews are white	Jews are black. There will be impostors who say they are Jews but are not. The current "Israelis" are gentiles not genetic Israelites	Deuteronomy 28:15-68 Songs of Solomon 1:5 Jeremiah 17:4 Lamentations 4:8 Luke 21:24 Revelations 2:9
9.	Virgin birth	Christ was an Israelite from the seed of David. The Virgin birth comes from pagan worship of the queen mother of fertility	Jeremiah 7:18 Mathew 1:1 Acts 2:29-30 Romans 1:3-4 Hebrews 2:16 Revelation 2:20
10.	Christ was a spirit	Christ was a man	Mathew 1:1 Galatians 4:4 Hebrews 2:18 1 John 4:3
11.	Christ is white	Christ is black	1 John 5:10 Mathew 24:24 Hebrews 7:14 Revelation 1:15

	Theology The church says	**Bible** The Bible says	**Precepts** Verses /Proof
12.	Christ changed the law	Christ was a high priest of the Israelites who did away with the need for the law of sacrifice. No other law or commandment was changed other than the carrying out of punishment under the law	Mathew 5:17 John 15:10 Romans 8:1 Hebrews 7:28 & 9:22& 10:10 & 10:28 2 Corinthians 3:14 Galatians 3:13 Ephesians 1:7 Revelation 14:12
13.	Christ is not in the Old Testament	Christ is in the Old and New Testament	Isaiah 7:14 & 8:8 & 9:16 & 53:1-12 11:1& 53:1-12 Jeremiah 23:5 Mathew 1:23
14.	Christ was not about division	Christ was about division	Mathew 10:34 & 15:24 Luke 12:51
15.	The Israelites rejected Christ	The corrupt elders, Scribes, and Pharisees rejected Christ	Mark:8:31 John 8:32

	Theology The church says	**Bible** The Bible says	**Precepts** Verses /Proof
16.	Christ came for everybody	Christ came for the Israelites because the Israelites were given the law and would need a sacrifice under the law	Isaiah 59:20 Mathew 15:24 Mark 12:29 John 17:9 Acts 2:4 & 5:31
17.	You have a personal relationship with God	There is only one path	1 Timothy 2:9 Ephesians 2: 18 Ephesians 4:3-6
18.	Pray in public and in groups	Pray in private	Mathew 6:1
19.	Speaking in tongues means shouting in a made up languages	Speaking in tongues means speaking a known language that is unknown to the listener	Acts 2:4 & 2:5&2:8 1 Corinthians 14:26-28
20.	People only pay for their own sins	You must pay for the sins of your forefathers	Exodus 20:5 Leviticus 26:39-40 Numbers 14:8 & Isaiah 14:21 & 65:7 Lamentations 5:7

	Theology The church says	**Bible** The Bible says	**Precepts** Verses /Proof
21.	Don't judge people	You are commanded to rebuke (correct) your brother and show him his error so he does not suffer in sin	Leviticus 19:17 Mathew 18:15 Ephesians 5:11 Hebrews 3:13
22.	Nations should come together	Nations should be divided. When they do come together it will be under the rulership of the House of Jacob	Deuteronomy 7:3 & 7:6 & 32:8 Exodus 23:33 Leviticus 20:24 Amos 9:8-9 Revelation 2:25-27 & 7:4 & 13:10
23.	Love everybody	Love your own people	Leviticus 19:17-18 Proverbs 22:24 2 Esdras 6:56 Hebrews 12:10
24.	Trust your heart	Do not trust your heart	Proverbs 28:26 Jeremiah 17:9
25.	Everybody can be saved	Only a few will be saved	Isaiah 45:17 Mathew 7:14 Revelation 21:24
26.	Following man's law is ok	Follow only the law of the Israelites	Psalms 147:19 Jeremiah 17:5 Acts 5:29
27.	Symbols, crosses, beads, statues, pictures, paintings	No idols	Exodus 20:4 Psalms 115:4 Jeremiah 10:1 Revelation 13:15

	Theology The church says	Bible The Bible says	Precepts Verses /Proof
28.	Sunday is the day of worship	Saturday Sabbath is the Holy day of rest	Exodus 20:8 Exodus 35:2 Jeremiah 17:22
29.	Live and let live	Boundaries and separation must be kept	Romans 1:27 Revelation 22:18
30.	Except all religions	There is only One God	Deuteronomy 32:17 Revelation 22:19
31.	Continuation of pagan rituals and holidays	We are to observe the Sabbaths, High Holy Days and, Feast days that give thanks and remembrance to the God of our forefathers	Exodus 20:8 Leviticus 23:2 Isaiah 58:13 Jeremiah 10:1
32.	Eat anything	No pork or shellfish or animals not meant for human digestion	Leviticus 11:1-2 & 11:7-10 Hebrews 10:26
33.	Men and woman are equal	Men and woman are not equal. There is order to man-woman relationships	Genesis 3:16 Deuteronomy 22:5 Isaiah 3:12 1 Corinthians 11:3 & 14:34 1 Timothy 2:11-14

	Theology The church says	Bible The Bible says	Precepts Verses /Proof
34.	The Israelites are no longer the chosen	God will never put away His people	Isaiah 14:1 & 45:17 & 54:8 & 65:9 Jeremiah 23:6 & 31:31 Luke 1:71 Romans 9:7 & 11:1 Hebrews 11:1 Revelation 7:4
35.	It doesn't matter who is Israel	There is a distinction between Israelites and other people	Romans 11:16-21 James 1:1 Revelation 7:4 & 21:12
36.	The Apostle Paul was a Roman	Paul was an Israelite from the Tribe of Benjamin who was born in Rome	Romans 11:1 Philippians 3:5 2 Corinthians 11:22
37.	The Apostle Paul was teaching non Israelites	Paul was teaching dispersed Israelites that took on the customs of Greeks and other nations	John 7:35 Acts 21:21

	Theology The church says	**Bible** The Bible says	**Precepts** Verses / Proof
38.	The Apostle Paul contradicts the teachings of Christ	Paul was a converted Pharisee and an expert in the Law of Moses. He taught Israelites from whatever understanding that they had to convert them to the Law. He never contradicted Christ.	2 Peters 3:16 1 Corinthians 9:19-9:23
39.	Heaven is in the sky	Heaven is the last kingdom on earth. It will be ruled by the Israelites	Isaiah 14:1-4 & 14:3 & 60:12 Revelation 2:27 & 21:2 & 21:14& 21:18 & 22:24 & 22:18

The Scriptures show that Thus saith the Lord is vastly different from thus said the Roman Church.

John 3:16

To further highlight the deception embedded in theology, let's look at the most famous and misunderstood verse in the Bible, John 3:16.

> For God so loved the world, that he gave his only begotten Son, that whosoever believeth in him should not perish, but have everlasting life. - John 3:16

John 3:16 is probably the most well known verse in the Bible. The Christian church teaches that this verse means that Christ came to save everyone in the entire world. This is the doctrine that goes hand in hand with the false image of white Jesus. The white man as savior myth is a key component of the white supremacy agenda.

It is indirectly true that the Messiah came to set the whole world straight but specifically Christ came to save the House of Israel, his people. Ignoring the truth of John 3:16 helps create the religious climate that makes white supremacy possible. By making the Israelites insignificant in its doctrine, Christianity distorts the truth of Christ and the importance of the House of Jacob.

This false doctrine goes along with the false image of white Christ.

To get a proper understanding of John 3:16 you must understand that the whole Bible pertains to the House of Jacob. When John 3:16 says "world" it is talking about the world of the Israelites. The Bible explicitly says that Christ came to save the Israelites from their enemies.

John 3:16 was a part of a running conversation between Christ and a religious ruler Nicodemus.

> There was a man of the Pharisees, named Nicodemus, a ruler
> of the Jews: - John 3:1

In his conversation with Nicodemus, Christ was making a parallel, as he did many times, between himself and Moses.

In the Old Testament, Moses foretold of the coming of Christ.

> I will raise them up a Prophet <u>from among their brethren</u>, like
> unto thee, and will put my words in his mouth; and he shall
> speak unto them all that I shall command him.
> - Deuteronomy 18:18

In the Book of John, Christ was explaining to Nicodemus that because Nicodemus had shown that he did not fully understand the Law of Moses, he could not understand the teachings of Christ.

It is ironic that instead of learning from the mistake of Nicodemus, this very conversation is used by the unlearned to misrepresent the life and purpose of Christ.

Christ came to give atonement for sins under the Law of Moses. He became the High Priest and the sacrifice for the sins of Israel that has always been a part of the Law. Before Christ, this sacrifice was to be performed every year by sacrificing animals. For the most severe offenses the offender was put to death.

After Christ, belief in Christ became the sacrificial part of the law. The law and the consequences under the law are considered the whole law. Jesus fulfilled the sacrificial part of the law so no one has to be put to immediate death under the law. He is the sacrificial Lamb of God. Belief in Christ means that you understand that spiritual death is what you need to avoid.

The reference to Moses that Christ made in John 3:16 was from the Old Testament where Moses was able to save the children of Israel from dying after they received snake bites after God sent snakes against them for their lack of trust in God's word. The Israelites questioned that God would allow them to win in battle against the Edomites. After they were bitten by the snakes, the Israelites did not die as long as they stayed focused on a pole that God ordered Moses to make. This is the parable that Christ was expressing to Nicodemus.

Look at what Christ told Nicodemus in the verse before the "God so loved the world" statement:

> **And as Moses lifted up the serpent in the wilderness**, even so must the Son of man be lifted up: - John 3:14

This statement alludes to the precept in the Old Testament. In the Book of Numbers there is the account of Moses saving the Israelites from the snakes. John 3:16 is a parable that draws equivalents to the condition of Israel under the Romans (Edomites) and the pit of snakes that they dealt with in the time of Moses. The snakes were God's punishment for the Israelites fear of going to war with the Edomites.

> And they journeyed from mount Hor by the way of the Red sea, to compass the land of Edom: and the soul of the people was much discouraged because of the way. - Numbers 21:4

Here is the account of how Moses lifted up the pole in the Book of Numbers:

> 5 And the people spake against God, and against Moses, Wherefore have ye brought us up out of Egypt to die in the wilderness? for there is no bread, neither is there any water; and our soul loatheth this light bread.
>
> 6 And <u>the Lord sent fiery serpents among the people</u>, and they bit the people; and much people of Israel died. 7 Therefore the people came to Moses, and said, We have

sinned, for we have spoken against the Lord, and against thee; pray unto the Lord, that he take away the serpents from us. And Moses prayed for the people.

8 And the Lord said unto Moses, Make thee a fiery serpent, and <u>set it upon a pole</u>: and it shall come to pass, that every one that is bitten, <u>when he looketh upon it, shall live</u>. 9 And Moses made a serpent of brass, and put it upon a pole, and it came to pass, that if a serpent had bitten any man, when he beheld the serpent of brass, he lived. - Numbers 21:5-9

The serpent of brass is used as a medical symbol today. It is a symbol of healing. Christ was sent to heal the world, but this is only accomplished by healing the House of Jacob.

The "whosoever" and the "world" like everything in the Bible refers to Israel.

<u>And so all Israel shall be saved</u>: as it is written, There shall come out of Sion the Deliverer, and shall turn away ungodliness from Jacob: - Romans 11:26

If you read further in the Book of John you find the stance of Christ concerning the whole world. In John 17:9 Christ states:

I pray for them: <u>I pray not for the world</u>, but for them which thou hast given me; for they are thine. - John 17:9

The "them" in this verse pertains to the Disciples who were Israelites. Verse 17:6 shows this.

I have manifested thy name unto the men which **thou gavest me out of the world**: thine they were, and thou gavest them me; and they have kept thy word. - John 17:6

Here is one more definitive precept on the meaning of "world" and "salvation" and on the fact that the Old and New Testament are in total agreement:

But **Israel** shall be saved in the Lord with an everlasting **salvation**: ye shall not be ashamed nor confounded **world without end**. - Isaiah 47:15

If you do not study the precepts of the Bible you can easily get tripped up in misunderstandings. This is by design. The idea of precepts is what kept the Bible from being destroyed by the enemies of Israel. The hidden understanding of precepts is the reason why the enemies of Israel have brought forth the Scriptures to the Israelites even as they hold Israel captive. The prophecy of the Bible predicted that things would transpire just as they have.

What is the Church teaching?

> Her priests have violated my law, and have profaned mine holy things: **they have put no difference between the holy and profane**, neither have they shewed difference between the unclean and the clean, and have hid their eyes from my sabbaths, and I am profaned among them. - Ezekiel 22:26

The doctrine of the modern Catholic Church, and by extension, all so-called Christian Churches is actually the doctrine of Nicolas, a converted "Jewish" Edomite who was a follower of Paul the Apostle. Nicolas was not an Israelite, but a Jewish convert.

> And the saying pleased the whole multitude: and they chose Stephen, a man full of faith and of the Holy Ghost, and Philip, and Prochorus, and Nicanor, and Timon, and Parmenas, and Nicolas a proselyte of Antioch: - Acts 6:5

A proselyte is a Gentile Greek or Roman who was converted into following the laws and customs of the Israelites. They are the converts that we now call "Jewish".

> Now when the congregation was broken up, many of the Jews and religious proselytes followed Paul and Barnabas: who, speaking to them, persuaded them to continue in the grace of God. - Acts 13:43

> Phrygia, and Pamphylia, in Egypt, and in the parts of Libya about Cyrene, and strangers of Rome, Jews and proselytes - Acts 2:10

The modern Catholic and Protestant Churches are promoting this doctrine which does not match the doctrine of the Israelites or the followers of the Christ of the Bible. This doctrine is theology. It is religious theory not Biblically based.

The Messiah warned about what was happening with these converts:

> Woe unto you, scribes and Pharisees, hypocrites! <u>for ye compass sea and land to make one proselyte</u>, and when he is made, ye make him twofold more the child of hell than yourselves. - Mathew 23:15

Christ, in the Book of Revelation, admonished the church of Smyrna for promoting the false doctrines of Nicolas the convert.

> So hast thou also them that hold the doctrine of the <u>Nicolaitanes</u>, which thing I hate. - Revelation 2:15

We must accept the unfortunate conclusion that the modern Christian church has been high jacked by Satan. To understand this, you must understand the Bible as it is written.

Take away from this chapter:

1. The Bible is the history and Constitution of the Israelites, the House of Jacob. It was written by the ancestors of the so-called people of color.

2. The Bible can be validated by the many prophecies in it that relate to the state of the earth today.

3. There is a big difference between religious theories and philosophies and the actual words of the Bible.

> 1 My son, **forget not my law**; but let thine heart keep my commandments: 2 **For length of days, and long life, and peace**, shall they add to thee. 3 Let not mercy and truth forsake thee: bind them about thy neck; **write them upon the table of thine heart**: 4 **So shalt thou find favour** and good understanding in the sight of God and man.
> - Proverbs 3:1-4

11 Religion Reset
The unified definitions dilemma

> That this is a rebellious people, lying children, children that
> will not hear the law of the LORD: Which say to the seers,
> See not; and to the prophets, **Prophesy not to us right
> things, speak to us smooth things, prophesy deceits**:
> - Isaiah 30:9-10

1. How do we regain our spiritual power?
2. How do we develop a unified belief system?
3. What fruit does your belief system manifest?

Most religions are at best political organizations and at worst tools of
propaganda, oppression, and exploitation. This may sound like a harsh
criticism but we must face reality and examine the evidence in an
unemotional and sober manner.

Do modern churches teach a value system that helps us overcome the
unique problems that face our community? Is the doctrine of the
churches consistent with the wisdom of the Bible? Are religions based
on historical fact? Are religions based on the truth?

Do religions help us solve the problem of the triplets of racism,
materialism, and militarism?

Since none of the major religions recognize the identity of the true
historical Israelites, we know that the answer to all of these questions is
NO.

> **Who changed the truth of God into a lie**, and worshipped
> and served the creature more than the Creator.
> - Romans 1:25

The House of Jacob is not about religion, it is a mindset and a lifestyle.
The Bible does not discuss religion. It is a Book of laws and definitions
that lead to a natural lifestyle. These laws and definitions are the laws
and definitions of spiritual life and death.

The religion of white supremacy

> Behold, <u>I am against them that prophesy false dreams, saith the Lord</u>, and do tell them, and **cause my people to err by their lies**, and by their lightness; yet I sent them not, nor commanded them: therefore **they shall not profit this people at all, saith the Lord**. - Jeremiah 23:32

When you believe in white Jesus and the false doctrine that goes along with him, your belief system is white supremacy not the Bible. We have to face the fact that what we have been calling our religion is nothing more than slave teachings. The Bible shows this in clear detail.

Even after the atrocities of slavery and the murdering of great men like Martin Luther King, America is somehow still able to pull off its propaganda of being the world's champion of truth, justice, freedom, and "Christian values". Presidents and lawmakers take oaths on a Bible even as they openly seek to create their own philosophies that are most times the exact opposite of what the Bible teaches.

Why would anyone fight against a man speaking the words of Christ as Dr. King was doing? In spite of the propaganda about being a "Christian nation", America's past and current history shows that the real religion of America is white supremacy.

It's not just that religions don't follow the Bible; the irony is that they are obviously set up to directly oppose the Bible. All laws created by the governments that were set up by the religions of white supremacy also directly go against the Bible.

The Bible is a book of the law of the House of Jacob and the application of this law. In showing the application of the law, it became a historical record of the Israelites and prophesies about what will befall the Israelites in the future. There is no such thing as Catholic, Protestant, Baptist, Methodist, Mormon, or any other religion in the Bible.

There are more than 4200 religions in the world but none of them follows the Bible because none of them are controlled by the children of the House of Jacob.

The Bible has been used to spread Euro-centric pagan religions but it was not written for the purpose of religion and it was NOT written by Europeans.

The only consistent value system across all the major religions is paganism and white supremacy. The major religions either teach multiple gods, superstition, idol worship, or that the white man is god.

The truth is that white supremacy has not really created any culture or religion other than white supremacy itself. White supremacy has created an artificial culture by absorbing the knowledge and understanding of many other cultures. Once it absorbs cultural knowledge and understanding, white supremacy renders the previous culture powerless to resist domination by the white supremacy system. This is what has happened to the Israelites and many other nations.

All modern religions that dominate the world were either set up, promoted, encouraged, or co-opted by the House of Esau as a method of world wide rulership and control. These religions under white supremacy domination are political parties that mostly practice religious theories and philosophies that are not found in the Bible.

The point of the major religions is to get you to worship anything but the God of the Israelites – The Most High God that is expressed in the laws, statues, commandments, and judgments of the Bible.

White supremacy and all the sub religions that it has spawned is the religion of false authority. Following these religions will lead you to idolatry and spiritual domination which will ultimately lead you to spiritual death.

Consumerism religion

Idol worship through spectacle, illusions, and symbolism is the chief method of a "thing based" belief system. Beautiful artwork, grand church structures, and the allure of opulence is the hallmark of religious attraction. The religion of consumerism as a branch of white supremacy is no different.

The propaganda of consumerism has successfully merged white Jesus, Santa Clause, and the corporate beast into one treat providing entity in the minds of the indoctrinated.

Indoctrinated consumers never stop loving toys. They will do anything to prove themselves worthy of receiving the material things that the corporations can provide. They view debt as a gift from the gods of white supremacy and judge each other by their ability to borrow money. They think that they are experiencing spiritual freedom through the idea of luxury and "prosperity" but they are really just participating in idolatry and pagan illusions that are destined to fail.

Unnecessary material goods and debt tied to your labor are illusions of wealth and are the very definition of spiritual enslavement under the corporate plantation system.

Universal paganism

> But I say, that the things which the Gentiles sacrifice, **they sacrifice to devils, and not to God**: and I would not that ye should have fellowship with devils. - 1 Corinthians 10:20

Theology is a form of white supremacy science that seeks to overthrow the wisdom of the Bible. The Bible rebukes theology and the false teachings of all the major religions that are practiced on the earth today.

God did not give us religion; He gave us laws, statutes, commandments, and judgments that form the basis of a consistent value system that is based on the truth. Through these laws we can understand the true consequences of our actions. This knowledge is important because our emotions can manipulate us into making false connections between our actions and the consequences that result from those actions.

When you look at the major religions objectively you see why they have not helped in creating justice on the earth. They have, for the most part, done just the opposite by aiding in the spread of injustice, chaos, and confusion. To get at the truth, we must objectively look at the facts no matter how uncomfortable or painful they may be.

The major religions

> Howbeit **in vain do they worship me**, teaching for doctrines the commandments of men. - Mark 7:7

Catholicism is actually Babylonian pagan worship and it teaches that the laws of the Bible do not matter as long as you worship the white supremacy god that it created. The word catholic itself literally means universal. The rituals and holidays associated with modern Christianity all come from the Catholic Church; very few of these rituals are found in the Bible. In fact, many of these church rituals are directly denounced in the Bible. There is no Christianity in the Bible. Christ like all other wise Israelites taught and followed the laws, statutes, and commandments of the Old Testament.

204

Christmas, Easter, and Sunday worship are all examples of the continuation of Roman pagan traditions that were incorporated into one universal state religion of Rome--Catholicism. All of the thousands of so-called Christian denominations are just off shoots of this universal religion that openly practices white supremacy and blasphemy against the Bible.

Islam is the Turkish version of Catholicism. It claims to follow the teachings of the prophets of the Bible but also adds its own book, the Quran. Adding to the scripture is expressly denounced on the last page of the Bible.

> For I testify unto every man that heareth the words of the prophecy of this book, **If any man shall add unto these things**, God shall add unto him the plagues that are written in this book: - Revelation 22:18

Islam is Catholicism that is tailored to the Turkish Arab lifestyle. It was created to facilitate Arab control over Africa, the Middle East, and the Far East. What it has morphed into is Edomite Turks controlling the areas of the world that the white Christians can not.

Hinduism is the religion of the East Indians. It is an openly pagan religion with multiple gods. Hindus have been thoroughly conquered by white supremacy. At one time as little as 100,000 British ruled over the Indian nation of over one billion people. To show the power that white supremacy has over both religions; Britain split India in two by creating Pakistan, an Islamic country; and India, a Hindu country.

Judaism bills itself as following the customs of the Israelites but it uses the Babylonian Talmud, not the Bible as its "holy book". Judaism is interesting because it most closely follows the traditions of the Israelites eventhough the people who practice it are Edomites. By posing as Israelites these Edomites are able to gain extraordinary power over the rest of the House of Esau eventhough they are the smallest religion by number. This should show you the power that even the basic traditions of the House of Jacob can have over world affairs.

The new pagan mainstream movement

Beware lest any man spoil you through philosophy and vain deceit, after the tradition of men, after the rudiments of the world, and not after Christ. - Colossians 2:8

The latest pagan fad is the New Age movement. Many Christian Mega Churches have morphed into this New Age philosophy. Also many celebrities are spokes people for this philosophy. New Age mixes mysticism, eastern Hindu philosophy, self help, and materialism into one belief system of feel good emotionalism and vague rules. New age presents the ultimate manifestation of blurred lines and confused meanings. New Age philosophy encourages the idea of no boundaries, no separation of things, everybody has their own "personal relationship" with God, there are "many paths to God", and "no one can judge or be judged".

New Age draws people in because it sounds very righteous on the surface. The truth is that it is just another way to confuse the definition of right and wrong, which ultimately aids those who create injustice in the world. The white supremacy system loves any religion or philosophy that does not call for justice and fair compensation for its historical crimes against humanity or that encourages you to forget the past and ignore the negative and destructive things that are going on in the world.

In the end, all of these philosophies lead you to idolatry. New Age leads you to the worship of yourself and your so-called intellect. It encourages you to trust your own understanding through what you feel. Your supposed to "trust your heart" and all of these flowery high sounding ideals. Here is how the Bible clearly deals with this kind of philosophy:

The heart is deceitful above all things, and desperately wicked: who can know it? - Jeremiah 17:9

These deceptive philosophies have been around forever. Like all pagan belief systems New Age leads you to worship anything but the God of the Bible – the Most High God of the House of Jacob.

Science as religion

Many of us think we are being smart or intelligent by following Atheists who claim to be using science, human logic, and human intelligence as their guide. Atheism is itself a religion that is just another form of idolatry – the worship of creations instead of the Creator.

Each new "scientific discovery" is really an admission of the changing nature of mans understanding. Depending solely on the observations of man cannot be relied upon as fact or true knowledge because mans own ideas are the original source of his blindness to the truth that he claims that he has "discovered". Man must change in order to find the truth; the truth does not change to suit man.

Science does not create anything; it can only describe what already is and was before the "scientist" discovered the existence of a thing. In this respect scientific discovery is admission of ignorance. All science can do is try to understand cause and effect relationships. The Bible already describes these relationships going back to the beginning of time. For the most part, belief in science is nothing more than a white supremacy attempt to claim existing knowledge for itself.

White supremacy scientist will invent any story to keep the lies of white supremacy consistent. Consistency is the key to the white supremacy belief system. It does not matter whether something is true or false it only matters if it can be made to fit into the narrative of white supremacy.

The Bible explained many so-called scientific discoveries long before white supremacy scientists claim to have found out these things. Many thousands of years, before Einstein or any other scientist "discovered" anything, the Bible already gave us the truth and the proof behind what these so-called scientist claim to be discovering. The first three verses of the Bible sums up the inferiority of thousands of years of white supremacy so-called scientific discovery against the true science of the Bible.

The belief in one God is the first of all scientific concepts.

Even with man's admission of ignorance, misguided men still feel they can improve on the design that was already working before they arrived. It is a vain and useless attempt to modify and overthrow the natural order set by God.

The ironic thing is that all so-called science is predicated on the "faith" of constant cause and effect relationships. Without an original cause there is no science, therefore all science eventually points back to a mind and a Creator.

Pagan domination

White supremacy dominates all other pagan belief systems because it is the newest form of pagan belief on the earth. The founding fathers of white supremacy borrowed the false teachings from all the other pagan belief systems that have existed throughout history.

The false idea of skin color supremacy is the only real innovation of the white supremacy religion. This simple deception has allowed white supremacy to overtake all other pagan belief systems. Eventhough this assumption is clearly inconsistent with reality; the simple idea of "white is right" gives white supremacy paganism a consistent unifying force that is able to trump all other pagan beliefs.

Not only has white supremacy been able to dominate the Israelites who stopped following the laws of their God; but white supremacy has also dominated the Egyptians, Persians, Hindus, Arabs, Asians, and any other group that believes in pagan idol worship and multiple gods. The forefathers and promoters of white supremacy have taken the pagan philosophies from all these conquered peoples and mixed them together to form their own pagan religious theology.

The secret to white supremacy success is that they found out that once you subscribe to a false or inconsistent belief system, you can easily be confused, corrupted, and dominated by those who take a consistent approach, even if that consistent approach is not based on the truth.

Returning to the truth

No religion, philosophy, or history that has been taught to us in our captivity explains why we were captured and brought to the Americas to have our whole history wiped away.

None of these religions or philosophies explains why seemly wicked people are allowed to rule the world and plunge the world into turmoil, death and destruction while no force seems to be able to stop them to create lasting peace.

The Bible explains these things in glaring detail if you actually read what it says instead of taking other peoples word for what it says.

The Bible clearly exposes white supremacy religion with its false idols for what it is, an integral part of the global corporate racket.

Take away from this chapter:

1. All religions that claim to use the Bible are false since they do not correctly identify the Israelites on the earth today. The Bible does not speak of religion and is not a book of religion.

2. Paganism is the chief religion across the earth. The white supremacy system is the dominant pagan belief system that currently controls the earth.

3. The Israelites are still in captivity because they are under the influence of false belief systems.

The Lord shall bring thee, and thy king which thou shalt set over thee, unto a nation which neither thou nor thy fathers have known; **and there shalt thou serve other gods, wood and stone.** – Deuteronomy 28:36

12 Definitions Reset

The rulership dilemma

> Thy righteousness is an everlasting righteousness, and thy
> **law is the truth**. - Psalm 119:142

1. Where do the people who rule over you get their authority?
2. What is the alternative system to white supremacy?
3. How do you convert liabilities into assets?

To convert liabilities into assets, or problems into solutions, or unproductive activity into productive activity requires a change in the definitions that you are using. Using these new definitions, you can shape a new vision.

In the evolution of the House of Jacob, we have all the evidence that we need to correctly divide things into their proper categories. We have the Scriptures to guide us plus we have the historical evidence that the Scriptures are the truth.

Many people get thrown off by the words "commandment" and "law". But the commandments and laws are just the definitions set forth by the Creator. They are the definitions of prosperity, peace, happiness and all the other positive emotions. The laws of The Most High God are the definitions of life. In fact they are the definitions of everlasting life.

The only question is will you follow the definitions of the Scriptures or will you believe in your own understanding. The condition of our community should be proof positive that our own understanding is not the truth. Understanding this is the beginning of the transformation of our community.

Natural definitions and duality

> Jesus answered and said unto them, **Ye do err, not knowing the scriptures, nor the power of God.**
> - Matthew 22:29

Contrary to what is taught in modern society, the Scriptures tell us that you must think in duality. This means that you must recognize that we live in a world of opposites. It is hard for many of us to understand that evil is contained in blurred lines and the false idea of "oneness".

> So then because **thou art lukewarm, and neither cold nor hot**, I will spue thee out of my mouth. - Revelation 3:16

Most of the confusion that exists in the world today comes from vague, ambiguous and false definitions, a lack of clarity about what things mean. The Bible is proven ancient wisdom that defines what may be otherwise difficult to define concepts. What is love? What is right? What is success? What is happiness? What is the purpose of life?

These concepts can only be understood by comparing and contrasting them with their opposites. You cannot define love without also defining its opposite, hate. You cannot define good without defining evil. Opposites give meaning and clarity to the world in which we live.

> **And he shall speak great words against the most High**, and shall wear out the saints of the most High, **and think to change times and laws**: and they shall be given into his hand until a time and times and the dividing of time.
> - Daniel 7:25

To be mis-educated means that your ability to properly define and categorize things has been impeded to the point where you cannot understand the natural definitions set by the Most High.

Simple decision making

When you understand the dual nature of our existence, decision making becomes much easier. You come to understand that everything in life must be broken down into a series of yes or no questions.

> But let your communication be, Yea, yea; Nay, nay: **for whatsoever is more than these cometh of evil**.
> - Matthew 5:37

As the above verse shows, evil comes when you go away from simple yes or no answers to questions. The truth is contained in yes or no, or true or false. That is it. That is the logic of God.

There are only two choices that we must be concerned with: Good or Evil. How you define these two opposite concepts determines whether you are acting wisely or foolishly.

If you think this way, you always have a 50-50 chance of being correct. If you find proof that you are incorrect, all you have to do is immediately repent to the opposite way of thinking. If both ways are proven to be incorrect, you know that you have not correctly chosen two opposites but have been fooled into choosing between two falsehoods; you have not rightly divided the word of truth.

When you have this mindset, even when you are wrong, you are still receiving valuable information because the more evidence that you have of what is false, by the process of elimination, the closer you get to the truth.

Slavery or freedom through definitions

> And ye shall know the truth, and **the truth shall make you free**. - John 8:32

If you are using the definitions of people who oppose you, your enemies, you become their slave and your own worst enemy. You can instantly free yourself from this enslavement by changing the definitions that you are using. The Bible is the reference that contains the true definitions that we should be following.

> **For the commandment is a lamp**; and the law is light; and reproofs of instruction are the way of life: - Proverbs 6:23

If you are still following the customs and definitions of the descendants of slave masters, you are still a slave. If you are not using the definitions that are given by the wisdom of the Scriptures, you are, without a doubt, operating under the inferior definitions given by men who are under the influence of Satan.

> But I say, that the things which the Gentiles sacrifice, **they sacrifice to devils, and not to God**: and I would not that ye should have fellowship with devils. - 1 Corinthians 10:20

Competition, greed, theft, militarism, and all other forms of covetousness and negative emotions are the power behind the empire that is currently ruling the earth. This empire is set up under the rules and definitions of Satan to go against God and God's people. Like all other empires that were set up in a similar manner, this one too will fail miserably.

> And the great dragon was cast out, that old serpent, called the Devil, and **Satan, which deceiveth the whole world**: he was cast out into the earth, and his angels were cast out with him. - Revelation 12:9

Satan's empires always lead to destruction because the further you go away from the definitions and natural uses set by the Most High God, the more stress you create and the closer you come to having your works being destroyed.

> **He that trusteth in his own heart is a fool**: but whoso walketh wisely, he shall be delivered. - Proverbs 28:26

If you do not rely on the definitions that are contained in the Scriptures, you will be enticed by Satan to lean on your own understanding and feelings. Under this mindset, you can easily be manipulated and controlled by evil. You will even begin to identify with, and justify evil.

> **He that justifieth the wicked, and he that condemneth the just**, even they both are abomination to the Lord.
> - Proverbs 17:15

Once you are under the possession of the false definitions of Satan, you will begin to falsely believe that these false definitions are who you are. You become enslaved by these false definitions.

To end this enslavement, we must do two things:

1. Agree on the truth
2. Correct ourselves according to the truth

Everything must be labeled as either good or evil. The inability to find choices that are good, and the seemingly endless availability of choices that are evil, shows the corrupt state of our society.

Conversion and transformation by definitions

Once it has been confirmed that a path that you have taken is not correct according to the natural definitions of the Most High, you must return to the opposite definition to get back in order. This is how you convert liabilities into assets. Everything can be changed by repenting to the proper definitions.

> And said, Verily I say unto you, **Except ye be converted, and become as little children**, ye shall not enter into the kingdom of heaven. - Matthew 18:3

Transformation comes through redefining the rules and concepts by which we operate. When you change your definitions, you become proactive instead of reacting to outside forces. Definitions create the reality that we live in. New definitions create a new consciousness.

> **The law of the Lord is perfect, converting the soul**: the testimony of the Lord is sure, making wise the simple.
> - Psalm 19:7

The Bible is the Book of Life. Without these definitions you get the chaos and strife that dominates the world today.

Rulership by definitions

> Thus saith the Lord; **Cursed be the man that trusteth in man**, and maketh flesh his arm, and whose heart departeth from the Lord. - Jeremiah 17: 5

You can never be ruled by people, you can only be ruled by ideas. Rulership comes through ideas, which means that rulership is determined by the definitions that you accept. When the Bible speaks of a change in rulership, it is speaking of a change in the accepted definitions of what things mean.

What is promoted to be the good life under the current system is actually the definition of spiritual death. By not considering spiritual death, those who appear to be prospering despite breaking God's definitions will eventually have to pay the price for their temporary gains. When you seek gain by breaking God's definitions you are most likely prospering by causing the unnecessary suffering of others. The price for this kind of gain is physical and spiritual death. That is justice.

No matter how men try to play around with definitions, the final provider of reward and punishment is God because God set the definition of reward and punishment from the beginning.

Those who go against God and God's people are only living "the good life" relative to the state of God's chosen people. Those who prosper from evil can only live this way at the expense of the House of Jacob.

The good news is that the current state of the world will not last. Justice, peace, and prosperity will be restored to the earth as was intended since the beginning.

The oppressive rulership over the earth will come to an end. More and more people are waking up to the fact that it must come to an end. The" kingdom of Heaven is at hand" means that the proper definitions will be returned to earth. The Scriptures tell us that Heaven is a new kingdom under the House of Jacob that will be ruled in righteousness.

> Thy kingdom come, Thy will be done **in earth, as it is in heaven**. - Mathew 6:10

The unrighteous and unwilling to submit to the definitions of God will be destroyed so that the new and everlasting kingdom can come to power.

We are living in the time that was prophesized where we have only two choices in belief systems. The choices are either the belief system of Jacob or the belief system of Esau. It was prophesized that these two national belief systems would usher in a new social order. Humanity would fall under one or the other and be judged according to that choice.

> **For the Lord will have mercy on Jacob, and will yet choose Israel**, and set them in their own land: **and the strangers shall be joined with them**, and they shall cleave to the house of Jacob. - Isaiah 14:1

Justice will come into the world when the House of Jacob returns to the natural definitions set by God. The Scriptures tell us that when the House of Jacob is restored, rulership under wicked kingdoms and their false definitions will stop, those who have refused to return to the definitions of God will be destroyed, and everlasting peace and prosperity will rein over mankind.

The question is which side of it will you be on?

You can protect yourself from this correction by being on the proper side of the equation. You must practice the right formulas in order to neutralize the influence of the House of Esau over your daily affairs. This requires economic as well as a spiritual repentance. It also requires that you recognize the power of your nationality.

The fall of the definitions of the House of Esau

The good news of the Scriptures is actually bad news for those currently in rulership, and those who agree with them. Justice demands that those who gain from causing suffering and evil must be punished.

> O Lord, my strength, and my fortress, and my refuge in the day of affliction, the <u>Gentiles</u> shall come unto thee from the ends of the earth, and shall say, **Surely our fathers have inherited lies, vanity, and things wherein there is no profit.** - Jeremiah 16:19

The false definitions given under the white supremacy system is the major stumbling block of the House of Esau. The competitive based law of the House of Esau breeds constant stress. The fear caused by an unnatural lifestyle is what brings on this unnecessary stress. A proper belief system defends you against the constant threats, competition, envy, vanity, and other negative emotions that are embed in the artificial lifestyle that is forced on us under the House of Esau.

Will people under this belief system of white supremacy accept the truth of the identity of the Israelites and the black Messiah?

> **For thy violence against thy brother Jacob shame shall cover thee,** and thou shalt be cut off for ever. - Obadiah 1:10

By blocking the truth, and misappropriating God given assets, the House of Esau has created for itself a liability with God. This is why the global corporate system is destined to collapse like all other empires. Justice means that the House of Esau must fall from rulership over the earth.

The economic system of the House of Esau blocks God given assets and creates new illusionary liabilities through unnecessary luxuries. This artificial control creates an imbalance in the ledger that is only corrected by destroying the blockage. This is the story of the rise and fall of all empires throughout history.

Most of us have no real knowledge of history so we cannot understand that there were many nations that appeared to have the upper hand that disappeared overnight. The current ruling kingdom of the House of Esau is built on the ashes of these failed philosophies.

The House of Esau has absorbed a massive liability from all other empires because it has sought to control the entire world. According to the prophecy of the Scriptures, because of its conquests The House of Esau has absorbed the liabilities of all the other empires throughout history and will therefore suffer the most dramatic fall of all.

> **He that leadeth into captivity shall go into captivity:** he
> that killeth with the sword must be killed with the sword.
> Here is the patience and the faith of the saints.
> - Revelation 13:10

The belief system that is forced on us is not built to relieve fear and worry; it is built to create it.

If you look closely at the laws set up under the House of Esau, you find that most of them go directly against the Bible. This is done in the name of "personal freedom".

The U.S. Constitution, the United Nations, and the European Union are not the will of God. Following these things put you in direct opposition to God because the white supremacy system does not follow the natural order set by God.

Because something is legal under white supremacy we are made to think that there is no other judgment that will take place.

Both Garvey and King became a problem to the U.S. government because they were espousing a different law than the U.S. law. They were speaking of a higher law-- the law that is based on truth and justice, not propaganda. The higher law destroys the global illusion.

The rise of the definitions of the House of Jacob

Many of us go along with the status quo eventhough we don't agree with it. This is because we falsely believe that there is no other choice. If you do not understand the Bible and the alternative philosophy of the House of Jacob this is true. When you decide that you will spiritually separate from the House of Esau, you must have another belief system to take its place.

The House of Jacob is the set of definitions, belief system, rules, and principles that bring about peace and prosperity. The problem with returning to the proper definitions is that we live under another belief system that is based on false definitions.

> I say then, Have they stumbled that they should fall? God forbid: but rather through their fall salvation is come unto the Gentiles, for to provoke them to jealousy. **Now if the fall of them be the riches of the world**, and the diminishing of them the riches of the Gentiles; how much more their fulness? - Romans 11:11-12

The above verse shows that the rulers of the earth are ruling by default because the definitions of God have been discarded by the House of Jacob. As the House of Jacob returns to the proper definitions, the earth will be put back into order. The fall of the definitions of the House of Esau will mean the rise of the definitions of the House of Jacob.

> But unto the wicked God saith, What hast thou to do to declare my statutes, or that thou shouldest take my covenant in thy mouth? 17 **Seeing thou hatest instruction, and casteth my words behind thee.** - Psalm 50:16-17

There is no way to change anything using the false definitions of African American, West Indian, Haitian, Dominican, Puerto Rican, or any other fictional label. These fictional names come along with false definitions and a false belief system that allows the enemies of God's definitions to rule the earth.

> 40 **If they shall confess their iniquity, and the iniquity of their fathers, with their trespass which they trespassed against me**, and that also they have walked contrary unto me;

> 41 And that **I also have walked contrary unto them**, and have brought them into the land of their enemies; if then

their uncircumcised hearts be humbled, and they then accept of the punishment of their iniquity:

42 **Then will I remember my covenant with Jacob**, and also my covenant with Isaac, and also my covenant with Abraham will I remember; and I will remember the land.
- Leviticus 26:40-42

The verses above promise that if we find ourselves oppressed in the land of our enemies, we should understand that it is a sign that our ancestors discarded the definitions of God and we are continuing in their error. But if we turn to the definitions set by God, He will return power to us.

And the kingdom and dominion, and the greatness of the kingdom under the whole heaven, <u>shall be given to the people of the saints of the most High</u>, whose kingdom is **an everlasting kingdom**, and all dominions shall serve and obey him. - Daniel 7:27

The House of Jacob is the eternal kingdom. When it comes back into power, the definitions that it uses will rein forever. Thus saith the Lord.

Grace, repentance, reward, and punishment

What shall we say then? **Shall we continue in sin**, that grace may abound? - Romans 6:1

The Christian church has been very effective in convincing people that the laws of God can somehow be done away with. Along with this false doctrine comes the idea that grace means that there is no sin and that you can do anything that you want and still be favored by God.

The truth is that the law equals the commandments plus the consequences.

Before Christ, the consequence of breaking the law was animal sacrifice or physical death. After Christ, you have grace to repent in his name instead of animal sacrifice or being put to physical death. When you repent and acknowledge your transgression of the law you are able to obtain forgiveness through Christ.

Question: How can you repent if you don't know what law you have broken?

Answer: You can't, that's why they are written in the Bible in the first place, so you can know what to do and what not to do.

> For **God shall bring every work into judgment**, with every secret thing, whether it be good, or whether it be evil.
> - Ecclesiastes 12:14

Because we have been tricked by religious philosophy, we are being controlled by oppressive laws created by unrepentant wicked men instead of the freedom produced under the natural laws of God.

Take away from this chapter:

1. The white supremacy system has gained rulership by distorting the natural definitions that were set by God. The earth is being ruled by falsehoods instead of the truth.

2. You cannot be ruled by people, you can only be ruled by the definitions that you accept.

3. Freedom comes by ignoring false white supremacy definitions, and returning to the truth of the natural laws and definitions that were set by God.

Thus have ye made the commandment of God of none effect by your tradition. - Matthew 15:6

13 Emotional Weapons Reset

The feelings dilemma

> Where there is no vision, the people perish: but **he that keepeth the law, <u>happy is he</u>**. - Proverbs 29:18

1. How do your definitions get mixed up?
2. How do you control your emotions?

Emotion is the chief weapon used to rule the earth. Emotional manipulation through false definitions is the number one method of control that is used by the House of Esau. The militaristic nature of the white supremacy system has unleashed confusion across the earth through aggressive, destructive, negative emotions.

The Bible is the book that shows you how to control confusion and stress by overcoming these emotions.

> **Put on the whole armour of God**, that ye may be able to stand against the wiles of the devil. - Ephesians 6:11

The white supremacy system has assumed its rulership over the earth through negative emotions, and can <u>only</u> rule through the proliferation of fear, competition, and other destructive emotions. The masses of people are manipulated into the overuse of negative emotions through the white supremacy media and educational systems.

You must be able to neutralize these aggressive and destructive emotions in order to have peace and prosperity.

To neutralize these destructive emotions you must be able to rightly divide emotions into their proper purposes and causes. God is the dividing line that separates the positive emotions from the negative emotions. You must understand the natural laws of God in order to rightly divide your emotions. This is the purpose of the Bible.

To neutralize those who are operating under negative emotions you must be able to understand the emotions that are driving them. If you are not able to do this, you will become just as corrupt as those who you are fighting against, which only continues the problem.

But if I cast out devils by the Spirit of God, then the
kingdom of God is come unto you. - Mathew 12:28

The Bible offers the wisdom that is needed to solve the problem of
empire and control without tipping the scales of justice against you.

Emotion and perceived value

Let's go back to the wealth and value formula and further break down
perceived value.

Wealth = real value + <u>perceived value</u>

Perceived Value = Imagination x Emotion

The above formula means that what you believe (imagination) and how
strongly you believe (emotion) equals what you will value.

We are really in a war of emotions and imaginations. Because the seed
of activity is first sown in the mind, all economics begins in the mind.

Your imagination is the starting point of all activity. Perceived value
comes from your perception which is just your imagination. Your
perception is really your prediction about what the future holds and
how strongly you believe in this prediction.

What you can imagine is controlled by the definitions that you use. The
definitions that you use will determine what you think is possible which
ultimately controls your actions.

Emotions

He that is slow to anger is better than the mighty; and he
that <u>ruleth his spirit</u> than he that taketh a city.
- Proverbs 16:32

In general, positive emotions are assets and negative emotions are
liabilities. These opposing emotions make up the dilemma of human
nature. Wisdom means knowing how and when to apply these
opposing emotions. How you call on these emotions is defined by your
identity and the definitions that go along with your identity.

The negative emotions are associated with individualistic survival goals.
The drive for survival causes stress. Positive emotions are associated

with peace and harmony.   The drive for harmony causes faith. What you have faith in determines your social behavior.

To rule over your emotions you must be in tune with the Spirit of the Most High. How do you do this? By staying in tuned with the definitions of God, you become the ruler over your emotions and a person of unlimited power.

Imagination

> But they hearkened not, nor inclined their ear, but **walked in the counsels and in the imagination of their evil heart**, and went backward, and not forward. - Jeremiah 7:24

The House of Jacob is in economic captivity because our vision has become blocked by our own thoughts and imaginations. Of course this has been induced by the trauma of slavery and oppression, but we must realize that no matter the physical circumstances, all we need to do is turn back to the right definitions, the truth, and everything will change.

> **And they said, There is no hope**: but we will walk after our own devices, and we will every one do the imagination of his evil heart. - Jeremiah 18:12

We are still captives because we cannot see past the artificial world that has been created for us by the enemies of our people.

> Casting down imaginations, and every high thing that exalteth itself against the knowledge of God, and **bringing into captivity every thought** to the obedience of Christ;
> - 2 Corinthians 10:5

To control your perception you must be able to control your imagination. The key to doing this is to understand that your imagination is not reality...yet. But the more you focus on something, the more likely it becomes that that circumstance will eventually come into your experience. This works for both desirable and undesirable circumstances.

There is no need to imagine a situation that you feel that you cannot change. That is a waste of your energy and a waste of your imaginative power.

With your imagination you are free to create ANYTHING that you want. Why would you waste time creating undesirable circumstances? Why would you waste your time imagining circumstances where you or someone else is harmed? Why would you not spend your energy imagining the best possible circumstances and circumstances that bring about peace and prosperity? This is a choice that no one can take from you. It's always your choice as to how you direct your imagination.

Knowing which visions to focus on and which visions to discard will determine the direction of your life. What you focus on through your imagination becomes your perception of the world.

Emotionalism

> 3 But if our gospel be hid, it is hid to them that are lost: 4 In whom **the god of this world hath blinded the minds of them which believe not,** lest the light of the glorious gospel of Christ, who is the image of God, should shine unto them.
> - 2 Corinthians 4:3-4

Through New Age philosophy, many people are being deceived into mistaking emotionalism for spirituality. When you take the rules that come along with truth and justice out of emotions, you are left with emotionalism, flattery, and infatuation. These are superficial and situational emotions that are based on temporary opinions and changing preferences.

> **Woe unto them that call evil good**, and good evil; that put darkness for light, and light for darkness; that put bitter for sweet, and sweet for bitter! - Isaiah 5:20

The only god that does not require rules for emotions is Satan, who is the god of the temporary worldly realm.

> **And that ye may put difference** between holy and unholy, and between unclean and clean; - Leviticus 10:10

Winning the spiritual war means that you recognize that God put a difference between the clean and unclean, the holy and the unholy. This requires rules that separate things into their proper categories and functions.

And this is love, that we walk after his commandments. This is the commandment, That, as ye have heard from the beginning, ye should walk in it. - 2 John 1:6

The false New Age doctrine that says that there is "no difference between things" and "we are all one", is not love but the main weapon of spiritual warfare. When you take on this doctrine you are practicing emotionalism, not love. This is a Satanic doctrine that seeks to deny that judgment will come to the wicked.

Understanding how to rightly divide things into their proper place insures that your emotions are directed properly.

A time to love, and a time to hate; a time of war, and a time of peace. - Ecclesiastes 3:8

As the above verse shows, all emotions have a place and time. Knowing the time and place to use emotions is the definition of wisdom.

Neutralizing spiritual attack

Negative emotions call the negative spirits into existence. These negative emotions manifest the urge to steal, kill, and destroy. If the destructive spirits can get you to fight back with negative emotions, you have not neutralized the spirits but increased their power over yourself and other people.

43 **When the unclean spirit is gone out of a man**, he walketh through dry places, seeking rest, and findeth none.

44 Then he saith, I will return into my house from whence I came out; and when he is come, he findeth it empty, swept, and garnished.

45 **Then goeth he, and taketh with himself seven other spirits more wicked than himself**, and they enter in and dwell there: and the last state of that man is worse than the first. Even so shall it be also unto this wicked generation. - Matthew 12:43-45

The idea of fighting a spiritual war is to avoid inadvertently invoking the spirit that you are trying to neutralize. Since the destructive spirits are invoked through negative emotions, they must be neutralized with positive emotions.

This is what Dr. King was doing when he developed the non violent approach to dealing with the violent system of white supremacy. He showed that non violence does not mean non resistance.

The healing of these spirits means that they are neutralized. You can not neutralize them by invoking the same emotions that caused them in the first place.

> Be ye angry, and sin not: let not the sun go down upon your wrath: - Ephesians 4:26

The idea of justice always neutralizes the negative spirits. Seeking justice without crossing the line into the negative emotions that invoke these spirits is the challenge confronting all of those who seek to heal themselves and others from these spirits.

In the spiritual world you can not fight fire with fire. You have to neutralize negative emotions using positive opposites. If not, you will just move the negative spirit off of someone else onto yourself or another person.

Spiritual health means that you can deal with problems without causing more problems. This is the very definition of wisdom.

Emotional intelligence

> For as he thinketh in his heart, so is he: - Proverbs 23:7

Controlling your emotions starts with understanding that positive and negative emotions cannot exist at the same time. The existence of one means the absence of the other. The idea of controlling your emotions ends with the understanding that there is a second spiritual death that you must try to avoid at all costs. If you cannot understand the concept of everlasting life and spiritual death, you can easily lose track of what is important and your belief system will become corrupted.

The point is to shut off the negative, destructive emotions and develop the positive emotions. How do you do this?

> **But whoso hearkeneth unto me shall dwell safely**, and
> shall be quiet from fear of evil. - Proverbs 1:33

The only fear that you should have is of the Most High God. The Most High is the only real authority and controls all other authority. If you

226

only fear God, you will never have any other fear. The fear of the Most High is the healthy fear that eliminates unnecessary stress.

The Most High has specific and definite rules that do not change. These rules eliminate chaos and cause peace and prosperity to exist at the same time. The two opposites of individual desires and group desires no longer oppose each other but are one under the Most High. This is the everlasting kingdom that the Bible speaks of.

Just as a parent is the protector of a child and tries to show the child how to be happy and healthy, so is it with the Most High God. He is our Father in Heaven. His definitions protect us from our own vain imaginations, from fear, and from our destructive thoughts. Through the wisdom of this protection, our positive dreams and visions can be manifested.

The goal is to maximize emotional assets through positive emotions and minimize emotional liabilities that stem from negative emotions. We must be protected from our own negative emotions at all costs. To do this requires rules to properly govern our perception.

Opposite emotions

> There is no fear in love; but perfect love casteth out fear: because fear hath torment. **He that feareth is not made perfect in love**. - 1 John 4:18

Spirituality is expressed in terms of these positive and negative emotions. Understanding the time and place for the various emotions is what defines wisdom.

> No man can serve two masters: **for either he will hate the one, and love the other**; or else he will hold to the one, and despise the other. Ye cannot serve God and mammon.
> - Matthew 6:24

Since all emotions have opposites, the absence of one means the presence of the other. The absence of hate is love, and the absence of love is hate. Each opposite emotion defines the other. This is the simple way to understand and define emotions.

> **The fear of the Lord is to hate evil**: pride, and arrogancy, and the evil way, and the froward mouth, do I hate.
> - Proverbs 8:13

Love and hate are reconciled in the fear of the Most High. To love the Most High means that you hate evil. This is the proper use of negative emotions because you are using negative emotions in the advancement of truth and justice. Without the compass of the guidance of God, man has no way to tell if he is advancing justice or being a destructive force. This is the meaning of rightly dividing the word of truth.

Negative emotions

> An angry man stirreth up strife, and a furious man
> aboundeth in transgression. - Proverbs 29:22

All sin is the result of the over use of negative emotions. These emotions work from the left hand of the Most High and create only temporary energy followed by some form of destruction.

Negative emotions eventually cause stress. The main cause of stress is fear.

> **The fear of man brings a snare**: but whoever puts his trust
> in the LORD shall be safe. - Proverbs 29:25

Fear and imagination go hand in hand. Fear is actually an imagined threat that has not happened yet. The key is that what you fear has not happened and may never happen because fear can only exist in your imagination. It is a creation of your own mind. By focusing on what is feared instead of possible solutions, you are actually bringing what you fear out of your imagination and into your present circumstances. It is all a matter of perception.

As we have already discussed, when you fear only the Most High and accept His definitions, no other fear can overtake you. The fear of the Most High puts your imagination in check and focuses you on the truth that it is your own negative emotions that are blocking you from overcoming whatever it is that you may be fearing.

Positive emotions

Positive emotions free you from the stress, fear and worry of the negative emotions. These emotions work from the right hand of the Most High and create lasting energy.

> **For we are saved by hope**: but hope that is seen is not hope: for what a man seeth, why doth he yet hope for?
> - Romans 8:24

Positive emotions, like negative emotions, work through your imagination. As the above verse shows, we are saved by hope and hope is faith in that which is not yet seen, but exists in the imagination.

> For whatsoever things were written aforetime were written for our learning, **that we through patience and comfort of the scriptures might have hope.** - Romans 15:4

There are no rules that govern negative emotions, but positive emotions require definitions, boundaries, and rules. To reap the benefits of positive emotions, you must sow your thoughts according to these definitions, boundaries, and rules.

> 22 But **the fruit of the Spirit** is love, joy, peace, longsuffering, gentleness, goodness, faith, Meekness, temperance: against such there is no law.
> - Galatians 5:22-23

The laws, statutes, and commandments of the Bible are the laws of positive emotion. They spell out how to keep good order and shut out the destructive nature of negative emotions, both in the individual and amongst a nation.

The laws of emotion

> For the word of God is quick, and powerful, and sharper than
> any two edged sword, piercing even to the dividing asunder of
> soul and spirit, and of the joints and marrow, and is **a**
> **discerner of the thoughts and intents of the heart**.
> - Hebrews 4:12

The laws of the Bible are really the laws of emotions. They are intended
to steer you away from unproductive thoughts.

The law is meant to give us the power of discernment, not to restrict us,
but to free us from unproductive activity and emotions.

It is important that we understand the components of the law so we do
not make the mistakes of the past by striving in the law and
misunderstanding the purpose of the various components.

The basic laws of emotions are called the Ten Commandments. They
are found in Deuteronomy chapter 5 and also in Exodus chapter 20.
These laws have been born out through history and our current
condition as being the true definitions of the ways of prosperity and
peace. They are the laws of life.

1. Thou shalt have no other gods before me.
2. Thou shalt not make unto thee any graven image.
3. Thou shalt not take the name of the Lord thy God in vain.
4. Remember the Sabbath day, to keep it holy.
5. Honor thy father and thy mother.
6. Thou shalt not kill.
7. Thou shalt not commit adultery.
8. Thou shalt not steal.
9. Thou shalt not bear false witness against thy neighbor.
10. Thou shalt not covet any thing that is thy neighbor's.

Summation of the basic law

Christ gave the final clarity on how to view and apply the law. When he
was asked what are the greatest commandments, he replied by
restating the Law of Moses:

> 29 And Jesus answered him, The first of all the
> commandments is, **Hear, O Israel; The Lord our God is one**
> **Lord:**

> 30 And thou shalt love the Lord thy God with all thy heart, and with all thy soul, and with all thy mind, and with all thy strength: this is the first commandment.
>
> 31 And the second is like, namely this, **Thou shalt love thy neighbour as thyself**. There is none other commandment greater than these. - Mark 12:29-31

This account of Christ is also told in Mathew 22:37-40. The summation of all the laws, statutes, and commandments is:

1. Know and love <u>your</u> God
2. Love <u>your brethren</u> by resisting the instinct to covet his portion

All the other laws are meant to express these two ideas. These two commandments also again show that the God of Israel is separate from all pagan gods and differentiated by totally different definitions and customs.

By believing in the truth of one God, you not only love God but your brethren who also believe in the truth of one God. By doing this there is no need to resort to using negative emotions. The absence of negative emotions in dealing with each other is what brings about peace and prosperity.

This is the unifying idea that will rebuild the House of Jacob and bring lasting peace and prosperity into the world, the everlasting Kingdom.

The first part of Christ's answer is the exact wording in the Old Testament in Deuteronomy 6:4. This is one of the most important verses in the Bible because it shows that Christ was teaching the laws, statutes, and commandments that were given to Moses. Nothing changed except that he himself was to be the sacrifice that is required under the law. Christ came to provide the complete understanding of the law and the reason why sacrificing was required under the law – to remember the truth.

Christ clarified the purpose and the function of the law and showed that the purpose and function is more important than traditions that may confuse the purpose and function. Today instead of just blindly following the priest and scribes like the past, we all have the Scriptures at our finger tips. We are able to study day and night to get the understanding of the definitions. We are able to remember daily.

The definitions that the laws are meant to express have not and will not ever change because the truth does not change.

What laws are we following?

When we go through the basic laws of the House of Jacob we see how we are so easily dominated and deceived. Under the laws of the House of Esau we are under definitions that are directly opposite to the laws given to us by the Most High.

1. Thou shalt have no other gods before me.

> Thou shalt have no other gods before me. - Exodus 20:3

Many Black and Hispanics do not even believe in God. And if we do, we act as if the enemies of our nation are more powerful than our God. This puts the spirit or god of these other nations before the Most High God of our nation.

All the major religions of the world are based on worship of some lesser god other than the Most High God of the Bible.

Christianity attempts to make a false white image of Jesus God. Islam worships a stone in Mecca. Judaism is not really based on the Bible and has its own books the Talmud and the Kabala that seem very demonic at best.

Our collective lack of understanding of the Bible causes even the most sincere people of our community to worship a god other than the God of our forefathers which is the God of Truth.

2. Thou shalt not make unto thee any graven image.

> Thou shalt not make unto thee any graven image, or any
> likeness of any thing that is in heaven above, or that is in the
> earth beneath, or that is in the water under the earth.
> - Exodus 20:4

We have been tricked through religion into worshiping crosses, beads, false pictures of Christ, Popes, prophets and all manner of graven images.

Through the economic system we have been made to worship money, material goods, celebrities, logos, and all sorts of demonic symbolism. One of the most popular T.V. programs ever is actually called American Idol. It doesn't get any plainer than that.

Through false nationalism we have been made to salute and hold flags and national symbols as sacred.

3. Thou shalt not take the name of the Lord thy God in vain.

Thou shalt not take the name of the Lord thy God in vain; for the Lord will not hold him guiltless that taketh his name in vain. - Exodus 20:7

Taking oaths on the Bible, handling contracts ie money that invoke the name of God are all forms of using the Lord's name in vain deceit by the wicked societies in which we find ourselves.

All religions force us into this because they are not truthful about what they are actually founded to do, namely control different tribes of people under a belief system that benefits a ruling power. This misuse of power constitutes taking the Lord's name in vain.

4. Remember the Sabbath day, to keep it holy.

Remember the sabbath day, to keep it holy. - Exodus 20:8

This is one of the most obvious and easy to see deceptions. The Sabbath day is the last day of the week which is Saturday NOT Sunday.

Sunday worship is a part of Roman pagan worship of the sun and is in direct opposition to the teachings of the Bible.

But the seventh day is the sabbath of the Lord thy God: in it thou shalt not do any work, thou, nor thy son, nor thy daughter, thy manservant, nor thy maidservant, nor thy cattle, nor thy stranger that is within thy gates:
- Exodus 20:10

We are supposed to rest on Saturday and refrain from any strenuous activity. Our churches have used every rationalization to justify breaking this commandment week in and week out.

5. Honor thy father and thy mother.

Honour thy father and thy mother: that thy days may be long upon the land which the Lord thy God giveth thee.
- Exodus 20:12

We honor the so-called forefathers of America, the kidnappers and murders of our people more than we do our true ancestors.

It is impossible to honor your ancestors if you don't know who you really are to begin with. This is why identity is so important.

6. Thou shalt not kill.

> Thou shalt not kill. - Exodus 20:13

Not only do we kill in the military conquests of our oppressors, we routinely kill each other in our own communities. This commandment was meant to apply to murder within the Israelite nation. It did not mean that the Israelite nation can not defend itself in war or that capital punishment could not be handed down.

7. Thou shalt not commit adultery.

> Thou shalt not commit adultery. - Exodus 20:14

This is another commandment that we are routinely encouraged to break by the rulers of our captivity. Dating is not in the Bible. Sleeping with someone means that you are married according to the Bible.

8. Thou shalt not steal.

> Thou shalt not steal. - Exodus 20:15

The last three commandments allow us to see the wickedness of the nations that have held us captive. Every colonial nation constitutes and act of theft. These people brought these very commandments with them as they committed theft and murder to create their countries.

9. Thou shalt not bear false witness against thy neighbor.

> Thou shalt not bear false witness against thy neighbour.
> – Exodus 20:16

Lying about who we are and who the people of the Bible really are is the greatest atrocities of false witness that the world has ever seen.

10. Thou shalt not covet anything that is thy neighbor's.

> Thou shalt not covet thy neighbour's house, thou shalt not
> covet thy neighbour's wife, nor his manservant, nor his
> maidservant, nor his ox, nor his ass, nor any thing that is
> thy neighbour's. - Exodus 20:17

Capitalism and colonialism is actually built on coveting other people's goods, lands, and lifestyles. Competition and jealousy are built into the system. Our community is infected with this mindset. It is a mindset of scarcity. Everyone is made to believe that they cannot get what they want without competing with the next person to get it.

A covetous man's eye is not satisfied with his portion; and the iniquity of the wicked drieth up his soul. - Sirach 14:9

The power of the laws of Jacob

For this is the love of God, that we keep his commandments: and his commandments are not grievous.
- 1 John 5:3

When you operate outside of the rules of God, you are left to deal with the negative emotions on your own. Most times this means that you will wind up choosing "the lesser of two evils".

Under the proper definitions of God, instead of choosing the lesser of two evils, you reject evil. You resist evil because you know that replacing one negative emotion for another does not solve the original problem.

Ask yourself, what is it that you are trying to do that the laws of the Bible will not let you do? Then ask yourself, what is the normal outcome of such behavior? When you look at it this way, you will see that the law is there to stop you from being seduced into things that are of no profit to you, that will eventually cause you pain.

Take away from this chapter:

1. Your definitions can get mixed up when you follow your emotions instead of reason.

2. Positive emotions create prosperity; negative emotions create chaos and destruction.

3. The laws of God shut off the overuse of destructive negative emotions.

For we are saved by hope: but **hope that is seen is not hope**: for what a man seeth, why doth he yet hope for?
- Romans 8:24

14 Lifestyle Reset
Personal prosperity dilemma

> And I heard another voice from heaven, saying, **Come out of
> her, my people**, that ye be not partakers of her sins, and
> that ye receive not of her plagues. - Revelation 18:4

1. How do you reconcile the dual nature of our existence?
2. How do you reconcile real value with perceived value?
3. How do you measure a successful lifestyle?

The word "lifestyle" encapsulates everything that we have discussed so
far. The word "lifestyle" contains the concept of duality that we have
talked about throughout the book. Lifestyle is a combination of two
words, "Life" and "style".

Total value = real value + perceived value

Life is real value, style is perceived value. This concept translates into
needs versus wants. How you deal with needs (real value) versus wants
(perceived value) determines the quality of your life.

Through deception and propaganda the idea of needs and wants is
totally confused in the minds of the majority of those who are being
ruled by the definitions of white supremacy. The greatest deception of
the white supremacy system is to confuse style with substance through
false definitions.

White supremacy is a self absorbed system that induces negative
emotions as a way of life. The idea of creating problems and then
offering a so called solution is at the heart of the white supremacy
economic system. When we look at the giant triplets of racism,
materialism, and militarism we see that these ideas induce negative
emotions. They induce a self-destructive spirit.

> Envy thou not the oppressor, and choose none of his ways.
> - Proverbs 3:31

The good life

> Be not deceived; **God is not mocked**: for whatsoever a man
> soweth, that shall he also reap. For he that soweth to his
> flesh shall of the flesh reap corruption; **but he that soweth
> to the Spirit shall of the Spirit reap life everlasting.** And
> let us not be weary in well doing: for in due season we shall
> reap, if we faint not. - Galatians 6:7-9

Living a good life is not about money or having things. Living a good
life is about being free from stress, worry, and fear. This is the true
measure of freedom.

Negative emotions are the forces that lead to spiritual corruption. A
person who is not encumbered by these negative emotions is free to
create whatever he wants without restriction.

You must understand that under the false authority of the House of
Esau, you are being ruled by anxious people who are full of worry. Why
else would people who are already rich, create war and destruction
instead of enjoying their so-called wealth?

Because this so-called wealth has been gained by using negative
emotions, it is completely under the destructive power of Satan.

> **No man can serve two masters**: for either he will hate the
> one, and love the other; or else he will hold to the one, and
> despise the other. Ye cannot serve God and mammon.
> - Matthew 6:24

The proof is all around us that the artificial lifestyles heaped on us by
the white supremacy system are not the truth. The evidence also
proves that the white supremacy system itself will shortly be destroyed
along with anyone who builds their life around the false thinking that it
produces. The destruction will not only be a physical destruction, but a
destruction and extermination of the very thinking that produced the
white supremacy based kingdom.

True success means that you can solve problems without resorting to
prolonged worry or stress.

How do you live a life without fear or prolonged worry? Simple. Never
ever worry about anything. How can you do this while functioning in a
chaotic world? You have to realize that you can be concerned about

circumstances and analyze issues and problems but never worry about the outcome. Trusting the process set up by the Creator is the essence of faith. You must come to the understanding that outcomes are automatic when you do things in the proper order.

Lifestyle of duality

A double minded man is unstable in all his ways. - James 1:8

To manifest the power of God, you must live a life of duality. You must always be rightly dividing things into clean and unclean, productive and unproductive. This is what it means to be a spiritual person.

To do this you must recognize that you must live in two worlds at once. You must be able to function in the world that we currently live in, but you must simultaneously focus on building the world that is to come. We must live under the current system and at the same time be creating the alternative system that will render the current system powerless and irrelevant. The blending of substance with style is the key to manifesting this power.

The main question that you must answer is, would you rather?

1. Have what you want?
        Or
2. Do what you want?

This is the daily lifestyle dilemma that must be reconciled.

For the flesh lusteth against the Spirit, and the Spirit against the flesh: **and these are contrary the one to the other**: so that ye cannot do the things that ye would. - Galatians 5:17

To reconcile the dilemma of having or doing, you have to start with what you want to do and use those goals to get what you want to have.

What you want to do is directly tied to who you want to be. Who you want to be goes back to your identity.

The idea of nationhood solves this dilemma. Your identity under the House of Jacob reconciles this dilemma. The ultimate thing that you want to do is experience everlasting life under the Kingdom of the House of Jacob. This should be the overarching goal to whatever you find yourself thinking or doing. This puts you in alignment with God and in alignment with the truth.

Vision

> **Where there is no vision, the people perish**: but he that
> keepeth the law, happy is he. - Proverbs 29:18

The goal of this book is to help you expand your vision. Many of us cannot envision a world where black and brown people are not controlled by white people. Many of us think that the world has to be corrupt. Many believe that that's the way it has to be. As long as this is the collective vision of humanity, the world will continue to be in chaos. The small minority will continue to oppress the majority of the world's population. People will feel that they have no choice but to go along with the corrupt nature of the rulers of this world. You have to develop a full mental picture of what life can be.

Substance and faith

> **Now faith is the substance** of things hoped for, **the
> evidence** of things not seen. - Hebrews 11:1

Faith is where style and substance are linked. It is a vision of the future. This vision exists purely in your own imagination and in the imagination of those around you.

Faith is an imagined outcome that is not yet seen. A lifestyle of faith is a lifestyle based on converting problems into solutions. It is a conversion through vision. In this conversion substance is uncovered.

Faith can only be developed when you have a strong and clear picture of what you want to happen.

Success redefined

> This book of the law shall not depart out of thy mouth; but
> thou shalt **meditate therein day and night**, that thou
> mayest observe to do according to all that is written therein:
> for **then thou shalt make thy way prosperous, and then
> thou shalt have good success**. - Joshua 1:8

If you consider yourself prosperous in this world and have not or do not follow the ways of the Most High God, you must accept the reality that the power that you are receiving is coming from the god of this world (Satan), not the Most High God. The god of the carnal material world is

Satan. The power you are receiving is coming from a destructive force and will eventually lead to your own spiritual destruction.

<u>What the corrupt world defines as prosperity and freedom is really a form of demonic possession</u>. Can you accept this fact?

When you set goals, they must be suitable goals. Suitable goals must be consistent with your purpose. They must be consistent with each other. They must be consistent with your identity.

If you consider yourself prosperous and you are using principles that don't line up with the Scriptures your apparent success is coming at the expense of your spiritual health. You are flirting with spiritual death.

Becoming converted

> **Repent ye therefore, and be converted**, that your sins may be blotted out, when the times of refreshing shall come from the presence of the Lord. - Acts 3:19

To repent means to convert ourselves back into the definitions of truth.

Under the definitions of the House of Jacob you develop an identity based on hope, courage and faith. These positive emotions allow you to extinguish the destructive force of any of the negative emotions. This is the lifestyle of peace and prosperity.

The lifestyle of the House of Jacob

> Wherefore come out from among them, and **be ye separate, saith the Lord**, and touch not the unclean thing; and I will receive you. - 2 Corinthians 6:17

The following are the basic principles of the lifestyle of the House of Jacob. These principles shut out negative emotions and promote unlimited creative power.

1) <u>One God</u> – There is only one God, one faith, and one Spirit that is above all others. You should have no other fear other than the fear of the Most High.

2) <u>Proper separation</u> – The Most High God is not the author of confusion. The Most High separated things into their own

particular purpose. Humanity is separated into nations based on bloodline. Everything is separated into clean and unclean.

3) The law is The Holy Spirit of God – The laws, statutes, and commandments given to the House of Jacob ensure that they respect proper divisions.

4) Sin - Is the transgression (breaking) of the law.

5) Vision - Positive vision is necessary in order to activate positive emotions.

6) Everlasting life - This means that a second spiritual death is possible. We are both physical and spiritual beings. Justice requires that because of sin, we can experience two deaths, one that is temporary, and one that is permanent and everlasting.

7) Regeneration - Belief in the resurrection. Salvation of the world through the reincarnation of the Messiah of the House of Jacob. This shows faith that the law stands past physical death.

8) Spiritual over the physical - The priority is on the everlasting truth versus the temporary illusions of the physical world.

9) Justice - Justice is inevitable and is not limited to a physical lifetime. Descendants are responsible for the transgressions of their forefathers because the spirit of their forefathers is regenerated through them.

10) Repent - To repent is to turn back to the law and the proper definitions. To ask for forgiveness and change. Generational curses stand until the next generations repent.

11) Grace - There is a grace period which means that you will not immediately suffer the penalty of spiritual death for breaking the law. You have an unknown time frame to turn back to the truth.

12) Rebuke - We should encourage one another to keep the law and the proper definitions. We must try to correct ourselves and our brethren to remove the danger of spiritual death. This is not judging which would mean that we would enact a penalty on one another for breaking the law.

The understanding of all of these concepts comes from reading the Bible as it is written.

To straighten out our definitions, we must concentrate daily to:

1. Know yourself and your nation
2. Know the enemy
3. Reprogram yourself to see the truth
4. Use the truth to destroy the programming
5. Reinstate proper boundaries

Knowing what to do

He that obeyeth me shall never be confounded, and they that work by me shall not do amiss. - Sirach 24:22

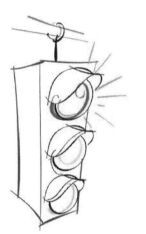

We must reduce all activity into two categories, productive and unproductive activity. Productive activity produces tangible and intangible assets. Unproductive activity produces tangible and intangible liabilities.

When we look at our daily activities this way, things start to come in to clear focus.

Knowing what to do is as simple as being able to correctly categorize things as either assets or liabilities, productive or unproductive. Every decision can be put into one of these two categories.

Thinking in these simple terms can eliminate fear and worry. By using a consistent system, you can avoid the uncertainty that results in emotionalism, regret, and other negative emotions that you have been programmed to feel when things seem that they are not going your way. In the end, you are only choosing one thought or another.

If you chose the wrong thought initially, you simply must repent by changing to the opposite thought.

Eliminating ambiguous thinking is a sign that you are operating under the wisdom of a consistent belief system. A consistent belief system eliminates worry and stress.

Fasting

> This is the bread which cometh down from heaven, that a
> man may eat thereof, and not die. - John 6:50

Fasting means that you are boycotting something, foregoing something. Any physical or spiritual ailment or affliction can be overcome by fasting. Fasting is the number one way to abstain from evil.

Fasting was a major part of how the prophets of the Bible were able to receive knowledge. Moses fasted for 40 days. The prophet Elijah fasted for 40 days. Christ fasted for 40 days. All the prophets were able to receive the knowledge of God through their suffering and self discipline.

Fasting detaches you from your dependence on the physical world. By afflicting yourself in the physical world, you become more aware of spiritual things. When you fast, you cleanse yourself of unnecessary attachments that can become a veil over your vision. By fasting you gain a heightened awareness, energy, and vision that brings you to the truth.

Prayer

Prayer is a meditation on the truth. It involves focusing on the correct definitions as given by God. Christ gave us the proper way to pray. He told us that we should NOT pray in public to be seen, but pray in private. He went so far as to say that you not only should pray in your own house but pray in a closet where no one can see you.

> 6 But thou, **when thou prayest, enter into thy closet**, and
> when thou hast shut thy door, pray to thy Father which is in
> secret; and thy Father which seeth in secret shall reward
> thee openly. - Matthew 6:6

Christ explained what we should pray for and how we should pray:

> 9 After this manner therefore pray ye: Our Father which art in heaven, Hallowed be thy name.

> 10 Thy kingdom come, Thy will be done in earth, as it is in heaven.

> 11 Give us this day our daily bread.

> 12 And forgive us our debts, as we forgive our debtors.

> 13 And lead us not into temptation, but deliver us from evil: For thine is the kingdom, and the power, and the glory, for ever. - Mathew 6:9-13

This prayer is all the religion that you need. It is also all the wisdom and motivation and hope that you need to live a lifestyle of success and prosperity.

Take away from this chapter:

1. The dual nature of life seems to be a trade off between substance and style (real value and perceived value).

2. Returning to the definitions set by God reconciles substance and style.

3. Returning to the definitions set by God lead to a lifestyle of prosperity without resorting to corruption and negative emotions.

> And he said unto him, Why callest thou me good? there is none good but one, that is, God: but **if thou wilt enter into life, keep the commandments**. - Matthew 19:17

15 Nation Building Reset

The community arrangement dilemma

> **But the saints of the most High shall take the kingdom**,
> and possess the kingdom for ever, even for ever and ever.
> - Daniel 7:18

1. How do we organize ourselves to resist false authority and artificial reality?
2. How do we rebuild our nation?
3. How do we achieve power as a nation?

You must come to the realization that through the trauma of slavery and the continued oppression of your people, you have been given a false impression of nationality. The truth is that you have been de-nationalized from your true natural nationality and have been given a false identity by those who have carried out the slavery and oppression.

Since nationhood is the chief instrument of wealth and personal power, you cannot achieve any real wealth or power as long as you are operating under a confused idea of nationhood.

When you define yourself by your ability to associate with the colonial nations that have committed theft and genocide against your ancestors, you do yourself, your ancestors, and your future generations a disservice. You become your own worst enemy. This is where we are today as a people. By pretending that there is no other choice, you deny the truth of God.

We have shown throughout this book that you have the God-given right to a nationality that is not controlled by the historical enemies of your people. You have a right to live your life under the truth. No person or government has to grant you this right, and no one can take it away from you because no one can control the definitions that you will accept, but you. This is your natural right to self-determination under the truth of Thus saith the Lord.

You must realize that history shows that the nations that are currently ruling under the House of Esau defy natural definitions and are nothing more than artificial political fictions that are doomed to fail. No real power can be manifested by submitting yourself to being the physical and spiritual subjects of these fictitious nations.

By complying with the false definitions that they put forth and aligning yourself with the failed strategies of these corporate fictions, you can become seduced into living an artificial, individualistic, and nonproductive lifestyle.

But even when you are seeking personal, individualistic goals, you cannot get around the truth behind nationhood. Who you are, what you think, what you can own, where you can receive help, and how you will be able to overcome your personal challenges are all filtered through the structure of the nation.

Our economic and personal problems persist because our nation is in a state of total disrepair. We are in a national crisis.

As we have shown, individuals and nations are ruled by definitions, not by people. To rebuild our nation, we need to educate ourselves on how to return to using proper definitions. Using these definitions we must then institute the standards and rules that bring about justice.

When we take this approach, we will realize that we have all the wealth that we need and the real problem is that our wealth is being syphoned off because we have not focused on building a national infrastructure to resist spiritual and economic attack.

Our focus has been on trying to unnaturally gain access into other nations instead of rebuilding our own. These nations are just political statuses that were created to protect the genocide and land theft perpetrated by the Edomites who are now calling themselves Europeans. Again, a nation is a bloodline, not a landmass or physical location.

The purpose of nationhood

> **Gather yourselves together**, yea, gather together, O nation not desired; - Zephaniah 2:1

The number one job of our nation is to seek justice, not equality. Seeking justice automatically puts us on the path to solving our own problems from within our own community. Seeking equality puts us on the path to a perpetually subservient position because seeking equality validates the false standards and definitions that are put forth by the white supremacy system.

We are a separate nation and should operate as such. This means that we must view our assets and liabilities from the standpoint of our nation first. We must view productive and unproductive activity from the standpoint of whether the activities that we are engaged in will help or hurt our nation.

We are a developing nation, and developing nations need strict rules and clear definitions in order to take advantage of its unique resources and protect itself from outside threats. We must return to the natural definitions and avoid colonial customs and methods as best we can.

The key benefits of nation building are:

1. It eliminates weak formations that take away your personal power
2. It institutes strong formations that increase your personal power

Agreeing under Thus saith the Lord

Can two walk together, except **they be agreed?** - Amos 3:3

A nation that is free from injustice and strife is the goal that we should be aiming for. This can only be done by forming ourselves under the truth of Thus saith the Lord.

If you are comfortable under the current system it is probably because you have been taught to agree with it. This is a very dangerous mentality. Only through brainwashing and the belief in illusions could you be made to believe that you are benefiting from living under a system of injustice. Under this programmed mindset, you will never see the certain destruction that is coming to the system and the certain destruction that is coming to those who agree with the system, including yourself.

He that justifieth the wicked, and he that condemneth the just, even they both are abomination to the Lord.
- Proverbs 17:15

You must choose between the wicked and the just. There is NO in between. The just follow Thus saith the Lord. The wicked follow their own feelings, which actually means that they are following the programming put on them by the white supremacy system. They are therefore following thus said some white man who has undoubtedly been operating under the influence of Satan.

3 **For what if some did not believe?** shall their unbelief
make the faith of God without effect?

4 God forbid: yea, **let God be true, but every man a liar**; as
it is written, That thou mightest be justified in thy sayings,
and mightest overcome when thou art judged.
- Romans 3:3-4

This is the reality that you are living under whether you want to believe
it or not.

The chief operating procedure of the House of Jacob

The operating procedure of the House of Jacob can be found in the
following scripture:

Prove all things; hold fast that which is good. Abstain from
all appearance of evil. - 1 Thessalonians 5:21-22

1. When you say that you are benefiting from the current system,
   you must be able to prove it.
2. To prove it, you must have a clear understanding of what is
   good and what is evil.
3. You must then prove that you are engaging in good and
   shunning evil.

This is the chief operating procedure of the House of Jacob. You must
be able to rightly divide things. Clarity and order eliminates injustice
and evil. This is the basic foundation of a strong national formation.

We should not under any circumstances use our own opinions to judge
these things. We must use the evidence and the wisdom of thousands
of years that is contained in the Scriptures.

If any man speak, **let him speak as the oracles of God**; if
any man minister, let him do it as of the ability which God
giveth: that God in all things may be glorified through Jesus
Christ, to whom be praise and dominion for ever and ever.
Amen. - 1 Peter 4:11

We have at our finger tips the proof of ancient wisdom that has already
settled every matter that we will deal with. All we have to do is listen to
it.

Common purpose

> Now I beseech you, brethren, by the name of our Lord Jesus
> Christ, **that ye all speak the same thing, and that there be
> no divisions among you**; but that ye be perfectly joined
> together in the same mind and in the same judgment.
> - 1 Corinthians 1:10

To rebuild our nation we must get our spiritual and economic house in order. We must engage in transformation through the commonality of purpose. That purpose must be truth and justice.

Anything that we are confused about must be examined and must be proven to be either good or evil - an asset or a liability, productive or unproductive. If it is found to be good or can be converted into something that is productive, it can continue. If it is found to be evil or unproductive it must be rooted out.

Confusion about race and what it means

> And he said unto them, Ye will surely say unto me this
> proverb, **Physician, heal thyself**: whatsoever we have heard
> done in Capernaum, do also here in thy country. - Luke 4:23

There is no question that all people should be for their race first. There is nothing wrong with that. Somehow when so-called people of color choose this logical stance, it becomes something that is criticized.

There is no such thing as having love or charity for other races when you are not paying attention to the problems of your own. Charity begins at home. Dignity and pride in ones own self, family, and race is the first law of love.

Whether we are talking about entrepreneurship, charity, or attention, we must focus on our own nationality first.

The vulnerable of our nation

> And Adam was not deceived, but the woman being deceived
> was in the transgression. - 1 Timothy 2:14

There are two lines of defense that the men of the House of Jacob must overcome before they can even begin to have any real economic or spiritual struggle against so-called white men, the House of Esau:

1. The women of the House of Jacob
2. Fearful, brainwashed, or effeminate men of the House of Jacob

These two groups are the first lines of defense that will do the bidding of the House of Esau. They can often be vicious in their protection of the false authority of white supremacy. Why? Because white supremacy transfers some level of false authority over to these two groups. They are made to feel strong and powerful by their association with the false authority of white supremacy.

The damage that continues to be done from these two groups is hard to defend against because the attack may appear to have nothing to do with white influence. Because they are under a false doctrine of equality and oneness instead of justice, these two groups are tricked into attacking anyone who seeks to bring the House of Esau to justice. They are emotionally manipulated into acting against their own self-interest.

Mothers, daughters, sisters, and wives have to be spiritually protected or they can be confused through their emotions into becoming an open enemy of the men of the House of Jacob. Christ recognized that people in spiritual rebellion have to be dealt with just as any other enemy of the truth. In speaking about family Christ said:

> And he answered and said unto them, **My mother and my brethren are these which hear the word of God, and do it.**
> - Luke 8:21

Although it is operating totally under a wicked spirit, we have to realize that the House of Esau has really not transgressed any law because it was not given the Law in the first place. Until the members of the House of Esau are confronted with the truth, they can continue on in what they are doing. It is the House of Jacob that is in total rebellion against the Laws of God by not seeking to institute truth and justice.

We have to get the emotionally vulnerable members of our own culture to see that justice not equality is the will of God. Those who will not hear are doomed to spiritual destruction under the false authority of the House of Esau. The Scriptures tell us that two thirds (.666) of our people will not stop following false authority and be destroyed.

Confused personal relationships

The first thing that we must do as a group is to deal with the broken state of our relationships and our confused family roles.

> As for my people, **children are their oppressors, and women rule over them.** O my people, they which lead thee cause thee to err, and destroy the way of thy paths.
> - Isaiah 3:12

Confused and dysfunctional man-woman roles is one of the first indications of a spiritually destroyed community.

The men of the House of Jacob are the main targets of economic and spiritual warfare. Because of this, the men of the House of Jacob are at the lowest end of every society that has been taken over by white supremacy.

Because their fathers, sons, and brothers are being targeted, the women of the House of Jacob have been tricked into believing that they are acting independently when in actuality they are totally dependent on the system of white supremacy.

Man-woman relationships (the beginning of power)

The Bible exalts the so-called men of color. It places the Israelite man at the head of all people on the face of the earth (Deuteronomy 7:6). Many people have a problem with this fact including the women of our community. Most of our women have bought into the brainwashing and false equality doctrine of the white supremacy system. The low state of our community is the most direct proof that the man has to be returned to his natural role as leader and protector of our nation.

The men of the House of Jacob are the true targets of spiritual and economic warfare because they are the leaders of the nation. As long as the leaders are in a low state, the rest of the nation will remain destroyed. As long as the men are spiritually weak and effeminized, the nation has no defense against economic and spiritual attack.

Spiritual leadership involves setting and keeping the standards, rules, and definitions that keep good order. This is a job. It is not an indication of superiority or inferiority. The Bible is clear on who is most suited to fill this role and how leadership should be set up:

> But I would have you know, that the head of every man is Christ; **and the head of the woman is the man**; and the head of Christ is God. - 1 Corinthians 11:3

The natural order is:

1. God
2. Christ
3. Man
4. Woman
5. Child

This is Thus saith the Lord.

Many of our women will rebel against this logic. They do not understand that subjecting yourself to order is not the same thing as occupying a lower position. We must maintain order at all times. Confusion is an indicator that we are losing the spiritual war.

When a man is unable or unwilling to lead, of course our women are forced into these unnatural roles. This is one of the main tactics of spiritual attack on our community. Once a nation has been conquered, the natural leadership of the men of that nation is replaced with foreign rulership over the women. We must recognize role reversal as what it is: an indication of a community in spiritual crisis. Role reversal should be seen as a temporary emergency tactic; it should not and cannot become a lifestyle.

> The tender and delicate woman among you, which would not adventure to set the sole of her foot upon the ground for delicateness and tenderness, **her eye shall be evil toward the husband of her bosom, and toward her son, and toward her daughter,** - Deuteronomy 28:56

Just as women must be protected from physical domestic abuse and violence, they must that much more be protected from spiritual abuse because the spirit is much more valuable than the physical body.

The Bible is very clear on this matter but because of "thus saith the white man" and the brainwashing of the House of Esau, clearly many of the men of the House of Jacob will have major difficulties trying to implement Thus saith the Lord in these important relationship issues.

From the story of Adam and Eve in the Old Testament to the writings of the Apostle Paul in the New Testament, the guidance remains the same:

> 11 Let the woman learn in silence with all subjection.
>
> 12 But I suffer not a woman to teach, **nor to usurp authority over the man**, but to be in silence.
>
> 13 For Adam was first formed, then Eve.
>
> 14 And Adam was not deceived, but the woman being deceived was in the transgression.
>
> 15 Notwithstanding she shall be saved in childbearing, if they continue in faith and charity and holiness with sobriety.
> - 1 Timothy 2:11-15

Common sense should tell you that no nation can be led into battle by the women of that nation. The women are meant to bring forth life and nurture life not to struggle in competitive situations that can lead to the loss of life.

We must understand that in the captive position that we are in, our men and women are forced into roles that are totally unnatural. This is the key weapon in producing spiritual corruption throughout our community. The Scriptures are clear on the natural order. Our lack of man-woman order is the key indicator that we have a broken and weak formation that is unnecessarily draining the energy of each one of us.

Leadership

> **For the leaders of this people cause them to err**; and they that are led of them are destroyed. - Isaiah 9:16

Real leadership is not about controlling people. It is about accepting the job of keeping good order. This can only be done by having a correct understanding of what needs to be done and the knowledge of how to accurately define success and failure.

The men in leadership roles must be well studied in Thus saith the Lord. They must be in total submission to the truth of Thus saith the Lord or they will not have the proper foundation, methods, courage, or power to effectively lead under the current disadvantaged circumstances that our community finds itself in.

Because the men do not have the understanding of how to take on the leadership role, our women are being led by the men of another nation. As much as our women like to claim that they are being independent and making it on their own, they are really just submitting themselves to the men of another nation out of perceived necessity.

The spiritual and economic enemies of our nation encourage our women to be "independent" because they know that this only means that our women will wind up submitting their energy to foreign economic schemes that do not benefit their own nation.

> And the Lord God said, It is not good that the man should be alone; **I will make him an help meet for him**.
> - Genesis 2:18

The energy of our women belongs in our nation. The wife is meant to be a help meet to the husband and or the men of her nation. A wise man does not restrict his wife's abilities but allows her to use her natural gifts and realize her full potential. The man however must keep the family and the community focused on the boundaries and natural laws that will keep the community safe from emotional attack.

Emotional attack is more likely to be successful against the women; therefore they must receive their guidance in the Law from the men. The man's job is not to be superior but to stay focused on the emotional stability and physical protection of the family and community.

> **Withhold not correction from the child**: for if thou beatest him with the rod, he shall not die. - Proverbs 23:13

Children are a liability to the family and society until they are nurtured into becoming productive members of society. They must be guided and taught the proper definitions and values that will allow them to become assets to themselves and their community.

Finally, we will list another Scripture that will prove if we are serious about fixing our community structure with Thus saith the Lord, or if we are just using the Bible to further our own worldly desires through thus said the white man or thus said the white man's religion:

254

33 **For God is not the author of confusion**, but of peace, as in all churches of the saints.

34 **Let your women keep silence in the churches**: for it is not permitted unto them to speak; **but they are commanded to be under obedience as also saith the law.**

35 And if they will learn any thing, let them ask their husbands at home: for it is a shame for women to speak in the church. - 1 Corinthians 14:33-35

How many of our so-called Christian women will adhere to these verses. How many believe the women's liberation propaganda that they should be able to do anything that a man can do? I think you already know the answer? Our churches are in total spiritual rebellion against Thus saith the Lord and are full of women who conveniently skip over these verses in the Bible.

And the Lord hath sent unto you all his servants the prophets, rising early and sending them; **but ye have not hearkened, nor inclined your ear to hear.** - Jeremiah 25:4

Waking up the world

And I will make of thee a great nation, and I will bless thee, and make thy name great; and thou shalt be a blessing: **And I will bless them that bless thee, and curse him that curseth thee**: and in thee shall all families of the earth be blessed. - Genesis 12:1-3

As long as the world is in denial as to the truth about the House of Jacob, the earth will remain in turmoil. As long as so-called Christians exalt another people over the natural bloodline of Jacob, the wicked will rule the earth in false authority.

18 **Boast not against the branches**. But if thou boast, thou bearest not the root, but the root thee.

19 Thou wilt say then, The branches were broken off, that I might be grafted in.

20 Well; **because of unbelief they were broken off**, and thou standest by faith. Be not highminded, but fear:

21 <u>For if God spared not the natural branches</u>, **take heed lest he also spare not thee.** - Romans 11:18-21

The above Scripture makes it clear that the true children of Israel must be recognized. The Israelites have gone into captivity because they became arrogant and rebelled against the definitions of God. Those who are in rulership now are in their position because the natural leaders went into captivity. Those who will recognize this truth may be spared but those who continue to perpetuate and believe lies will not.

Christ spoke this in a parable:

> And other **sheep I have, which are not of this fold**: them also I must bring, and **they shall hear my voice**; and there shall be one fold, and one shepherd. - John 10:16

The voice that the other nations must heed is the true Messiah who was a black man from the tribe of Judah, not the false white supremacy created Jesus and the false doctrine that goes along with it.

Trying to deny this fact or saying that it doesn't matter puts you in total rebellion against the truth and the word of God.

Waking up our people

> And go, get thee to them of the captivity, unto the children of thy people, and **speak unto them, and tell them, Thus saith the Lord God; whether they will hear, or whether they will forbear**. - Ezekiel 3:11

Waking up our people is not an easy task but it is an act of love. To love your brother is to reprove and correct him according to the definitions of the Scriptures (Leviticus 19:17). We are commanded to do this so that we are not allowing our brethren to suffer in sin. So you must try to reach those who are still asleep whether they will hear or not. Once you have done this, it is between them and God whether they will hear or continue on in rebellion.

You must understand and take refuge in the truth of the Bible in order to withstand the sometimes vicious attacks that will come from within our own community. All the prophets including Christ have dealt with the same rebellious spirit that currently has a hold over our people.

3 And he said unto me, Son of man, I send thee to the children of Israel, to a rebellious nation that hath rebelled against me: **they and their fathers have transgressed against me, even unto this very day.**

4 **For they are impudent children and stiffhearted**. I do send thee unto them; and thou shalt say unto them, Thus saith the Lord God.

5 And they, whether they will hear, or whether they will forbear, **(for they are a rebellious house,)** yet shall know that there hath been a prophet among them.

6 And thou, son of man, **be not afraid of them, neither be afraid of their words**, though briers and thorns be with thee, and thou dost dwell among scorpions: be not afraid of their words, nor be dismayed at their looks, though **they be a rebellious house**. - Ezekiel 2:3-6

Today through the oracles of the Bible, we have the benefit of the prophets and Christ. Couple this with the thousands of years of prophecy that has come to pass since the Bible was written and you can be 100% sure that we already know what the outcome will be.

If someone at this point in history cannot see that the Bible is the truth, it is only because they do not understand the Bible. Those who are shown the proper understanding of the Bible and choose to ignore it were never meant to know the truth in the first place. If a person is too stiff necked to hear the solution to their problems and the problems of their people, this person is under a demonic spirit. You should really pity that person. Again this is difficult because a person under the influence of Satan will often become vicious in their attacks on the truth and anyone speaking the truth.

And the servant of the Lord must not strive; but be gentle unto all men, apt to teach, patient, **In meekness instructing those that oppose themselves**; if God peradventure will give them repentance to the acknowledging of the truth; **And that they may recover themselves out of the snare of the devil**, who are taken captive by him at his will.
- 2 Timothy 2:24-26

Those who know the truth must aggressively show our people the truth but they should not teach with strife. Your job is to expose the truth and try your best to instruct your people in the truth, but God will determine whether a person is meant to see the truth.

Solomon's prayer for our people gives us the understanding of the condition of our nation and our people:

> 47 Yet if they shall bethink themselves in the land whither they were carried captives, and repent, and make supplication unto thee in the land of them that carried them captives, saying, We have sinned, and have done perversely, we have committed wickedness;
>
> 48 And so return unto thee with all their heart, and with all their soul, in the land of their enemies, which led them away captive, and pray unto thee toward their land, which thou gavest unto their fathers, the city which thou hast chosen, and the house which I have built for thy name:
>
> 49 Then hear thou their prayer and their supplication in heaven thy dwelling place, and maintain their cause,
>
> 50 And forgive thy people that have sinned against thee, and all their transgressions wherein they have transgressed against thee, and give them compassion before them who carried them captive, that they may have compassion on them:
>
> 51 For they be thy people, and thine inheritance, which thou broughtest forth out of Egypt, from the midst of the furnace of iron:
>
> 52 That thine eyes may be open unto the supplication of thy servant, and unto the supplication of thy people Israel, to hearken unto them in all that they call for unto thee.
> - 1 Kings 8:47-52

Standards and definitions

> **Righteousness exalteth a nation**: but sin is a reproach to
> any people. - Proverbs 14:34

We must always seek Thus saith the Lord as the standard of behavior
and in judging and correcting the behavior of the members of the House
of Jacob. The following questions and answers can be used to discuss,
teach, and instruct on the understanding that is contained in the
Scriptures.

Who does the Bible say so-called people of color are?	The lost sheep of the House of Israel. The bloodline of Abraham, Isaac, and Jacob. The House of Jacob	Mathew 15:24 Job 30:30 Song of Solomon 1:5 Lamentations 4:8 Lamentations 5:10
What is the purpose of the Law of the House of Jacob?	To shut you off from the prolonged destructive nature of negative emotions	Leviticus 10:10 Proverbs 29:18 1 John 5:3
What is love? What is Hate?	Rebuke your brethren and not suffer sin upon your brother	2 John 1:6 Leviticus 19:17
What is sin?	Sin is the transgression of the law. Thus saith the Lord, not thus said the white man	1 John 3:4 1 John 5:3 Proverbs 28:13-14
Who pays for sin?	Sins of the forefathers are visited on the next generations until they repent. This proves reincarnation of the spirit. This is justice	Exodus 20:5 Isaiah 14:21 Revelation 13:10
What is spirituality?	Things must be rightly divided into true and false; productive and unproductive; creative and destructive	2 Timothy 2:15 Mathew 5:37

What is the mission of our nation?	Rulership and everlasting life. Rulership or captivity on earth is Heaven or Hell	Isaiah 5:14 Isaiah 58:14
What is the operating method of our nation?	Prove all things. Hold on to the good (productive), shun evil (unproductive)	1 Thessalonians 5:21-22
What is the final authority on right and wrong?	Thus saith the Lord	Ezekiel 3:11 John 8:32 Proverbs 1:7
What is the Bible?	The governing constitution and definitions of the House of Jacob	Isaiah 30:8 Isaiah 58:1 1 Peter 4:11
Why is understanding the House of Jacob important?	The bloodline of Jacob was given the understanding of laws of life	Psalms 147:19-20
What are the physical characteristics of Israelites?	People of color	Jeremiah 14:2 Job 30:30 Songs of Solomon 1:5-6
What is the spiritual characteristic of Israelites?	Israelites were given the law but have not been following it therefore they are in captivity	Ezekiel 3:7 Deuteronomy 28:15
Why does our true identity matter?	Because of our spiritual make up we are bound by the law	Deuteronomy 7:6 Deuteronomy 6:4 Joel 2:9
Why are we still in captivity?	We are not following the definitions given by God. We are following the definitions of the enemies of God	Amos 3:2 Isaiah 5:13-14 Jeremiah 23:1 Hosea 4:6 Proverbs 17:15

What is the identity of those who are ruling over us?	Edomites. The House of Esau	Ezekiel 7:24 Romans 9:13 Genesis 25:23-25 Obadiah 1:1-2
Who is Christ?	An Israelite from the tribe of Judah	Hebrews 7:14 Mathew 1:21 Mathew 5:17 John 1:1
What did Christ look like?	It was a dark skinned man like all Israelites from the tribe of Judah	1 John 4:2 Revelation 1:14 Daniel 10:6
What is justice?	You reap what you sow	Revelation 13:10
How do we end injustice and gain prosperity?	We must go back to the laws and definitions of prosperity as found in the Scriptures	Revelation 22:14 Isaiah 58:1
What are the basic instructions?	Love the God of your ancestors, love your brethren, love yourself	Mark 12:29-31
What is the structure of the House of Jacob?	Order stops confusion	Isaiah 3:12 1 Corinthians 11:3
How do we accomplish real progress and change?	Become converted back into the proper definitions (repent)	Acts 3:19 Ezekiel 3:11 Mathew 18:3

Take away from this chapter:

1. Returning to the natural definitions set by God requires that you return to your true nationality.

2. The definitions that are found in the Bible create the alternative system to the false definitions of the white supremacy system.

3. When the definitions of the House of Jacob are implemented, the world will experience peace and prosperity.

Submit yourselves therefore to God, Resist the devil, and he will flee from you. - James 4:3

16 Economic Strategy Reset

The collective prosperity dilemma

> **But seek ye first the kingdom of God**, and his righteousness; and all these things shall be added unto you. - Matthew 6:33

1. How do we overcome outside dominance over the economic affairs of our community?
2. What is the right individual economic strategy?
3. What is the right collective economic strategy?

The first thing that we must do to reclaim our nationality is to take matters into our own hands. We must cease being willing participants in unjust schemes. We must direct our boycott at the institutions of white supremacy and not at our own business community.

To start with, we should redirect our projected trillion dollar buying power into supporting more productive and responsible enterprises. This one maneuver by itself would immediately change the system quicker than any political participation or plea to charity.

We must view every purchase we make as an investment decision. Every time we go to the cash register we are choosing to provide support to some set of investors and entrepreneurs. We must be aware of the consequences of these choices and the intended and unintended results that go along with these decisions. We cannot continue to fund the destruction of our own community.

We need a conscious, sustained, grassroots effort in order to create a real change. Above all, we must not allow the habit of economic apathy to be passed down to future generations.

Leadership through entrepreneurship

A good man leaveth an inheritance to his children's children:
and the wealth of the sinner is laid up for the just. - Proverbs 13:22

Our view of entrepreneurs and entrepreneurship must change. Small business and entrepreneurship is the key to addressing the devastated economic and spiritual condition of the House of Jacob.

Entrepreneurship is the only way that we are able to solve our own unique problems. We must use our own methods and create our own social arrangements that are based on the truth of the word of God, not on the false authority of white supremacy.

We must all think like entrepreneurs even if we are not. We must make decisions like right thinking money managers in order to counteract the propaganda and distortions of the white supremacy system.

Entrepreneurs create perceived value. They make a value proposition that is either accepted or rejected by a group of people. The value proposition is a proposed solution to a real or imagined need or problem. If a group of people deems that what is being offered solves their need or problem, they will trade money for the proposed solution.

Entrepreneurial innovation and problem solving

Our businesses need to be more responsive and responsible to solving the problems of our community.

We need to structure our enterprises in a way that encourages opportunity and income mobility as well as value to customers.

As customers realize the far reaching benefits of organizations that serve more than just a narrow group of capitalist, they will come to see the greater benefit in doing business with these more economically just organizations.

As an entrepreneur you are attempting to either solve a physical problem or a mental problem for some constituency of people. Problem solving should ALWAYS start within your own nation and your own households. If another nation is dominating the physical resources, as is currently the case, we need to concentrate on controlling our mental resources.

We need to leave the artificial world created by the global corporate empire and return to natural configurations and processes.

We don't have to necessarily invent new products, we only need to come up with new ways to accomplish the same thing. The innovation is in providing better alternatives to the harmful system that we are forced to deal with.

Any business or idea that helps defeat the triplets of racism, materialism, and militarism is an innovation and deserves the full backing of our community.

The small entrepreneur versus the global empire

> And all this assembly shall know that the **LORD saveth not with sword and spear**: for the battle is the LORD'S, and he will give you into our hands. - 1 Samuel Chapter 17:47

Because entrepreneurship is heavily involved in shaping the culture and perceived value of a society, it is a mandatory building block in restoring our nation. The yoke of unjust economics is a major stumbling block in our spiritual progress. As long as our people can be bribed away through fear of poverty, they can be easily manipulated into acting against their own best interest.

Since most of the economics of The House of Esau deals in perception, we can easily build a market for our own products and services through changing the perception of our people.

The key to overcoming the seemingly overwhelming dominance over our economic affairs is to again focus on the definitions and formulas that we are using and see what formulas can be employed to counteract and neutralize the power that our historic enemies have over our affairs.

The Biblical story of King David's defeat of the supposedly invincible foe Goliath gives us the guidance of how to deal with a foe that seems to be invincible. David used his faith and his vision to see the weakness in the so-called invincible foe.

The global corporate empire is the Goliath but as the Scriptures show, Goliath can be beaten using the proper strategy. Just as our ancestor King David was able to defeat a foe that no one thought could be beaten, the House of Jacob when organized properly, can overcome any obstacle.

The Old Wealth of the House of Esau has major problems because it is not based on the truth. It is just a rehash of failed kingdoms. This again is why the Scriptures are so valuable. They help you cut through the illusions to see things for what they are.

> The thing that hath been, it is that which shall be; and that which is done is that which shall be done: and **there is no new thing under the sun.** - Ecclesiastes 1:9

The key to defeating Old Wealth is to create a large number of small enterprises. This is the exact opposite of Old Wealth. Old Wealth is a small number of large enterprises that take the energy from the great majority of the people in the world.

By doing the opposite of this we can protect and distribute energy based on the truth. The truth is that all energy comes from the Most High. Everything that is life sustaining and valuable is abundant on the earth just as the Creator planned it.

Economics under the House of Jacob will combine the two types of technology (physical and spiritual) to solve the problems created by Old Wealth.

The role of politics

> Envy thou not the oppressor, and choose none of his ways.
> - Proverbs 3:31

Politics redistributes real assets for the benefit of the controllers of white supremacy. Engaging in politics under white supremacy is akin to asking a thief to share his stolen wealth. It is an insane notion that has proven to offer little more than forcing a shift in the tactics of attack against our nation.

All the mechanisms of politics under the white supremacy system were built by the robbers of the land to protect the robbers of the land. Your vote is not going to change that. Ask any person who believes that voting changes things to explain to you how the Electoral College works and see what response you get?

White supremacy under the power of Satan has convinced people that they can vote out the will of God. This is an absurd idea and shows the depth of spiritual corruption that we are living under.

> **For the leaders of this people cause them to err**; and they that are led of them are destroyed. - Isaiah 9:16

There is no way to vote out the thief when he himself did not gain power through a vote. The thief stole the resources. You are not going to vote back the resources that he continues to steal. His false authority will be rendered powerless but this will never come from participating in his fantasy of authority.

Any politics that does not seek to reinstitute the laws of truth is a waste of time and will only serve to exalt the false authority of white supremacy. The only political aspiration that we should have is to institute truth and justice. If we are participating in politics as a way to try to institute "equality" we are not operating from the truth.

The definitions used under white supremacy politics are all based on falsehoods and false authority and once you in any way use these false definitions in your analysis, you are taking a futile and powerless position and wasting your energy and resources.

All rights are God given and have nothing to do with voting. It is a delusional notion to believe that you can vote to change the truth. The truth cannot be voted in or out.

Entrepreneurship is the leadership of a nation not politics. Politics only serves entrepreneurs who are focused on an organized objective.

The economic formulas used in the white supremacy system are destined to fail. In fact, the economic system of the white supremacy collapsed in real terms as soon as our people came out of physical slavery.

Lifestyle economics

Your lifestyle and economics are always linked. This means that your identity is always integrated with how you get money. Proper lifestyle economics means that you seek to match your consumer and business activity with the best interest of you and your community. It means that you focus your economic activity on rightly dividing things into unproductive and productive activity based on the truth. You are constantly focusing on assets and liabilities and who gets the benefit from your activity.

You should be seeking to invest time and invest money instead of spending time and spending money. When you invest time you are building an asset. When you do this you will be able to convert liabilities into assets.

Income, on the income side, lifestyle economics involves getting paid for things that you are already doing in your free time or that fit your personal values, beliefs, and interests.

Expenses, on the expense side you are looking to entrepreneurs from your own nation to solve problems for you. It should be clear after 30 or more years of trying to assimilate into the white supremacy system that our problems are not going to be solved by entrepreneurs that are outside of our community. Government is owned by entrepreneurs not by the vote of consumers. There is no way to vote out the economic dominance of these corporations over the governments that were created to serve them.

As a consumer, you should be looking to support those things that will eventually advance the causes and interests of your nation. By doing this you stay focused on building even when you are dealing with liabilities.

As business people, we have already stated, we need to use business to transform our nation. Our businesses must be set up in accordance with our spiritual values which are based in historical truth. We must create businesses that line up with the definitions of God and avoid copycatting the mistakes of those who appear to be in power positions.

Lifestyle business

A lifestyle business is a business that enables you to practice your beliefs and advances the interests of your family, group, or nation.

It enables you to fund your lifestyle without conflicting with your core beliefs. You set the rules and the parameters that the business must adhere to, to be considered successful. A profit is necessary but is not the most important factor in determining success of a lifestyle business.

The ultimate goal of lifestyle businesses should be to help convert the liabilities of our community into assets. To do this, each one of us must look to create business by looking to solve the problems of our own community. Everyone must think like an entrepreneur.

With a lifestyle business mentality, you become your own profit center. You think like a business person in everything that you do. Families should operate like partnerships and the community should operate as a series of joint ventures.

Arranging ourselves as profit centers will provide the backbone that will create the alternative economy to the white supremacy economic system.

This arrangement would reconcile the needs of each individual with the needs of the group. It would take on the characteristics of profit centers that are networked and arranged properly to defeat the self centered, inefficient, and monopolistic economic system of the House of Esau.

The basic operation of a lifestyle business is to:

1. Convert the minds of the community into the proper definitions
2. Direct unused resources
3. Transform liabilities into assets
4. Transform unproductive activity into productive activity

In short, lifestyle businesses deal in creating high perceived value. This perceived value is used to uncover real value.

The lifestyle entrepreneur

As a lifestyle entrepreneur you are looking for either passive income, that is income that is not tied to your time, or income from doing things that you enjoy or are already doing in your free time. Any of these kinds of activities that can be shown to solve the problems of other people is a lifestyle business opportunity. You are investing time instead of spending time and you are investing money instead of spending money. You may even work much more than the average person in the beginning but even still, the time you spend doing things that you find distasteful is many times less than the average person.

You are also looking to avoid overconsumption of anything. If you do deal in luxury, it must come from passive income and must involve furthering the interest of creating opportunity for other lifestyle entrepreneurs of your nation.

The first hurdle in developing this kind of business is to focus on taking care of your real liabilities. These are your basic health and safety needs.

Duality and lifestyle entrepreneurship

A lifestyle business is a business that is built around your belief system, interests, and identity.

Business is about solving problems. A lifestyle business solves not only your own personal problems but helps solve the problems of the people and the causes that you care about – your true nation.

A lifestyle business is built around your current lifestyle, the lifestyle that you want to live, or the way that you would like to see the world.

Most people are forced to build their lifestyles around businesses that they would not necessarily agree with if there was no money involved. This is how our people are coerced into indentifying with unjust and evil schemes. Plain and simple, they are bribed into a counterproductive identity. The only way they can reconcile what they know to be behavior that is harmful to themselves and their community is to justify it by using money as the measure of success (materialism).

Spiritual failure can never be considered success no matter how much money is attached to it. We spent the entire book talking about how you define a successful lifestyle.

> Prove all things; <u>hold fast that which is good. Abstain from all appearance of evil.</u> - 1 Thessalonians 5:21-22

Being controlled by money leads to an inconsistent corrupted lifestyle, period. This is because those who control the current money system are corrupted and wicked white supremacists. If you can't admit this to yourself, there is no hope for you. If you justify the wicked, you are just as wicked and are an enemy to yourself and your own people.

A lifestyle business is a business that is integrated with your identity. It is a business that solves a problem and creates a high real and perceived value for a particular group of people.

The point is to make a low stress way to create spiritual and economic freedom. The goal is to tailor business around your life instead of tailoring your life around some business that does not even belong to you or a member of your nation.

If you find yourself in this position (as most of us do) you must reset your definitions and repent daily. You must spiritually disconnect from the identity that justifies the wicked.

> And I heard another voice from heaven, saying, **Come out of her, my people**, that ye be not partakers of her sins, and that ye receive not of her plagues. - Revelation 18:4

You must recognize that what you are doing may be necessary in the short term, but it is NOT YOUR IDENTITY. You should view what you are doing as work that must be done in order to gain the resources to rebuild YOUR nation. You are working outside of your nation and are behind enemy lines whether you want to admit it or not.

The simple point of lifestyle business is to do what you enjoy to create income. Your skill and your interest are intangible assets that can be used to solve the problems of your nation.

The problem is that we have been conditioned to enjoy things that are not in our best interest. This is the point of focusing on the definitions that we are using.

Ultimately you can only do what you care about. You cannot sustain any healthy lifestyle by constantly doing things that you do not care about. The danger is when you contort your thinking to convince yourself that you care about things that are self destructive. This is a corrupted stressful lifestyle. This is where spirituality meets economics.

Lifestyle economics forces you to focus on necessary expenses versus luxuries. If you want luxury, you need to increase your passive income. This way you focus your attention on protecting the most important asset that you have, your time. This forces you to look for positive cashflow businesses instead of simply trading time for money at a job.

Thinking this way puts you in the right mind frame to rightly divide your activities into productive and unproductive.

If many people are doing this, the overall effect on the system is to reclaim time and redirect it to best satisfy everyone's interest and talents. Free time is the end result. The more free time that people have the more opportunity there is for other lifestyle businesses to fill that time with things that the providing entrepreneur enjoys doing while he provides products and services that make other people's lives more enjoyable.

The ultimate path to lifestyle economic freedom is to match monthly income with monthly expenses through passive income. You are investing your time instead of trading time for money.

When you focus on these things, you can clearly see that the quickest path to wealth is to create value by solving the problems of your own community.

Nationhood and lifestyle economics

> Then shalt thou delight thyself in the Lord; **and I will cause thee to ride upon the high places of the earth, and feed thee with the heritage of Jacob thy father**: for the mouth of the Lord hath spoken it. - Isaiah 58:14

We must understand that nationhood is the most important factor in regaining power over the activity of our community. Nationhood is the defining factor of wealth, power and prosperity.

There is massive opportunity for lifestyle entrepreneurs of the House of Jacob. So many problems have been forced on our community that other nations capitalize on, that there is a massive need for entrepreneurs from our own nation who can understand the needs of our people far better than anyone else.

This is the point of developing an incorruptible value system as an entrepreneur and leader. We do not need any more "black capitalist" entrepreneurs or politicians in our nation who only mimic the exploitation that they have learned by idolizing the corrupt businessmen and politicians of the House of Esau.

The key indicators of productivity and success

> Keep therefore and do them; for this is your wisdom and your understanding in the sight of the nations, which shall hear all these statutes, and say, Surely this great nation is a wise and understanding people. - Deuteronomy 4:6

To focus on real progress and real innovation, we must return our attention to the giant triplets of racism, materialism, and militarism. When we approach our analysis by looking at assets and liabilities we find that the triplets are intangible liabilities that drain the wealth of our community.

If we are in any way shape or form operating under the triplets, there is NO progress; no matter what things may appear to be on the surface.

Money, individual achievements, or social status do not necessarily create progress against the triplets.

How we are dealing with the triplets is the key indicator of productivity. Understanding the triplets as a productivity indicator is key in uncovering intangible assets and untapped wealth. By focusing on the triplets, we have a common measure of what is productive and what is unproductive.

Again everything must be rightly divided according to the truth.

Take away from this chapter:

1. The competitive nature of the white supremacy system forces you to recognize economic enemies.

2. Your spiritual and economic realities must be aligned in order to experience true freedom.

3. Entrepreneurship is the key activity in creating economic and spiritual freedom.

Ask, and it shall be given you; seek, and ye shall find; knock, and it shall be opened unto you: **For every one that asketh receiveth; and he that seeketh findeth;** and to him that knocketh it shall be opened. - Matthew 7:7-8

Conclusion

Let us hear the conclusion of the whole matter: Fear God, and keep his commandments: **for this is the whole duty of man**. - Ecclesiastes 12:13

The true nationality of so-called people of color is Israelite, the House of Jacob. The true nationality of so-called Caucasian Europeans is Edomite, the House of Esau. History bears out these distinctions.

The reason for the oppressed state of the world is that the balancing force to the oppression is not present. That balancing force is the alternative system of governance that is contained in the concepts and systems of the House of Jacob. This system is documented in the Holy Bible.

The spiritual system of the Bible deals with perceived value while the economic system deals with real value. These two come together to create the idea of wealth, power, and prosperity.

The House of Jacob and those who side with it will recapture all of the energy that has been blocked by the short sighted systems created by the House of Esau. To get this understanding you must understand the power of intangible assets and liabilities. You have to constantly stay focused on whether your activity is productive or unproductive. To do this you need to be able to properly separate and divide things into their proper categories using correct definitions. This process creates a transformation. This transformation is needed to change the low state of our community.

To transform our community we must concentrate on two things:

1. Transforming our spiritual system
2. Transforming our economic system

How do we reverse the economic and spiritual enslavement of our community? We must simply throw out the false definitions that were put on us by slavery and oppression. This costs nothing and is the most revolutionary thing that you can do.

When you realize that justice, and therefore God, is on the side of the oppressed, you see that the House of Jacob has the most potential power in the history of the world. But the real House of Jacob is still in captivity and under heavy oppression. This will continue until they wake up to their true identity and return to the natural order that was established since the beginning of time.

Because we have been operating under false identities, many of us have been tricked into total rebellion against God and into disordered, dysfunctional, artificial lifestyles. Too many of us are willing to accept a lifestyle built around obvious lies. This ultimately creates a belief system that is powerless and dependent on the institutions of white supremacy.

Despite what is professed in public, many of our people do not believe in God at all—at least not the God of the Bible. Yet these same people do believe in the false authority of the white supremacy system. Those who are operating under this spell are being controlled, manipulated, and judged at the whims of unjust schemes

When you become deceived about God your sense of justice becomes warped and altered. This makes you easily controlled and manipulated. Sound decision making becomes nearly impossible because when you deny God, you are denying that justice is a certainty. Likewise, if you have a false idea of God, you will develop a belief system that allows you to rationalize your behavior and harmonize with evil and injustice. This is the essence of spiritual warfare.

We are the chosen people of ancient wisdom, but we have been cut off from that wisdom because we do not realize our true identity. That wisdom is our inheritance. That wisdom is the basis of all wealth, prosperity, peace, and happiness. These things come through the structure of nations, not the pursuits of individuals.

This ancient wisdom and the application of it is chronicled in a book that many of us dismiss in our attempt to seem intellectual and logical: The Bible.

The Bible is NOT a religious book, but a book of history and the application of the laws statues and commandments that make us aware of the definitions of God. The world is in turmoil and God's people are in a low state because these definitions have been discarded to build an unnatural kingdom.

The good news is that the last wicked kingdom on earth will soon come to destruction. The only question is, will you be destroyed with it?

Guns and violence will not win this war or end this war. Nor will "humanitarian" efforts. The ONLY threat to the system is when the children of The House of Jacob reclaim their true identity. It is our spiritual awakening that will heal the destruction that is going on in the earth. It is this truth that will set us free. This is the truth that you cannot see as long as you are under the spell of the white supremacy system.

We are the balancing force that will free the world from the grip of chaos and injustice. As long as the House of Jacob is ignored and in disrepair, the people of the world will suffer under the bondage of the House of Esau. When we wake up and reassemble our House, EVERYTHING WILL CHANGE.

You must side with justice in order to free yourself from the certain judgment that must take place in order to bring the injustice to an end.

The only way to wake up from your altered state and brainwashed mentality is to think, act, and live "Thus said the Lord "instead of "thus said the white man".

> Enter ye in at the strait gate: for **wide is the gate, and broad is the way, that leadeth to destruction**, and many there be which go in there at: Because strait is the gate, and **narrow is the way, which leadeth unto life**, and few there be that find it. - Matthew 7:13-14

You only have two choices; will you join the rebelling spiritual force that will destroy the system of oppression or will you believe in the system and ultimately allow yourself to be destroyed with it?

The choice is yours.

Appendix 1 - Identity Survey

You can get more information about this survey at
TheSocietyofJacob.com

1.	Do you know what federal reserve notes are?
2.	Do you think money is used to control people?
3.	Do you agree or disagree: If people are being controlled by money, you need to watch who you give money to because you are giving them control?
4.	If money was no object, what would you be doing right now? Why aren't you doing it?
5.	Do you think economic inequality exists in your country?
6.	Is there enough food to feed the world? Why, why not?
7.	Do you believe that your ethnic community is the victim of economic exploitation?
8.	Do you believe that you can do something about economic inequality? Why, why not, how?
9.	Do you think economic unity among an ethnic community is important?
10.	Do you believe that your ethnic community has economic enemies? Why?
11.	Do your think wealthy people should do more to help their own ethnic community?
12.	How do you define wealth?
13.	Do you think that it is important to support entrepreneurs from your ethnic community? Why?
14.	Do you know what percentage your ethnic group makes up of the total population of your country?
15.	Do you think that your ethnic group spends this percentage of their money within your ethnic community?
16.	Do you yourself spend this percentage within your ethnic community? Why or Why not?
17.	Do you think that it is wise to spend the bulk of your money outside of your own ethnic culture?
18.	Do you think that boycott is an effective economic and political strategy?
19.	Do you agree that not spending within your own ethnic community is the same as boycotting your own businesses and stores? What effect does this have?
20.	When was the last time that you bought something from a person from your ethnic community?
21.	Do you and your family try to create wealth together? How?

22.	**Do you believe that your ethnic community shares a common belief system?**
23.	What is your ethnic nationality? How do you identify yourself?
24.	Do you believe that you have been mentally programmed by a culture that is foreign to your ancestors?
25.	Do you believe that you have been brainwashed?
26.	Is the earth round or flat? How do you know?
27.	Do you believe in God? Why or why not?
28.	Do you believe the Bible is a Holy Book? What does Holy mean?
29.	Have you read the Bible? The last time you read?
30.	Do you know your Biblical nationality?
31.	Do you read books? Last thing you read?
32.	What religion do you believe in (follow)?
33.	Do you and your immediate family share the same belief system?
34.	What is fear? What are you afraid of?
35.	Do you believe in justice? Is justice the same thing as equality?
36.	What is spirituality?
37.	Does the Bible speak of more than one God?
38.	Is Jesus God?
39.	Does the Bible say celebrate Christmas?
40.	Does the Bible say to celebrate Easter?
41.	Does the Bible say celebrate birthdays?
42.	Where do these holidays come from?
43.	Do you attend church? How often?
44.	Does the Bible say that we should correct one another?
45.	**Was Jesus a white man with blond hair and blue eyes? Does it matter?**
46.	Are there people who are enemies of God according to the Bible?
47.	Do you know what bloodlines are at war in the Bible?
48.	Do you think that the Roman Catholic Church is a powerful force in the world?
49.	Is the Pope a man of God? Why or why not?
50.	What race of people did Jesus descend from?
51.	Does the Bible say that we should judge each other under certain circumstances? Do you believe we can?
52.	Does God put curses on people according to the Bible? Who and When?
53.	What group of people's history does the Bible chronicle?
54.	Why does the U.S. support Israel?

55.	What race of people do the Jewish people descend from?
56.	Where are all of the descendants of Jacob today?
57.	Where are all of the descendants of Esau today?
58.	Were the European Jewish people enslaved in Egypt at one time?
59.	Can you tell the difference between the truth and a lie? What is the difference? Does it matter?
60.	Do you believe that there is an objective truth?
61.	Do you think that Satan exists?
62.	What do you consider the work of Satan?
63.	Do you believe that people sin? What is sin?
64.	Do you think that people worship Satan or can be put under the power of Satan?
65.	How do you determine what is evil?
66.	How do you know you are worshiping God and not Satan?
67.	**Do you understand the table of nations in the Bible? (Genesis chapter 10)**
68.	Do you think that the nation you come from has an impact on your development and quality of life?
69.	How do you define power?
70.	Does your nation dictate your customs, tastes, and desires?
71.	Do you believe that nations revolve around physical locations?
72.	Do you know what a multinational company is? Can you name a few?
73.	What formation makes a nation? Who decides?
74.	Are parents responsible for teaching their children?
75.	Are parents supposed to teach their kids the truth?
76.	Do you know the name of your grandfathers? Great?
77.	Do you think that it is natural for families to stick together?
78.	Is history important?
79.	Does it matter to you what happens to the members of your family? Why or why not?
80.	Do you think that supporting your nation is important?
81.	Do you think there are evil nations? Who, Why?
82.	What nation do you pledge your support to? Based on what reason?
83.	Do you consider a person educated who doesn't know his history?
84.	Did your ancestors plan to come to the western world?
85.	How were they chosen to come to the western world?
86.	Do you believe that wisdom comes with experience?
87.	**What is wisdom?**

88.	Do you believe that two lifetimes can contain more experience than one?
89.	What is inheritance?
90.	Is inheritance important? Why? Why not?
91.	Do you believe that wisdom is worth more than money?
92.	Does everyone start out in life with the same opportunity? Why? Why not?
93.	Does God bring justice?
94.	Does the nature of God change?
95.	Does the truth change?
96.	Do you believe that there is "no new thing under the sun"?
97.	Do you believe in the Ten Commandments?
98.	Do you believe that God is more powerful than man?
99.	Are you following God or man? How do you know?
100.	Do you believe that you can follow God and man at the same time?

Appendix 2 -Table of Nations

The explanation of the original nation bloodlines are listed in Genesis beginning in chapter 10. The genealogy in Genesis chapter 10 deals with the original nationalities of ALL people. Every person on the planet belongs to one of these bloodlines. THESE NATIONALITIES DO NOT CHANGE.

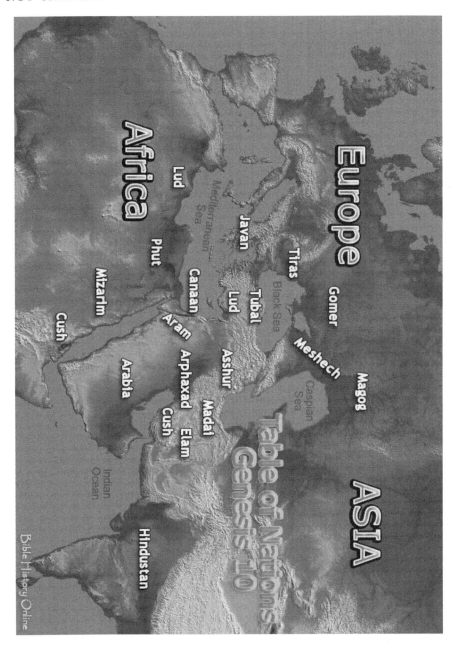

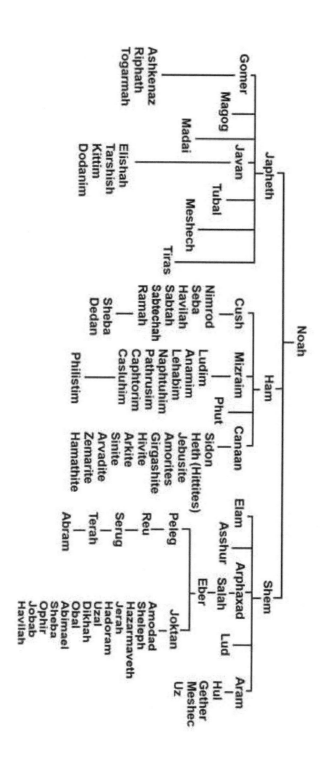

Appendix 3 - Lifestyle business formula

Go to TheSocietyofJacob.com to get the complete breakdown explanation of this diagram.

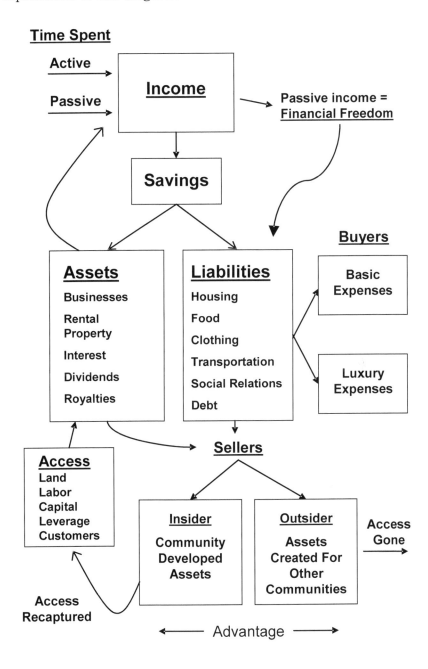

A Model for Action

Here is the basic approach to economic problem solving:

1. **Look at our under utilized resources.** Start with our unemployed and underemployed, vacant commercial property, and vacant residential neighborhoods.

2. **Look at our wasted resources.** We must examine our taste for things that waste our energy (money). We should count any money that we spend unnecessarily enriching other cultures as a complete waste. We must make the connection between this wasteful behavior and the opportunity that we are providing for other cultures at the expense of our own.

3. **Take an inventory of the things that we are wasting our resources on.** This is a personal assessment that each of us must take on. But things like alcohol, drugs, lottery tickets, gambling, and other so called "sin" items should be at the top of the list. Also included are unnecessary items that we purchase from other cultures like carry outs, over shopping at suburban malls, and purchasing worthless so-called luxury items. There is no excuse for spending on these things BEFORE we have taken care of our own community and businesses.

4. **Commit to creating the demand for black made products.** We need to make at least a mental commitment to look for alternatives to products and services that enrich other cultures. We need to ultimately replace these things that we buy from other cultures with products and services owned and controlled by people from the black community (at least at the 12% of our income level).

5. **Find out where we can produce our own products cheaply.** Places that have been blighted by unemployment and have vacant and abandoned buildings and factories could offer the manpower and the physical resources to produce competitive black-made products that are demanded by the black community. Our demonstrated demand for these products will create the financing vehicles to bring them to the marketplace. Placing some kind of sustainable business in an area automatically buoys other businesses and the housing market.

6. **Identify and mobilize expertise from within our culture.** We need to identify professional people who understand the

importance of giving their own culture just as much of their talent as they give to other cultures.

7. **Create fair organizational structures.** Using a systematic stakeholder approach to building companies is not only the right thing to do, but it could lower start up cost by showing workers a path to ownership. Utilizing innovative organizational structures that distribute profits more fairly are a must. Previously unemployed people can be given not only a paycheck but a sense of pride and loyalty by offering them full participation in ownership of what they produce.

8. **Think outside of traditional capitalistic models.** For example, in places where the housing market has collapsed, workers may work simply for ownership of a decent home. This work and homeownership combination could lower the cost of hiring employees and could provide opportunities to increase the value of blighted neighborhoods. The point is that we should craft strategies based on the resources that we already have and not wait for traditional wisdom to dictate how development should take place.

9. **Use crowdfunding to organize demand and provide start up capital.** With a large enough base of people who care (the crowd), any business can be financed with the money that we have been wasting and have been giving to other cultures. We must build a "willing crowd" that can be called on to create the massive leverage that can create the massive change that we need.

10. **Build up businesses around products and services.** Crowdfunding allows us to test the demand for products before we build business structures. We need to focus on innovation first before we engage in the traditional red tape involved in the capitalistic model. With the proper demand for a product, further investment and the administrative support that you need can easily be found to service the demand.

In the end, we must view our businesses as systems that can capture and better utilize our wasted resources. We must understand that we are already capital providers through our spending habits. We must reorganize the power of our capital and use it to create sustainable, fair, and just systems.

Areas of Focus

This section contains a reference list of things that you can do immediately in various areas.

Getting involved in solving the problems that are listed here could create more than enough employment for the black community. Each one of us benefits from any effort that is made in solving any of these problems, we are all stakeholders. Each one of us can take some action that can aide in solving these problems.

We should focus on at least one of these things daily and also be involved with some sort of group effort that is dedicated to solving one or more of these issues.

Economically

1. We must not freely give our wealth away to other cultural communities while neglecting our own.
2. Build our own market for our own products.
3. Become job producers instead of job seekers.
4. We must create our own physical and virtual economic communities.
5. We must create new models for economic interaction within our community.
6. We must practice more efficient uses of our capital.
7. We must pool our creative, knowledge and economic resources.
8. We must own and control businesses in markets where we spend most of our money.
9. We must start businesses in markets where we are the dominant population.
10. We must hold on to the money that we draw into our community through labor and employment from other cultures.
11. View money as a means to accomplish temporary goals and to solve temporary problems that can take us to higher values; we should not be attached to money outside of this temporary ability.

Mentally

1. We must discard falsehoods.
2. We must always look to raise our awareness/consciousness.
3. We must seek balance in our mental state.
4. We must identify first with our own cultural/social group before attempting to identify with or emulate anyone else's.

5. We must seek greater information about our social environment (always ask why things are the way they are).
6. We must face the truth about our condition.
7. We must look inward to look outward.
8. We must learn to trust each other as a matter of necessity.

Educationally

1. Teach kids how to decode their environment.
2. Teach kids that black people must be producing something and we must buy from each other.
3. Teach kids that our dollars should circulate 8 to 12 times within the black community.
4. Teach kids to never blindly except the status quo.
5. Teach kids to always question what is going on around them.

Culturally

1. Never adapt ourselves to corrupt, oppressive societies.
2. We must cease worshiping false idols just because they appear to have money or influence.
3. We must always ask, what is the right thing to do in this situation? Not what is the right thing for ME in this situation?
4. Recognize that trust comes from a sense of community.
5. Channel social frustrations into concentrated economic effort.
6. Remove the illusion that consumerism is the same thing as equality.
7. Put knowledge before money.

Politically

1. Audit all politicians and leaders on the basis of what they accomplish economically, not socially.
2. We must confront the origins of the current problems.
3. We must always be skeptical of anyone who represents the status quo.
4. Organize and move as a group.
5. We must assume everything that we see or hear from the establishment is propaganda meant to maintain the status quo.
6. We must stop cooperating with our own enslavement.
7. We must look inward to our own community for the answers to our problems.
8. Use boycott and non-support as a weapon against oppressive economic schemes.

Health and Safety

1. Understand that the criminal justice system is designed as a new form of slavery.
2. Do not intentionally harm members of our community.
3. Put people before money.
4. We must focus on our needs before our desires.
5. Use our own organized resources to protect the community from racism and brutality.
6. Use our economic resources to relieve the suffering that exists within our community.
7. Use truth as the only authority over you.
8. Cure disease within our community by curing the mindset that created the disease.

Finally

Each one of us must make a commitment to give our ongoing repeat support to black business just like we do with cell phone companies, and cable companies. Just like we do with lotto and slot machines, cigarettes, fast food joints, clubs, liquor stores, and foreign owned carry outs.

We can't continue to internalize self destructive behavior and call it culture. That is not our culture, that is the culture that was forced on us through colonialism and white supremacy.

We should also know by now that the government is fully owned by capitalist and we will never be able to vote money back that we have thrown away.

We have no excuse. If we have money to spend on destructive things, we have the money to change the economic condition of our community. Through our desire to assimilate into foreign cultures and value systems we have lost our way and have been tricked into enriching other cultures at the expense of our own.

We must remove our support from rule by capital systems and instead place our attention and focus on creating just and fair systems of our own. No one else will ever treat us fairly if we are not treating ourselves fairly.

References

King James 1611 Bible with Apocrypha

The Book of Enoch

The Book of Jasher

The Book of Jubilees

Antiquities of the Jews
By Flavius Josephus (94 AD)

The Hope of Israel
By Menasseh Ben Israel
R. I. for Hannah Allen, at the Crown in Popes-head
Alley (1650)

The Roman Empire the Empire of the Edomite
By William Beeston
George Cox (January 1, 1853)

Ancient And Modern Britons: A RETROSPECT Vol. I
By David Mac Ritchie
LONDON: KEGAN PAUL, TRENCH & CO., i PATERNOSTER SQUARE.
(1884)

Complete Works of Tacitus. Tacitus (. Alfred John Church. William
Jackson Brodribb. Sara Bryant. edited for Perseus. New York. : Random
House, Inc. Random House, Inc. 1873

Babylon to Timbuktu - A History of Ancient Black Races Including the
Black Hebrews
By Rudolph R. Windsor
AuthorHouse (August 18, 2011)

The Thirteenth Tribe: The Kazar Empire and Its Heritage
By Arthur Koestler
Fawcett Popular Library (June 1978)

Nature Knows No Color-Line: Research into the Negro Ancestry in the
White Race
By J.A Rogers
Helga Rogers; 3rd edition (June 1, 1980)

Hebrewisms of West Africa
 By Joseph J Williams
Kessinger Publishing, LLC (September 10, 2010)

WHO IS ESAU-EDOM?
By Charles A. Weisman
Published by Weisman Publications (December 1991)

American Holocaust
By David Stannard
Oxford University Press (1992)

CHARISMATIC CHAOS
By John F. MacArthur, Jr.
Zondervan Publishing House, Grand Rapids, MI,
(1992)

About the author

Anthony B. Cornish CPA, MBA

Who am I?

I am an entrepreneur, investor, risk taker, and creative finance expert. This is the second book that I have written concerning the economic, mental, and spiritual health of the so-called black community.

Over the course of my business career I have created multiple million dollar deals, always with the goal of uplifting the economic condition of my race and my culture.
I was born in Washington D.C. in the same year that Martin Luther King Jr. was assassinated. I grew up in D.C. during the 80's when drugs, murder, and prison were our main career tracks.

Through determination and good fortune, I was able to side step most of the sea of trouble that existed all around me, I even managed to get a decent education.
I attended D.C. public schools up until the 10th grade and then to a predominately white school 10th through 12th. I note this because before I attended this white high school, I had never personally known one white kid by name (I was 14 years old when I first interacted with white kids of my own age).

I then volunteered to the United States Marine Corps right out of high school and returned to D.C. to go to Howard University business school one year later. I spent my whole undergraduate college career in the Marine Corps reserve and worked various jobs to get through school over the next six years.

When I graduated from Howard, I went straight into trying to start a business. That business focused on helping black businesses find customers from within the black community. It was eye opening, to say the least. After seeing the condition of our business community, I figured I needed more education.

I went on to become a Certified Public Accountant and earned a Masters in Business from George Washington University in Washington DC.
So from the mid 1970s to the year 2000 I spent time bouncing between black schools and white schools with the Marine Corps sandwiched in

the middle. I always viewed my educational pursuits as a means to help my community and my culture.

As I moved through my educational experience, it became clear to me that the social problems in the black community really stem from economic problems, and that those economic problems stem from the system that was created to enrich white people at the expense of black people.

With master's degree in hand, I again set out on the entrepreneurial path.
Once again, I set out to not just be an entrepreneur, but a black entrepreneur.
That was the year 2000 and since then I have been involved in many different business ventures with varying degrees of success.

Among other things, I have been involved in trading the stock and options markets during the tech bubble, real estate development through boom and bust, starting numerous businesses, investing in other businesses, and consulting with countless other entrepreneurs. I knew that I had to involve other black people in order to create an impact that would help change our economic relationship with the power structure.

I figured out that any other strategy would be a waste of time and energy. And here lies the problem. What I found disappointed me. I found that there is actually no culture to back up entrepreneurs like me. Even in the overwhelmingly black city of Washington DC, there seemed to be a hostile environment for black entrepreneurship, not particularly by white people, but by other black people.

Throughout my entire business career what I have encountered are black people who are absolutely hostile to the idea of black entrepreneurship.
Everywhere I turned, there were black faces creating roadblocks and, sometimes, out and out sabotaging the progress that I was trying to make.

I had to ask myself why?

There is no way to make any meaningful change in the condition of our community without the support, cooperation, and involvement of other black people. So I knew that I had to work on this problem before the strategies that I was trying to implement could be effective. Anything else would only serve to further the system that creates massive oppression for my race.

I told myself that before I did another deal or started any other projects; I would seriously analyze what was going on and try to come up with solutions to what I was seeing.

This book is that analysis and contains those solutions.
It is my sincere hope that this book can be used as a reference tool for creating, understanding, and implementing solutions.

You can go to **TheSocietyofJacob.com** to get more information and tools to help you start and manage your own lifestyle investments, and business. You will also see our plan to help spiritually and economically rebuild the House of Jacob. Thanks for reading and paying attention to this important information, I hope that you have gotten something out of this work and I hope to see you as a member of The Society of Jacob. Shalom.

Feel free to contact me: sevenfigures10@gmail.com

Made in the USA
San Bernardino, CA
11 September 2014